DISCOVER

TUNISIA

Terry Palmer

HERITAGE
HOUSE

DISCOVER TUNISIA

First published July 1988

ISBN 185212.0114

Typesetting by: Essex Phototypesetting, Pace Units, Stephenson Rd, Clacton-on-Sea, CO15 4XA

Printed by: Colorcraft Ltd, Whitfield Rd, Causeway Bay, Hong Kong

Distributed in the UK and major outlets overseas by Roger Lascelles, 47 York Rd, Brentford, TW8 OQP

Published by: Heritage House (Publishers) Ltd, King's Rd, Clacton-on-Sea, CO15 1BG

© Terry Palmer, 1988

Acknowledgement.*Lake in the Desert* by Jamie Skinner in *Birds*, the magazine of the RSPB, Autumn 1985.

Further titles in the "Discover" series include:

DISCOVER MALTA
DISCOVER TURKEY
DISCOVER THE GAMBIA
DISCOVER GIBRALTAR
Also by Terry Palmer: *THE CAIRO ALTERNATIVE (Heritage House)*

THE GHOST AT MY SHOULDER (Corgi)

£4.95 in the UK

CONTENTS

The world is full of surprises, as Terry Palmer found in his travels through Tunisia — half an hour after arriving in Tunis two young women invited him to a wedding! He continued his journey using train, bus, louage, hired car, taxi, hired cycle, boat — and his own feet.

WHY TUNISIA?

Gateway to Africa

TUNISIA IS THE ORIENT MADE EASY. It's a compact country on the sunnier side of the Mediterranean with its back yard extending into the vast emptiness of the mystic Sahara. For centuries it has been the meeting-place of many peoples; Phoenicians, Romans, Arabs, Ottomans and French, with a brief encounter between Monty's Eighth Army and Rommel's Afrika Korps.

It has at Carthage an ancient city that once ruled half the known world; it has at El Jem a Roman amphitheatre that is in better shape than the one in Rome; and it has Kairouan, the holiest city in Islam after Mecca and Jerusalem.

It also offers an intriguing cultural mix between Europe and Africa, between Christianity and Islam, and between the mystic Orient and the progressive Occident.

Peopled by Arabs, Moors, Europeans and around one percent of the original Berber stock, Tunisia's official languages are French and Arabic and its rest day is Sunday, though Friday is the holy day.

Politically stable, despite the recent 'retirement' of its life-president, Tunisia is also economically sound. Its weather is utterly predictable, its people friendly, its beaches broad and its cost of living low. It's therefore an ideal holiday spot if you want to laze on the beach for a fortnight, but it shares with the other Maghreb states of Morocco and Algeria the distinction of being the gateway to the Dark Continent of Africa on a tarmac road across the world's greatest desert.

Tunisia covers 154,530 sq km (63,170 sq miles) including 9,080 sq km of inland salt pans. With a population of around 7,000,000, it's slightly larger than England and Wales together and is twice the size of Portugal, yet it is small compared with other countries in Africa. Its most northerly point is the aptly-named white cliffs of Cap Blanc at 37° 22' north, the latitude of Richmond (Virginia) and Seoul (South Korea), and its most southerly point is at 30° 15' north, roughly equal to New Orleans and Suez — and to Durban in the Southern Hemisphere. The cities of Tunis, Kairouan and Gabes straddle the 10th line of eastern longitude which also runs through Hamburg in Germany.

From north to south, as the migratory swallow might fly, Tunisia stretches 789 km (490 miles),and its greatest width, from the Libyan frontier beyond Ben Guerdane to the Algerian border by Nefta, is 371 km (230 miles). Its highest point is the unspectacular 1,544-metre (5,098 ft) plateau of Jebel Chambi in the Tébessa Mountains west of Kasserine, and its lowest point is the little-visited Chott El Gharsa, 20m below sea level, but for most people it will be anywhere along the scores of miles of golden sands. Bienvenu à Tunisie!

BEFORE YOU GO

Passport control

THERE ARE FEW ARRANGEMENTS for Western Europeans to make before a visit to Tunisia. Your domestic driving licence will permit you to drive a hire car so there's no need for an International Driving Licence. There are no special health requirements, no inoculations, there is no need for anti-malaria tablets. Few people will need a visa, and as the export and import of Tunisian dinars is prohibited, you can't buy currency in advance — but you could purchase some traveller's cheques.

VISA REQUIREMENTS

All foreign visitors need a valid passport. Visas are *not* needed by citizens of Western European countries, Canada, Japan, South Korea and the USA; the US visitors will be allowed a four-month stay with three months for all others. Visas *are* needed, therefore, by holders of Australian and New Zealand passports; they're issued to Australians on arrival but the Aussie visitor should check he gets one valid for the length of his stay and not just a statutory week. At the time of writing, New Zealanders will be given a week without the option; if they need longer they must apply for a visa through a Tunisian consulate before departure.

Holders of passports issued in South Africa and Israel are *not admitted*, nor are people from other nations whose documents contain frontier stamps proving they've visited South Africa or Israel. If this applies to you, get another passport before you come. Israeli immigration officers are aware of this problem and willl stamp you in on a scrap of paper. But if you go across the land frontier into Egypt the authorities there will not be so considerate and an *Egyptian* border stamp can prove your downfall.

If you're planning to look in on Libya while you're in Tunisia, you'll need to have all details of your passport translated into Arabic before the Libyan authorities will consider granting you a visa. The country isn't geared to tourism and the sensible advice is to keep away.

Algeria doesn't demand visas from western Europeans but it does insist on everybody changing US$200 or equivalent into its own dinars at the frontier. You'll realise why when you see black market money changers on the streets offering up to three times the official exchange rate in return for hard currency. That two-day trip from Tozeur across the erg to Touggourt could prove very expensive.

EMBASSIES IN TUNIS

This is a selection of embassies based in Tunis:

Belgium: 47 rue du 1er Juin; **Canada:** 3 rue du Sénégal, Place Palestine, Belvédère; **Denmark:** 5 rue de Mauritanie; **Finland:** No address; phone 252.806; **France:** Place de l'Independance; **West Germany:** 1 rue Al Hamra, Mutuelleville; **Netherlands:** 6-8 rue Meycen, Belvédère; **Sweden:** 87 ave Taieb Mhiri; **Switzerland:** 10 rue Ach. Chenkiti; **UK:** 5 place de la Victoire (at east gate to Medina); **USA:** 144 ave de la Liberté.

The Algerian Embassy at 136 ave de la Liberté, Tunis, will issue visas for those who need them. The Libyan People's Bureau is at 48 rue du 1er Juin, next to the Belgian Embassy.

TOURIST OFFICES

The Office National de Tourisme Tunisien, ONTT, has branches in numerous countries including:

Belgium: Bureau du Tourism Tunisien, Galérie Ravenstein 60, 1000 Bruxelles (02.511.28.93); **France:** ONTT, 32 ave de l'Opéra, 75002 Paris (742.72.67); **Germany:** Fremdenverkehrsamt Tunesien Am Hauptbahnhof 6, 6000 Frankfurt am Main (0609.231.891); Fremdenverkehrsamt Tunesien, Graf Adolf Str 100, 4000 Düsseldorf (0211.359.414); **Netherlands:** 61 Leidsestraat 61, 1017 Amsterdam (22.49.71-72); **Sweden:** Engelbrektsgatan 19, 11432 Stokholm (00468.206.773) **UK:** Tunisian National Tourist Office, 33 Dover St, London W1 (01.499.2234); **USA:** Tunisian Embassy, 2408 Massachusetts Ave NW, Washington, DC 20008 (202.234.6644).

WHERE TO GO

Sun-seekers. Tourists seeking the sun and planning to spend the maximum time on the beach should opt for Hammamet, Sousse or Jerba Island as first choice. Hammamet is a smart and friendly holiday resort built around a gentle and picturesque bay but with little character of its own behind the impressive kasbah — fortress — with the hotels strung out along the beach in both directions.

Sousse has several miles of good, wide golden sands stretching southeast to Monastir and north to Port El Kantaoui, though nearer town there is one unpleasant drain crossing the beach. At this southern end you are within a few minutes' stroll of the town and its attractions, including the medina, souks and nightlife, but the further north you progress the more difficult access becomes. Most of the hotels are large — some are enormous — and they tend to become mini-resorts. There is a regular service along the promenade between Sousse and Port El Kantaoui operated by a tractor with a Toytown locomotive bodywork and towing a train of open carriages. The service is comfortably relaxed but rather expensive.

The hotels on Jerba cluster along the north and east coasts where the sand is at its best, and are from 10 to 16 km from the tiny town of Homt Souk. As a result each hotel has, as at Sousse, developed into its own mini-resort. There are good bus services covering Jerba but they all start from the town; the taxi service is not so good and could soon prove expensive.

Desert-isle escapism. For beach plus an uninhabited stay on the nearest thing to a desert-isle this side of Tahiti, try the Kerkenah Isles. These two inhabited islands, plus several uninhabited ones, are sometimes billed as the poor man's Jerba but among the low-key hotels are the hideaway homes of several people whose names once made headline news around the world.

Beach plus sightseeing. You want the beach but you also want to see something of Tunisia? Then try Hammamet or Sousse. Hammamet or its neighbour Nabeul is a good base for visiting Tunis and the sprawling ruins of Carthage while Sousse has it all on the doorstep as well as being a good base for exploring the holy city of Kairouan.

Monastir has a good beach but the town is suffering from its legacy of being the birthplace of ex-president Habib Bourgiba. The old medina has been demolished to make way for modern buildings and straight streets, though some charm has been retained, and elsewhere you'll find the sumptuous Bourgiba mosque and the family mausoleum which forms our cover picture. There's an interesting ribat and you can see the open-air set where several films have been shot, including *The Life of Christ*.

Monastir also has Tunisia's most classiest marina with associated apartments and maisonettes which are being promoted on the European market.

Tunisian character. Mahdia is a small resort with plenty of character and history but its beach is several kilometers away and served by a cluster of modern and characterless hotels. Mahdia is not a convenient base for seeing other parts of Tunisia as no excursions operate from here, the bus connections are poor and the train service to Sousse is slow. It's excellent as part of a two-centre stay or for a day or so on an independent itinerary.

Ancient ruins. The most famous is, of course, Carthage, for which Tunis or Hammamet are convenient bases, but the most spectacular if virtually unknown relic is the well-preserved colosseum at El Jem. The town is unfortunately starved of decent accommodation.

The other ruins of note, such as Bulla Regia, Dougga, Mustis, Sbeïtla and Gighti are scattered around the country and best seen either on an organised excursion or from your own transport, be it hired or brought over on the ferry from Europe.

The desert. The southern part of Tunisia exerts a charm of its own. The Sahara, formidable and fearsome as well as fascinating, has some of the more unusual attractions of Tunisia on its fringe, notably the oases of Tozeur and Nefta, the vast salt pan of the Chott el Jerid crossable by road since 1978, and the unusual cave-community of Matmata where the people live underground — and where you can join them for the night in the subterranean hotel used briefly in the film *Star Wars.*.

WHAT TO TAKE

On the beach. To be safe, take everything you need, though it's possible to restock on most items. Package tourists planning to spent the majority of their time on the beach need very little and can travel light: swimwear with bikini top, casual clothes for around the hotel, and a more modest attire for strolling into town.

Remembering that few Tunisian women show much flesh and that some show none at all, it is surely inconsiderate of European women to wander around the souks wearing only t-shirt and shorts; if you've come to see the Tunisian way of life you should respect it. Topless bathing is widespread although it's forbidden, so be prepared for a sudden local clamp-down.

Take all the film you need, for Tunisia is a photogenic country and local supplies may not have been stored under the best of conditions.

Excursions. For excursions a decent pair of shoes is essential; I prefer trainers with really tough soles. Sunglasses and a sunhat are not vital unless you're coming in midsummer or planning to go inland, but a heavy-duty plastic water bottle of at least one-litre capacity is far more important, filled with mineral water if the tap water is too chlorinated. I also find myself rousing for a drink several times during a Tunisian night.

Independent. If you're planning to see the sights as an independent traveller, either alone or with a companion, you'll need a lightweight rucksack and sleeping bag — few of the cheaper hotels supply sheets — and the usual personal items: toilet roll, a good knife which can't be mistaken for a weapon, and several plastic bags. These have a variety of uses from storing wet swimwear and carrying bread to keep it fresh for a few more hours, to being a convenient container in which to wash fruit — and that includes dates and grapes as well as tomatoes and oranges.

A map is always useful. The best on the market is the Michelin 172, Algeria & Tunisia, on a scale of 1:1,000,000 (1cm 10km). It has inset maps of Tunis and the Tunis area, and where there is a variation in the spelling of Tunisian place names it is this Michelin version we have followed.

Camping Gaz is strangely not available, making roadside brew-ups rather difficult, but you could carry an immersion heater to boil your individual cup on those mornings when you wake up in a less-than-perfect hotel. You'll almost always find a power socket but as it'll be of the Continental type you'll need a suitable adapter.

I have an invariable rule of carrying all my documents and money in a nylon zip-up waist belt, usually worn under the shirt, and I've yet to fault the system. Each document is in its own plastic bag to prevent damage from perspiration.

WHEN TO GO

Oases. No matter what time of year it is, there is some part of Tunisia which is at its best for visitors. Winter is the most favourable time to see the oases and the desert, when the daytime temperature is what you would find

Hammamet beach and the Hotel Yasmina

in northern Europe in spring although the nights can be cold, with occasional frosts on the Grand Erg.

North Tunisia and Tunis. Spring and autumn are the best times for travelling the northern interior of the country, avoiding the winter rains and the searing heat of midsummer; Tunis is also at its best at these times for the same reasons.

Coast. On the coast, the season begins at Sousse in March and in north-facing Bizerte in May, going through to early November and the onset of the rainy season up north.

Fruit harvest. If you want to see the fruit harvest, visit Tozeur and Nefta in November and December when the dates mature. The olives of Sfax and the Sousse area are ready around the same time, and the orange groves of the north are cropped in late winter and spring.

LANGUAGE

Language presents little problem in the tourist resorts where English is fairly widely spoken, and in Sousse a number of Tunisians have mastered German, Swedish or Norwegian as well.

Beyond the tourist fringe it is certainly an asset to be able to speak French, even if it is only the *français cassé* (broken French) of the older Tunisians. You'll find the 'tu' form in far greater use than in France itself. After all, it is *tu*nisia!

The further south you travel the less French is spoken and a number of Berbers know only their own language and Arabic — and not always the latter.

The country's official languages are Arabic and French, with the currency and road signs using both. The Arabic script تونس you see on all vehicle registration plates spells 'Tunis' or 'Tunisia,' which is the same word without its added vowels.

INDEPENDENT or PACKAGE?

Package. The package traveller will find that in Tunisia he has more control over his destiny than he might have in Spain. There is more scope for excursions, there is less commercialism, and the totally different nature of the country beyond the hotel gate invites exploration more than it does in Spain.

A conventional package to a major coastal resort will provide the sun, the sand, the bed and board, leaving the visitor free to make his own entertainment and adventure. Virtually all the major hotels organise their own tours and are agents for specialist expeditions, but you must remember that the hoteliers are in the business of making money which means they would prefer you back under their roofs each night.

Day trips are therefore very common; a coach ride from Jerba to the oasis of Tozeur, for example, but if you want to see more of Tozeur than a three-hour conducted tour including a set meal in a restaurant — if, for example, you want to experience sunset and sunrise in the desert — you have three options. The easiest is to take a two- or three-day excursion, which would result in your paying for rooms in two hotels simultaneously; you could shop around for a two-centre holiday divided between coast and oasis; or you could quit your hotel for the second week and see the country on your own.

Independent. This is undoubtedly the best way to see the real Tunisia.

Four people travelling together in their own vehicle or a hired car will find it only slightly more expensive than a package, and will have the freedom to go where they want. Tunisia is an easy country in which to drive as the roads are reasonably good and the traffic is light — but don't forget the high accident rate. If you're travelling with one companion or alone, public transport will be more appropriate though more restrictive.

Sahara solo. The only part of Tunisia which is impracticable to visit independently is the Grand Erg, which stretches south and west from the Chott el Jerid and runs deep into Algeria. It's foolhardy to walk more than a few hundred yards from an oasis into the trackless sands, and for the ultimate adventure there is no option to mounting your own fully-prepared expedition or joining a properly-organised safari. But this is beyond the interests of the average package tourist and the Sahara is certainly no place to take children.

European women travelling alone. The Tunisian woman is equal in law to her male partner but in practise she still takes a submissive role, particularly in the south. This makes it very difficult for a European woman to see the country on her own as many youths will assume she has no morals and is there purely for their benefit. She is highly unlikely to be raped or seriously molested but she will find incessant and irritating hassle which could range from the annoying to the frightening.

If she's young and attractive she should not consider travelling alone unless it be a day trip to the next town, although two such young women

Portrait of an ex-president: the one-dinar note

wearing shirts and slacks would have no more problems than at home in Europe.

In most instances the addition of a European male to any party means the women are under his protection, but in the south where it's considered immoral for a Tunisian woman to be in the company of a paler-skinned man, there could be disapproval of the raven-haired beauty with the deep suntan.

TOUR OPERATORS

Tunisia draws the greatest number of its visitors from France, its former colonising power; 769,000 French tourists arrived in 1985. Germany is the next in importance with 227,000, the United Kingdom coming third with 100,000. The list continues with Italy (83,000), the Scandinavian countries (67,000), the Netherlands (45,000), Switzerland (39,000), Belgium (36,000) and the United States with just 10,000. There were 769,000 Algerian visitors in 1985, but you couldn't call them all tourists by any stretch of the imagination.

In 1985 the country had 93,368 hotel beds, just two percent of Spain's capacity, but it plans to increase that figure to 165,000 by 1995, concentrating in the new projects for Jerba, Hammamet, and the Ghar El Melh 'Disney World' and Montazah Tabarka, both on the north coast.

This list of British tour operators for the 1988 season is compiled from several sources but cannot be considered exclusive.

Airtours (A)
Allegro Holidays (Al)
Cadogan Travel (Ca)
Club Méditerranée (CM)
Club 18-30 (C18)
Cosmos Air Holidays (Co)
Enterprise Holidays (E)
Flair Holidays (F)
Global Holidays (G)
Golden Days (GD)
Intasun (I)
Lancaster Holidays (L)
Martin Rooks Holidays (M)
Panorama Holidays (P)
Patricia Wildblood Holidays (Pa)
Portland Holidays (Po)
Skytours (Sk)
Sovereign Holidays (So)
Stallard Tours (St)
Sunbound Leisure (SL)
Sunspot Tours (Su)
Thomas Cook Holidays (TC)
Thomson Holidays (T)
Tjaereborg Holidays (Tj)
Top Deck Travel (TD)
Tunisian Experience (TE)
Tunsian Travel Bureau (TB)
Wings Holidays (W)

The Tunisian Travel Bureau offers by far the widest range of destinations: Bizerte, Carthage, Cedriq, Ez Zahra, Gabes, Gammarth, Hammamet, Jerba, Kerkenah Isles, Mahdia, La Massa, Nabeul, Nefta, El Kantaoui, Sidi Bou Saïd, Skanes, Sousse, Tabarka, Tozeur, Tunis and Zarzis.

Apart from that, if you're looking for a package to a particular resort, here's an indication of what's on offer:

Hammamet: A, Ca, Co, CM, C18, E, F, G, I, L, M, Pa, Po, Sk, SL, So, St, Su, TB, TC, TD, TE, W.
Jerba: CM, I, L, P, St, TB.
Kerkenah Is: P, TB, TE.
Korba: CM.
Korbous: Sk.

Monastir: Sk, St.
Nabeul: A, Al, C, TB.
Nefta & Tozeur: TB, TE.
Sousse & El Kantaoui: A, Ca, Co, CM, E, F, G, I, L, M, P, Pa, Po, Sk, So, Su, T, Tj, TB, TC, TE, W.
Skanes: Ca, CM, Co, F, G, I, Sk, SL, Su, T, TB, TE, W.
Tunis: St, TB.

DISABLED

Tunisia is not an easy country for people confined to wheelchairs, but a package holiday is possible with careful planning. Passengers leave the plane at Monastir Airport, the most popular one with tour operators, by stairs, but mechanical lifts are available. The airport also has a toilet designed for the disabled.

There would be little problem on the courtesy buses and a number of hotels have made some provision for wheelchairs by installing toilets and some bedrooms on the ground floor and by dropping wooden ramps in front of the few single steps that were incorporated in the design.

Access to the beach could be more difficult. The Esplanade in Monastir has fair access to the beach at its back door, but the hotels immediately to the north of Sousse have a wide dual-carriageway between them and the sands: I noticed one intrepid tourist negotiating this road with his wheelchair-bound daughter. Further north, towards El Kantaoui, access becomes better but the sands are wider.

Roads, pavements and kerbs present fewer difficulties in resorts, and a disabled person could see something of the country in a hire car though bus and train travel would be impossible because of the steps and other obstructions involved. The few wheelchairs in use in Tunisia look ancient, and I saw one elderly man in a bathchair that was probably 50 years old.

The Ribat at Monastir is part of a giant film set

MONEY MATTERS

The Tunisian dinar is a soft currency that may not be imported or exported, except for a nominal sum you can take into Algeria. Banks at the airports and the ferry terminal in Tunis will change traveller's cheques or banknotes into the local currency: look for the notice headed *devises* for the latest exchange rate.

The dinar is divided into 1,000 millimes but price tags of 2500TD are asking for only 2½ dinars; two thousand five hunded dinars is written as 2.500TD, with a full stop instead of a comma. The Central Bank of Tunisia issues notes in values of ½, 1, 5 and 10TD, alloy coins for 2 and 5 mill, copper-bronze 10, 20 and 100 mill coins, and ½ and 1 dinar coins in nickel. The dinar coin is so similar to the British 10p piece that it's worth checking your change every time.

There are 39 banking organisations in the country, including 7 offshore, but to buy the local currency you must find a bank carrying the word 'change,' and in small towns there may be only one such place.

Banking hours. Bank opening hours are not standard. The core time is 0800-1130 and 1400-1630 (or 1615) Monday to Friday, but some have 1330-1515 as their Friday afternoon hours of business and in high summer some banks don't open in the afternoon. To make it complicated, a bank in Gafsa opens 0750-1350 Monday to Thursday and 0750-1330 on Friday and they all trim an hour off the working day during Ramadan, but to make it all simple again — every bank is closed on Saturday and Sunday.

Tourist hotels will change notes and cash traveller's cheques at any time, including weekends, but they charge a slightly higher commission.

Credit cards. Credit cards can be used in the 'change' banks for buying dinars, again with a slightly higher rate of commission, but you may have to wait 20 minutes while the assistant phones head office in Tunis for authorisation. You'll not be charged for the call.

Few shops will accept credit or charge cards but a surprisingly large number of traders in the souks have gone into the plastic money business.

There is no obvious black market in foreign currency in Tunisia and if you find one, stay clear. You must keep the receipts from every currency transaction and be prepared to show them at the airport when you leave; you'll also need them for reconverting any surplus dinars into hard currency, provided it does not exceed 100TD or 30% of the money you changed into dinars.

Inflation. The dinar, which takes its name from the Latin *denarius*, is a relatively stable currency which fluctuated around parity with the pound sterling until early 1986 when it lost value. It rallied later in the year to 0.750 and then went into a shallow decline reaching 1.420 by February 1988. As the dinar is roughly equal to 10 French francs the popular name for 100 mill is 'un franc.'

Cost of Living. These sample prices were current in late 1987 and they give an insight into the Tunisian way of life:

Women's fashion shoes	13 — 17TD
Women's evening shoes	8 — 25TD
Men's ready-made suit	70 — 130TD
Men's quality shoes	18 — 35TD
Shelled almonds	3.800TD kg
Raisins	1.500TD kg

Melon, small	.150TD
Pomegranate	.350TD each
Tomatoes	.400TD kg
Grapes	1.200TD kg
Dates	.400 — 1.200TD kg
Standard loaf	.100TD
Honey: 470gm jar	5.280TD
Nestlé's condensed milk, 397gm	.565TD
Postage on card to Europe (not France)	.300TD
Postage on letter to Europe (minimum)	.350TD
Cigarettes: Tunisian Caravanes, pkt 20	.520TD
Cigarettes: imported brands, pkt 20	1.400TD

Drinks at cheap bar (add 20% for medium-class bar; double prices for smart hotel):

Coffee	.120TD
Coke	.140TD
Boga cidre (lemonade, despite name)	.140TD
Chweps (Schweppes)	.160TD
Gini (gin, small measure)	.160TD
Mineral water	(70cl) .300TD

Spirits in supermarket:

Courvoisier cognac	41TD
Grant's whisky, 75cl	35TD
Haig whisky, 75cl	29TD
Admission to cinema	.500 — 600TD
Bus fare, Gafsa — Le Kef	4.500TD
Train fare, Monastir — Mahdia (2nd cl)	.790TD
50cc Motobecane moped, new	514TD
Telefunken colour tv set	544TD
Bed, complete; extremely ornately carved in wood; might suit smart hotel in Europe with oriental theme	3,500.000TD
Rental for reasonable, average-size house in tourist area, per month	30 — 60TD
Purchase of smart house in Tunis	40,000TD
Ditto in Sousse centre	15,000 — 20,000TD
Basic wages of unskilled labourer	*120TD per month*

ISLAM

The word 'Islam' means submission to God's will and Islam is indeed a strict religion, demanding its followers show that submission in their daily life and prayers.

Islam is the faith propounded by Mahomet and gathered into the holy book, the Koran. Mahomet's zeal set Islam on its course and it now has more than 460,000,000 followers from Dakar to Dar-es-Salaam, from Istanbul to Indonesia, and among them is the vast majority of the population of Tunisia.

A key point in Islam, as in Christianity, is the belief in the resurrection and in a world and a life beyond this one; adherents believe that each person's life follows a preordained pattern and for a few this idea that "it is written" or "it is the will of Allah" can become an excuse for indecision or inactivity.

The five commandments of Islam are the need for faith, as defined in the muezzin's chant from the mosque; the need to pray five times a day; the order for the wealthy to give 2.5% of their income to the needy; the observance of Ramadan, the ninth month of the Islamic lunar-based calendar, by refraining from eating, drinking and sexual activity during daylight hours; and to make a once-in-a-lifetime pilgrimage to Mecca.

The Koran has 114 chapters each of 6,666 verses and could be considered as the final volume of a trilogy beginning with Judaism and continuing with Christianity, for the Koran mentions Abraham, Moses and Jesus as earlier prophets, but Mahomet is the last and therefore the greatest of them all.

The traveller in Tunisia will find Islam's influence all around: the veiled and submissive women; the men kneeling on their prayer mats; the calls of the muezzin from public address systems on the mosque minarets; and the mosques themselves which, like the Bourgiba family mausoleum in Monastir, shown in our cover picture, dominate the town skyline.

The actual times of prayer vary slightly day by day but begin around 0630 with Fajr, followed at 1400 by Suhr, at 1700 by Asr and at 1930 by Maghrib, with the last prayer Isha coming around 2030.

There is no insistence that people pray at these times, nor that they go to the mosque to do so, but on Friday, the holy day, they should comply if possible difficult though that may be as colonialism bequeathed Tunisia with Sunday as its day of rest.

The muezzin's chant is indecipherable to non-Arab listeners but he is proclaiming in Arabic what in English would be "God is almighty. I believe there is no god but God and that Mahomet is his prophet. Come to pray. Come for redemption. God is almighty and there is no god but God."

Mahomet was born in Mecca around 570AD; he began hearing the voice of God around 612 but when he tried converting the moon-worshipping Arabs they drove him from the city and it is this exodus, the *hegira,* which is the starting-point for counting the years in the Islamic calendar. The Gregorian calendar of 365¼ days now in use in Tunisia places the *hegira* 1,365 years ago, but according to Islam's lunar reckoning 1,409 years have passed since the event.

Islam is the religion of the state of Tunisia, but is not the state religion, but there is tolerance of other beliefs. The country has 20,000 Catholics and a scattering of Greek Orthodox, French Protestants, and Anglicans, with a few Jews still in Tunis and a small community on Jerba.

In 1972 the Tunisian Government reacted to the outrage of too many Europeans entering the mosques improperly dressed by passing a law banning non-Moslems from entering the prayer-chamber of any mosque. The law is so well supported that you will invariably need permission and an escort even to enter the outer hall, for which you should, of course, be suitably attired with arms and upper legs covered, and with women wearing something on the head.

The only exceptions to this rule are a select few mosques in Kairouan and Sousse which tourists may enter without escorts — but they must be modestly dressed and the prayer hall is still forbidden territory.

For a Christian, however, a mosque holds little interest beyond that first experience. The building is used solely for prayer and not for preserving any links with the community's past through memorial plaques, tombstones or written records.

GOING TO TUNISIA

Air and sea connections

THE OBVIOUS WAY TO GO is by air, but there are arguments in favour of taking the sea crossing for people planning a longer stay.

BY AIR

Monastir is the main airport for package holidays and charter flights, with Tunis taking the majority of scheduled services.

Monastir. Monastir's Habib Bourgiba Airport, code MIR, is a modern terminal equipped with banks, impeccable toilets (incuding one for the disabled accessible for departing and arriving travellers), a post office with international telephones and 'Rapid Post' agency, souvenir shops, offices for car hire companies and tour operators, a duty free shop, and a bar (thé au lait 400 mill, whisky 2.500TD).

There is no airport bus. Package tourists are met by coaches which take them to their hotels but independent travellers must rely either on the Métro train just outside the airport gate, or on a taxi. Time of day will dictate your option as the last train to Monastir stops at 2037 and the last to Sousse at 2120. It's a long wait until 0640 for the first train to Monastir (fare 210 mill) or 0650 for the first to Sousse (fare 300 mill), and there's no ticket office at the Aéroport station. The taxi fare to Monastir is 5TD and to Sousse 6TD.

Monastir has scheduled connections with Frankfurt and seven French-speaking cities in Europe.

Tunis. Tunis Carthage Airport, code TUN, receives scheduled flights from 22 cities in western Europe including London, Frankfurt, Copenhagen and Amsterdam, and transfer connections put it into the worldwide network.

Tunis airport is larger than that of Monastir — about the size of a hypermarket — and has similar amenities, but there is a regular bus service on route 35 to Avenue Habib Bourgiba, Tunis, for a fare of 500 mill. Don't make the mistake of thinking the Aéroport station on the TGM rail service to Carthage drops you at Carthage Airport: it doesn't.

Jerba. Jerba Airport, coded DJE as it's often spelled Djerba, has scheduled flights only to Frankfurt, Geneva, Luxembourg and Paris but with transfer connections, often at Tunis, is integrated into the world network. British and northern European tour operators bring some charter flights to Jerba, either direct or via a transfer, in this instance usually at Monastir.

By day the independent traveller can catch a number 15 bus for the 7km ride into Jerba's only town, Homt Souk; by night it's the taxi again.

Other airports. Sfax has scheduled links with Malta and Paris and connects with other services at Tunis while Gabes has links only with Tunis although it shares the status of international airport. Gafsa's airport doesn't feature in any schedules, having been eclipsed by Tozeur. There are no bus services from any of these airports.

Discount fares. The relative lack of scheduled services to Monastir means the market for discount fares inevitably lands you in Tunis. The market is small but to break into it try the Air Travel Advisory Bureau at 01.636.5000 (London), 061.832.2000 (Manchester), or 021.783.2000 (Birmingham). Tour operators often have spare seats on their flights and for one of these try your local travel agent.

SEA

Two or more people planning to spend at least two weeks in Tunisia and seeing the country by hire car may care to examine the economics as it might be cheaper to take their own car on the ferries from Europe.

Sicily — Tunis

Tirrenia and General National Maritime Transport operates ferries from Trapani (Sicily) to Tunis. The weekly service leaves Trapani 0900 on Wednesday arriving Tunis 1700; it sails from Tunis 2000 Wednesday arriving Trapani 0600 Thursday. The single adult fare in 1987 ranged from £39.50 to £74.10, with a car up to 4½ m costing £84.70. Return fares are double.

The ship also plies between Trapani and Cagliari in Sardinia with the Tunis — Cagliari fare only slightly dearer than the prices quoted, which *apply to the 1987 season.* It's advisable to make reservations if you have a car, but the service is seldom overbooked.

The UK agent is Serena Holidays of London (01.244.8422); the company has offices in Genoa at the Stazione Marittima, Ponte Colombo.

Marseille — Tunis

The Société Nationale Maritime Corse-Méditerranée (SNCM) operates this route year-round with a minimum crossing time of 22½ hours. High-season return economy class fares are £111.80 with cabin class being £184.60. Low season return economy fares (November to May inclusive) are £100.20 and cabin class £163.40. *These fares were valid for 1987 and applied only for two to five adults travelling with their car.* Return fare for a car up to 4m long is £210.40.

SNCM's UK agency is Continental Shipping & Travel, 179 Piccadilly, London W1V 9DB (01.491.4986). In France: 61 blv des Dames, 13002 Marseille (91.56.32.00). In Belgium: SNCM, Centre Internationale Rogier, Passage Internationale 2, Boîte 9B, 1210, Bruxelles. In the Netherlands: Sanara Bv, Scheepstimmermanslaan 37b, 3016 AE, Rotterdam. In Denmark: Vestjdsk Rejseburo, Norregade 51, DK 7500 Holstebro.

The Compagnie Tunisienne de Navigation virtually duplicates the service, and it has the same UK agency.

Make your reservations, both ways, as far ahead as possible, particularly for July and August crossings.

OVERLAND CONNECTIONS

This, in effect, means an African landfall in either Morocco or Algeria and coming in either by train on the Trans-Maghreb Express which is a harassing experience and definitely not for unaccompanied women; coming over by bus which is an adventure in itself in Algeria; or bringing your own car probably on SNCM's Marseille — Alger route. In view of the hassle with Algerian authorities it's not a practicable route for a stay in Tunisia.

TRAVELLING IN TUNISIA

Road, rail, sea and air

YOU HAVE A WIDE CHOICE of transport options for internal travel, including air, bus, train, taxi, hire car, ferry, or that marvel of Tunisia, the 'louage.'

INTERNAL AIRLINES

Tunis Air has the lion's share of the internal air routes, with around 30 return flights each week between Tunis and Jerba, seven a week between Monastir and Jerba, four weekly between Monastir and Tunis, and two a week on the Tunis — Tozeur and the Tozeur — Jerba routes.

Tunisavia runs a twice-weekly return service between Tunis and Gabès and a weekly service between Tunis and Sfax.

Flying times are less than an hour even in smaller aircraft, but reservations should be made as far ahead as possible. Single fares on the Tunis — Jerba flight range from 21TD to 27.300TD, which is reasonable by European standards.

BUS

Tunisia has a good bus service, complicated rather than improved by the rivalry between the national carrier SNTRI (Société Nationale des Transports Interurbains) and the several regional carriers such as the Société des Transports du Kef and the Société Régionale de Transport de Sfax, known as SORETRAS.

Sifsari in Sousse

Berber women in Kairouan

SNTRI's buses link Tunis and every main town on a daily service in each direction, some of the schedules being non-stop. This makes it easy to travel around the country on these radial routes, with the smaller companies supplying the cross-country connections.

The problem is that there is no integration whatever between any of the companies, each of which stoically refuses to accept the existence of any other carrier. This means that if you arrive at a *gare routière* (bus station) in a small town and ask an official for the next bus to Wherever, he will tell you only the time of his company's next bus. Where several companies operate from the same gare it's merely a question of taking the concensus of opinion or asking a fellow-traveller but in several towns, notably Sousse, the companies operate from different starting points.

SNTRI usually has its timetables posted up, but they are frequently incomplete and occasionally long out of date. Few of the other companies bother with timetables.

Most buses carry small cards in the front window, giving their destination, but in the south there is a frustrating habit of writing them only in Arabic.

Once you've located your bus and bought your ticket at the appropriate office, travel is easy. The vehicles range from articulated German hand-me-downs still proclaiming *Eingang nur vorn* on the sides, to the occasional luxury air-conditioned coach with adequate luggage compartments beneath the floor, and travelling conditions range from overcrowded to sheer luxury.

TRAIN

Tunisia's rail network inherited from colonial times shrank in the early years of independence to a simple network centred on Tunis. SNCFT, the Société Nationale des Chemins de Fer Tunisiens, now operates from the capital to Bizerte; to Tabarka on the north coast; to Jendouba and on to Alger; to Gafour and on to Kalaat Khasba near Thala on the western frontier; and down the coast (with a branch line to Hammamet and Nabeul) to Sousse, El Jem and Sfax to a junction at Grïba from where one line goes south to Gabès and another crosses to Gafsa and Metlaoui. From Metlaoui a scenic route twists through the Gorges of Selja to Redeyef and a straight line runs on to Tozeur, but passenger services on these latter links are very infrequent.

Tunisia has reversed the rail decline and is now building more lines. The recent link from Sousse to Monastir and its airport was extended in 1985 to Mahdia, though even in late 1987 none of the stations on this single-track line had a name-board. A new suburban line is slowly carving its way southward out of Sfax and another is moving north from Tunis towards the airport.

Timetables. Timetables are on display at main stations and in some of the newspapers, but this is a summary of the trains from Tunis.

To Bizerte: Three return trains daily; 1hr 50min.

To Jendouba: Five returns daily; 2hr 30min; one is the Trans-Maghreb Express, the only train in Tunisia to be designated 'express.'

To Gafour: Four returns daily; 3hr; three continue to the end of the passenger line at Kalaat Khasba.

The coastal route: Opposite is a condensation of the timetable in operation in late 1987; the schedule varies slightly according to seasonal demand.

Southbound

TUNIS	0710	1205	1305	1414	1420	1520	1730	1805	1840	2120
BIR BOU REKBA	0807	1303	---	1516	1540	1628	1823	1920	1943	2216
SOUSSE	0907	1404	1458	1619		1749	1927		2102	---
EL JEM	1009		1602	---			2029			0015
SFAX	1056		1649	1803			2116			0100
GABES	1317			2024						0410
GAFSA										0410
METLAOUI										0622

Northbound

METLAOUI										1953
GAFSA						0951			1555	2054
GABES						1200		1800		2247
SFAX				0620		1315	1220		1815	0145
EL JEM				0708			1403		1903	0233
SOUSSE	0520		0700	0807	1246	1410	1505	1812	2011	0333
BIR BOU REKBA	0603	0648	0809	0915	1359		1606	1919	2113	---
TUNIS	0709	0758	0903	1009	1453	1610	1701	2022	2209	0529

In addition to this basic timetable there are seven daily shuttles each way between Bir Bou Rekba and Hammamet — Nabeul.

SNCFT's trains are diesel-powered, and the rolling-stock of French design is modern and fitted with toilets. Entry is by steps at the ends of the carriages.

The Sousse — Monastir — Mahdia line, called the Métro, runs completely independently of the other SNCFT services although it uses similar, sometimes identical, trains. This is a popular service with tourists and offers a relaxed way of seeing something of this part of the country.

Departures from Sousse's Gare Bab el Jedid are: **0545**, 0625, 0715, 0755, **0810**, 0920, 1020, 1120, 1220, 1315, **1340**, 1423, 1520, 1620, 1735, **1820**, 1835, 1920, 2022. Every train stops at every station, but only those in **bold type** go on to Mahdia, with a total of 23 stations en route. Travelling time from Sousse to Monastir is 35mins; to Mahdia 1hr 44mins.

There are 15 departures daily from Monastir for Sousse, beginning at 0640 and ending with the 2110 train.

There are five daily departures from Mahdia for Sousse, beginning at 0540; in addition there are two daily trains from Mahdia to Tunis, departing at 1205 and 1600 and not shown on any of the schedules above.

Note that this is the Monday to Saturday schedule; there are fewer trains on Sundays and public holidays.

Getting to the airport The Métro is the cheapest and most convenient way for independent travellers to complete their journey to Monastir Airport, with a second-class ticket costing 210 mill from Monastir or 300 mill from Sousse. The stations from Monastir are La Faculté, L'Aéroport, Les Hôtels, Sahline Sebkha, Sahline Ville, Sousse Sud, and Sousse Bab el Jedid.

The restaurant at Les Bérbères Hotel, Matmata

The TGM Line. An excellent electric train operates between Tunis Nord to La Marsa via the smart suburbs along the Gulf of Tunis, including Carthage.

The line crosses the Lake of Tunis on a man-made dyke then calls at 15 stations along the short coast run. Smart aluminium rolling stock built in 1978 with few seats but with plenty of straphanging space has replaced the wooden carriages which operated on this route for decades; the coaches were more than 70 years old when they were withdrawn.

The first train leaves Tunis at 0300, the last at 0030, with departures every few minutes at peak times in the morning and evening; during the day the traffic is light. Stations along the route are Le Bac, Goulette Vieille, Le Casino, Khereddine, Aéroport — which is *not* the station for Tunis Carthage Airport — Le Kram, Salambo, then the stations which serve the vast Carthage site, Carthage Byrsa, C Dermech, C Hannibal, C Présidence — the presidential palace is nearby — and C Amilcar. The line continues with Sidi Bou Saïd, Sidi Dhrif, La Corniche and finally La Marsa. The single fare for the full journey is 500 mill.

Other railways. Other railways shown on maps, notably the link between Kalaa Khasba and Metlaoui, carry only freight.

The Red Lizard. Would you like to ride in a royal train through the most spectacular scenery in Tunisia? It might just be possible. The *Lézard Rouge*, the train of the former Bey (King) of Tunis, has been modified into a tourist train with 116 seats, a bar, restaurant and observation car, and in summer it makes a weekly expedition from Metlaoui through the Gorge of Wadi Selja, and back. Contact Transtours, 63 ave Bourgiba, Sousse (tel 20.041).

HIRED CAR

Tunisia is one of the more expensive countries in which to hire a car, no matter which company you use. In the 1988 season a Fiat Uno 5DR, one of the smallest vehicles available, cost £280 a week with Budget Rent-a-car, a considerable increase since 1987, even though it was for unlimited mileage. This price included comprehensive insurance, collision damage waiver, local taxes and personal insurance, leaving only the petrol as an extra.

The comparable price for a Mercedes 190 was £480 a week.

You may be able to reduce this outlay by agreeing to pay a mileage charge and limiting your forays; you certainly won't be able to drop off the vehicle at any place other than where you hired it, unless you're prepared to pay a hefty charge.

In fairness I should add that among other rental firms in Tunisia are Hertz, Europcar, InterRent, Avis, Africar (not to be confused with a firm of the same name which builds wooden-framed cars), and local firms such as Cartha Rent, Garage Lafayette, Garage Liberté and others, but there is little to choose between their prices.

The legal angle. It is contrary to Tunisian law for a motorist to carry more passengers than the vehicle was designed for, which usually means hired cars have a limit of three, but you're unlikely to come against this problem unless you're obviously overloading, and the law is certainly not applied to drivers of *louages*.

Your domestic driving licence is acceptable provided it is not for a learner driver, you've held it at least a year, and you're 21 or more. Check your insurance fully as Tunisia recently had the second-highest number of accidents per vehicle-kilometre of all countries in UNO.

Speed limits. The speed limit is 50 kph in urban areas, 70kph in rural Jerba, 100kph in rural areas on the mainland, and 110 kph on the motorway. The wearing of seat belts and crash helmets is not obligatory — many cars don't have belt anchor points fitted — and vehicles have yellow headlights, as in France. Traffic drives on the *right* and at roundabouts gives way to vehicles coming from the left.

Parking. Parking is easy except in the centre of Tunis, and in towns you'll frequently find attendants ready to help you park even if there's no apparent difficulty. The officially-appointed *guardiens* wear badges; those without badges are self-appointed but they all expect a fee of 100 or 200 mill.

Larger towns allow parking on alternate sides of the road. *Coté du stationnement jours pairs* means you can park on that side on even dates; *jours impairs* is for odd dates. There are very few parking meters in the country, the most noticeable being in Houmt Souk, Jerba (150 mill for 90 minutes), but with unrestricted and free parking only a few feet away.

Petrol. Super grade petrol cost 470 mill per litre in late 1987, with the normal grade, called just *essence*, priced at 450 mill and gas oil — diesel — at 270 mill. This puts the price of petrol below the average cost in Europe and well below French levels. Petrol stations are equipped with the latest pumps and are well distributed in towns, though there are many miles of secondary roads without services. Most stations are open on Sunday.

VOITURE DE LOUAGE

Louage means 'hiring,' but a louage is not a hire-car in the accepted sense. It is a shared taxi in which the driver will squeeze as many passengers as possible, and he'll set off when the car is full or when he despairs of waiting any longer.

Each louage driver is licensed to operate specific routes at fixed fares, thus giving him little scope for increasing his income. The vehicles therefore tend to be old and poorly maintained, and if you want to get out half way along the route you'll be expected to pay the fare for the full distance; you may find it difficult to continue your broken journey unless you care to become the eighth person in a Peugeot 404 designed to carry five.

It's impossible to follow a planned timetable when travelling by louage. The first passenger may have to wait an hour and a half while the last one is hustled aboard scarcely with time to take his seat. Fares are higher than on the buses, although many louages operate on routes that wouldn't be economical for bigger vehicles — and avoid the back bench seat if possible: it's uncomfortable.

Police checks. Throughout Tunisia, the *police de circulation* operates traffic checks, particularly on the roads around Medenine. All Tunisian drivers automatically pull into the verge whenever they see a policeman and though the checks are often cursory, on occasion the police will demand to see proof of identity of every passenger, which is a major frustration if you're one of 40 people on a bus.

The road network. Tunisia has 26,200 km of road, of which around 10,000 km is asphalted. The only motorway, the 63km stretch from Tunis to near Hammamet, is well maintained as are the other main routes from the capital to Bizerte, to Jendouba, to Kairouan and Tozeur, and the coast road through Sousse and Sfax to Gabès and the Libyan border.

Minor roads, such as the one from El Kef to Kasserine, quite often have a central tarred section large enough to take a lorry, and with wide verges of hard-packed red earth, the laterite so common in Africa. These verges are used when meeting or overtaking and the disturbed dust can reduce visibility to dangerous levels.

If you've a mind for more statistics, consider that Tunisia had 282,000 vehicles in 1982, divided equally between private cars and commercial vehicles.

BRING YOUR OWN CAR

If your length of stay makes this an economic option, check that your insurance can be extended to cover this part of the world. You'll also need to carry documents proving ownership of the vehicle. The car itself should have a thorough service before you set out, paying particular attention to tyres, suspension, ground clearance, door locks, steering and the cooling system. Fit yellow filters to your headlights but don't plan on driving by night; carry as many spares as possible, including fan belts, a foot pump and perhaps a spare tyre. And if the Sahara beckons, do your homework well in advance and come fully prepared.

TRAVELLING IN THE DESERT

We all know that the desert can kill, but it's amazing how quickly death can come to anybody who has not taken simple precautions. The lesson is: *never* go into the desert without planning every move, and letting somebody in authority know where you're going and when you expect to arrive.

This rule applies even if you're walking a mere hundred yards from one of the great oases; beyond the next dune and out of sight of civilization, you're on your own.

If you plan to drive south from Tataouine, even on the tarmac road to Remada, tell the Garde Nationale at either Médenine or Gabès of your plans and take their advice on the preparations and precautions necessary. And if you contemplate going on from Remada on the track towards Tunisia's southernmost tip or into the trackless dunes, plan the journey down to the last detail: take as many spare parts and as much water and petrol as your truck can carry — which rules out going by hire car.

Never travel alone, preferably have a convoy of at least two suitable vehicles, and if you have a breakdown, on no account set off across the desert on foot. The killer is not the heat nor the intense sunshine; it is dehydration.

Anybody seriously considering exploring the desert should read *Sahara Handbook* by Simon and Jan Glen (Lascelles, £18.95) which covers every aspect of desert lore from studying the wildlife to making emergency repairs on the truck and keeping alive.

FERRIES

Jerba. Tunisia's busiest ferry service links Jerba with the mainland at the tiny village of Jorf, with two diesel-powered vessels on an almost non-stop service. Departures from Jerba are at 0100, 0300, 0430, 0530, and then at every half-hour until 2030; again at 2130, 2230 and 2330.

Departures from the mainland slot into this timetable and the passenger fare is 500 mill. The ferry is busy as most of the traffic from the north and from Medenine uses it rather than take the longer route via Zarzis and the 7km causeway.

Kerkenah Isles. There are from two to five crossings a day each way between Sfax and the islands, the frequency depending on the season. The ferry can carry six cars or their equivalent and the 20km crossing takes a little more than an hour.

The ferry terminal at Sfax is near the Office Nationale des Pêches in the pleasure-craft basin (Bassin des Voiliers) and the service is run by Somvik, the Société pour la Mise en Valeur des Iles Kerkenah.

TOURIST EXCURSIONS

There is a wide range of organised excursions designed for visitors, usually bookable either through tour operators or the tourist hotels. The simplest excursion is probably a coach tour of Jerba for 5TD but this list looks at some of the more interesting possibilities, with 1987 prices quoted.

Kuriat Isles. These small isles lie 17km east of Monastir and hold little more than a lighthouse and the ruins of what are claimed to be the homes of Barbary pirates. The Sunday-only ferry service is purely for tourists to 'live like pirates for a day.' Reservations at local hotels or phone Monastir 60156; the all-inclusive fare is 10TD.

Tataouine and Chenini. From Jerba by Land-Rover and visiting the *ghorfas* of Medenine, the old Berber village of Chenini west of Tataouine, and the ruins of the Roman city of Gighti on the way back to the Jerba ferry. 20TD.

A *ghorfa* is a stone-walled grain silo around 5 metres high, its domed plaster roof moulded onto sacks of soil or sand which filled the silo during building. Few ghorfas now remain of the 6,000 or so in the Médenine area at independence. Chenini is difficult to reach as there is no public transport and the few taxis charge extortionate fares; an organised tour is the best way of seeing the village.

Tozeur and Nefta. Fly from Jerba to Tozeur, then explore this oasis and the one at Nefta by truck before crossing the Chott el Jerid for a night at Douz. Return via Matmata. 62TD.

Three-day Land-Rover safari. From Sousse, visiting El Jem, Gabès and Matmata; the second day takes you around Douz on a camel and then by truck across the Chott to Tozeur; the third day takes in the Roman ruins of Sbeïtla and the holy city of Kairona. 70TD.

One-week Land-Rover safari. Departing Jerba on Sunday or Gabès on Monday, this expedition goes via Gafsa and Tozeur to Nefta, exploring the oases, crossing the Chott to Kebili and Douz, then goes deep into the Grand Erg Oriental, the trackless sand-dune Sahara, before coming back to civilization at Chenini and Matmata. 150TD. Contact Saharatours, 5 Ave Farhat Hached, Gabès.

Cruises. Day cruises from Sousse to Monastir aboard a fishing vessel under sail (for 8TD) or motor (for 7TD). Two rival vessels, both berthed at Sousse port near the bus stand. Neither vessel lands at Monastir.

ACCOMMODATION

Luxury to budget

THE TOURIST EXPLOSION has led to the building of many large hotels and holiday villages since the early eighties, but there has been less activity among the better-class local hotels not tied in with tour operators. As a result, the independent traveller may occasionally find difficulty in renting a room in high season in the popular areas.

Away from the tourist circuit there is little problem though standards, like prices, are lower. But if all else fails, pray that somebody will offer you a bed in a private house; the Tunisians are so hospitable you won't have to pray for long.

Pension. The pension, a cross between a small hotel and a private house, is a concept that is slowly gaing ground in Tunisia though it still has a long way to go.

Self-catering. At the moment there are five self-catering establishments in the country: the Hammamet Residence, Residence Paradis and Residence Pyramides, and in Sousse the Nejma and the Maisons de la Mer. It would be a waste of time to look for your own self-catering flats on arrival; Tunisia isn't that sort of country.

Camping. Camping is a possibility provided you bring all your gear, including Camping Gaz cylinders (but not if you fly as they're forbidden aboard aircraft). The very few official camping sites are at Hammam-Lif, Hammamet, Nabeul, Gabès and Zarzis, but there are unofficial sites at Bizerte, Sousse, Sbeïtla, Tabarka and Tozeur. The fee is usually less than a dinar a night.

You may go 'camping sauvage,' pitching your tent on private land with the permssion of the owner, or on public land with the blessing of the Garde Nationale or the municipalité, the local council. Discretion is advisable and there should be at least one male in the party.

Caravanning. There are very few trailer or motorised caravans on the roads of Tunisia, but there is no reason why you shouldn't pioneer the idea — provided you plan to stay long enough to make the economics worthwhile. The caravanner won't find any organised sites but he'll have no problem in deciding where to pull up for the night.

Holiday villages. Club Méditerranée has virtually cornered the market with villages near Monastir, Korba and Tozeur, and two on Jerba.

Hotel costs. Tunisia has inherited the French complications in pricing hotel rooms by having up to three seasons and charging for extras.

High season (haute saison) is from 1 July to sometime in September; mid (moyenne) season is the remainder of September and October plus April, May and June. Low (basse) season is the remainder of the year, from 1 November to 31 March. The date for the change from high to mid season varies according to the locality.

Prices quoted are usually per person, not per room: watch for 'tarifs individuels d'herbergement' and add 50% for a double. Strangely, the cheaper the rate the more likely it is to be for the room, not per person, which makes the bargain hotels even more of a bargain for couples.

Taxes and service are always included, but watch for those supplements.

These sample prices from 1987 show the wide range available. **AY** is the all-year rate, **HS** is high season, **LS** is low season, **RO** is room only, **B&B** is bed and breakfast, **FB** is full board and **PR** is the price per double room; otherwise assume the price is per person.

JERBA

DAR JERBA 'A' **** 643 beds; LS B&B 25.000; HS B&B 35.000 (+ sgl supp 6000 YR)

SIDI SLIM ** 351 beds; LS FB 10.500; LS B&B 13.000 (+ sgl supp 6.000 YR)

TOURING CLUB unclass 160 beds; LS B&B 2.400; LS FB 6.600; HS B&B 3.800; HS FB 8.200 (+ bath supp .700)

LE KEF

HOTEL DE LA SOURCE unclass 20 beds; 6.000 RO PR YR

MAHDIA

JAZIRA unclass 24 beds; B&B YR 4.000

MATMATA

LES BERBERES (underground) unclass 80 beds; RO 2.000; FB 6.000 YR

MONASTIR

RUSPINA ** 502 beds; LS B&B 9.000; HS FB 20.000

MONDIAL ** 84 beds; LS B&B 8.100; HS FB 14.600

NABEUL

CLUB AQUARIUS ** 600 beds; HS FB 18.200 (+ sgl supp 4.000)

SFAX

MARZOUK ** 40 beds; B&B YR 6.500; FB YR 10.500

SOUSSE

HANNIBAL PALACE ****luxe 500 beds; LS FB 26.000; HS FB 41.000 (+ sgl supp 10.000 HS)

RESIDENCE FATIMA pension 18 beds; HS B*B 5.800 (+ sgl supp 2.000)

TOZEUR

OASIS *** 47 beds; B&B 16.000

ESSAADA unclass 35 beds; RO YR 3.600

TUNIS

AFRICA MERIDIEN ****luxe 302 beds; B&B YR 35.000; FB YR 52.000 (+ sgl supp 22.000)

INTERNATIONAL ****luxe; presidential suite 220.000 YR

RESIDENCE CARTHAGE ** 27 beds; LS B&B 9.000; HS FB 19.000 (+ sgl supp 3.500)

RITZA * 56 beds; PR YR 6.500

ESSAADA unclass RO YR 2.000 (sgl room); RO PR YR 3.000

RESIDENCE LA SIESTA unclass, bungalow of 2 dbl rooms, per month, LS 250.000

Fiche de Police Each time you register at a hotel, no mater how basic, you're required to fill in a questionnaire, the *fiche de police,* similar to the one in use in France years ago. You'll also be asked to show your passport as nobody seems to acknowledge the temporary identity card issued on your arrival.

DINING OUT

And nightlife

TUNISIA IS NOT A GASTRONOME'S PARADISE. Arab culture doesn't put much emphasis on the pleasures of eating out so the custom has developed purely as a result of being colonised by the French, who are among the world's greatest restauranteurs. Despite that, the best of Tunisian cuisine is as widely available in the tourist areas as are European dishes.

On the coast, a 'restaurant' is usually in the French image but inland, where it's also known as a *gargote*, it may offer a meat and veg dish that's been kept warm throughout the day, with consequent problems for delicate European digestive systems. The *rôtisserie* does more frying than roasting and its food is often greasy and spicy.

This is from a typical menu in a medium-class restaurant in the tourist fringe, with 1987 prices:

Soups:

Fish	1.000

Cold starters:

Tunis salad	.920
Mechouia salad	1.150
Octopus salad	1.150
Ham & butter	1.150

Hot starters:

Brik with prawns	1.550
Brik with tuna	.795
Omelette	.920
Cheese omelette	1.080
Ojja with prawns	1.550
Ojja with brains	1.080
Mixed ojja	1.320

Fish:

Grilled prawns	3.900
Prawns, sauce chasseur	4.600
Calamar (squid) & green pepper	2.645

Meat:

Veal cutlet	3.000
Lamb kebeb (sic)	2.250
Roast chicken	1.500

Sweet:

Melon & other fruits	1.500
Tunisian pastry	.920

Mechouia is a salad of tomatoes, peppers and onions, finely chopped and grilled, and seasoned with olive oil and lemon juice; it's often served with capers.

Ham and other pork cuts are available for Christians though Moslems consider it unclean meat. Wild boar (sanglier) hunted in the Atlas Mountains invariably end on the menu for foreigners.

Brik is a Tunisian favourite and well worth trying. It's a very thin pancake folded in half and fried with a variety of fillings, with egg the most popular. Brik à l'oeuf, like all briks, is eaten with the fingers and the challenge is to catch the egg before it catches you. Other briks contain minced lamb, chicken or fish.

Ojja is a dish of meat or veg with an egg or two broken over it, resulting in a wet omelette.

Couscous, which is cracked wheat or sometimes millet, steamed or boiled with a dash of turmeric, is the base to which meat, chicken, fish or vegetables, or a combination of them, may be added. I sat down to a meal in the Hôtel Les Berbères in Matmata with a travelling companion and we shared a bowl of couscous 15" (40cm) in diameter by 5" deep.

Tunisian cooking is much more spicy than European, and soups are among the spiciest. Chakchouka and tbikha are vegetable soups thickly laced with animal fat, while tajin is a mutton stew with egg, olive oil, cheese, root vegetables and occasionally some fish.

Among the sweets, baklawa (baklava) is a tasty pastry with honey and nuts, and makhroud is a semolina cake decorated with dates. Visitors who thrive on low-calorie, low-fat diets may prefer to live on bread and fresh fruit, which is perfectly feasible.

Bab Diwan, Sfax

Alcohol and other drinks. The national drink is green mint tea served boiling and laced with sugar, a taste which Europeans need time to aquire. Restaurants serve tea much weaker but still as sweet unless you specify *thé à l'anglaise* or *thé au lait* (tea with milk). Tunisian coffee, sold as a powder, is rough stuff, and Nescafé and its rival brands are scarce and expensive. You might consider taking your own.

There are numerous soft drinks on the market, notably Boga, available in several flavours though 'cidre' is not cider nor is it alcoholic; Pepsi and Coca-Cola are made under license.

Apla, an unfermented apple juice, is the most common of several brands of fruit juices, and among the mineral waters are Koutine, Safia, the carbonated Aïn Garci, Aïn Oktor and Melliti.

Alcohol is available, but access is restricted to the better class restaurants and hotels (though it's served in Matmata where no hotel warrants a star rating), and to the few licensed supermarkets. Locally-produced wine does not exceed 13% proof and is surprisingly cheap for a Moslem country, but some of it is rough. By contrast, imported spirits are prohibitively expensive.

Celtia beer, a light lager which some people don't like, is brewed under one license and sold under another, for 700 mill a small bottle.

Tunisia's strongest liqueur, boukha (pronounced boora), is distilled from figs and usually sold clear, though the producers on Jerba add colour and perfume. Thibar and thibarine are sweet brandies which have been fermented from local grapes since French monks introduced the method years ago, and sirop is a sticky-sweet liqueur produced from pomegranate or other fruits.

But if you want to try a truly unusual drink, look for lâghmi, the slightly sour sap of the date palm which the people of Jerba drink either straight from the tree or partly fermented.

NIGHTLIFE

The Tunisian version of nightlife outside Ramadan is a group of men in a soft-drinks bar, or a couple going to the cinema. Western style nightlife is confined to the tourist hotels and the avenues Habib Bourgiba in Sousse and Tunis.

Hotel activities concentrate on the predictable disco, bingo in up to three languages at once, Moorish dancing and the ever-popular belly dancing. If you don't like what your hotel has to offer, go and see what its rivals are doing.

Or go out on the town. For the eleven months of the year when it's *not* Ramadan, the choice is simple. In a short section of the Avenue H Bourgiba in Sousse you will find the entire after-dark activities — the unimposing Topkapi night club for drinks and belly-dancing; the Atlantik Pub (sic) next door for drinks on the pavement; the Big Mac Pizzeria and two or three decent restaurants. At eight o'clock everywhere is quiet, including the scant traffic, and by 9.30 everybody has gone home to bed.

ATTITUDES TO SEX

The macho image

TUNISIAN WOMEN WERE DECLARTED EQUAL to men in 1956, but many behave as if they've yet to hear the news. The laws of Islam, economic pressures, tradition, and the attitude of women themselves, are still barring the way to total equality.

Add to those factors the complications brought by the mixture of Berber, Arab, Moorish and European peoples in modern Tunisia, the Christian colonisation of a Moslem culture, the effects of Western television and European tourism, and the picture becomes extremely complicated.

For a start, the law states that women are men's equals in marriage, in divorce, in career opportunities, in education, in property ownership, and in the right to vote.

But the civil law is not all-powerful. For centuries Islam has persuaded men that they are the superior sex, and women have therefore grown up with an inbuilt inferiority which is next to impossible to dispel amid the older generation living remote from the tourist traffic.

If the wearing of the veil in any form is a symbol of submission, then a large minority of Tunisian women of all ages and classes — but excluding the Berbers — openly proclaim their subjugation. The *sifsari* is a creamy-white garment worn over the clothing, the bottom part caught in at the waist to form a second overskirt, the top part thrown over the head to leave the face exposed and then held tight by clenching it with the teeth and holding the ends across the chest with the hands.

The official line is that the sifsari is a protection against dust, but if that were so the men would scarcely have ignored its potential. In the desert areas the women wear a Lawrence-of-Arabia-style headcloth sometimes recognisable as a towel and drape the ends across their mouth only when necessary.

In Tozeur, by the Chott el Jerid, some women cover themselves completely with black cloth, leaving only their feet exposed. They peer through the thin-weave mesh but are totally unrecognisable to the rest of the world.

The burnous is perhaps an exception as its ornate embroidery and decoration make it a fashion garment and, draped as it is from head to ankle in one fall, it actually emphasises the beauty of the face, the only part of the female anatomy exposed to gaze.

The Berber women still follow the traditions of dress which they have maintained for centuries, draping themselves in a long woollen blanket which forms skirt and shawl but always leaves the face exposed. It's not unusual to see a Berber woman walking along the road with a baby at the breast, which further complicates the picture.

Polygamy was banned in 1960, but men who already had more than one wife, up to the maximum allocation of four, were allowed to retain them provided the women were properly maintained.

Habib Bourgiba's post-independence reforms also tried to banish arranged marriages, but even here age-old tradition has been reluctant to relinquish its grip.

Virginity was held in such esteem that as soon as the new husband was satisfied of his bride's purity, and had deprived her of it, he would ceremonially kick over an earthenware pot by the bedchamber door. If he stepped over the pot the bride's family were plunged into shame and might never receive the dowry.

Many things have changed rapidly since independence. In most cases the marriage partners choose themselves, but in rural communities it's still accepted that first cousins should wed to preserve family strength.

Yet certain things have scarcely changed at all. Women may have the right to job equality — you find them in banks, shops, offices, and even in the police — but when unemployment hits a town the women are the first to be dismissed. Women still don't patronise the pavement cafés with their menfolk; teenage girls don't join teenage lads on the streets, nor do you find them unchaperoned on buses or trains. It's as if all females go into purdah at puberty and emerge into public life only after marriage. But there are exceptions: see *The Personal Touch* on page 44.

Television and cinema have bombarded Tunisia with Western ideas on slack morality, but bare bosoms are still banned from public scrutiny: cinema posters have a dash of paint on the offending parts, Pirelli-type calendars aren't on public display, and pornographic magazines are black-market issue.

For European women, topless bathing is normal in tourist complexes and on beaches safe from the local gaze — at Club Méditerranée's locations on Jerba, for instance — but it is not permitted on beaches close to towns where the Tunisian way of life could be offended, as at Sousse. Yet the ban isn't always enforced and Tunisian youths on the promenade eye the visitors dressed in nothing but skimpy bikini bottoms while half a mile away their own womenfolk are shrouded in sifsaris.

I can't help feeling this inaccessibility of Tunisian women has a connection with male homosexuality which is openly on offer in any backstreet, whether or not you're looking for it.

Tanit. Tanit was the principal Punic goddess. Also known as Astarte, Ashtoreth in the Old Testament (1 Kings xi and 2 Kings xxiii), or Venus to the Greeks, she and her male counterpart Baal were the protectors of Carthage from the 5th cent BC. Her symbol was found on many Punic objects and is now used throughout Tunisia as motif on anything from key rings to tourist souvenirs.

FACTS AT YOUR FINGERTIPS

What, where and when?

AFFILIATIONS

Tunisia is a member of the United Nations Organisation, the Organisation of African Unity, the Islamic Conference and the Arab League. It has no connections with the EEC although it does levy Value Added Tax.

ARMED FORCES

There is selective conscription for one year for males on reaching their 20th birthday, with officer cadets being trained in France.

The Army has 30,000 men in two infantry brigades, two armoured reconnaissance units and three field units. It has 68 main battle tanks and 55 light tanks.

In addition there is the part-military Gendarmerie with 3,300 men and the Garde Nationale with 7,000; these troops supplement the normal police force and are most often seen manning the road checks.

The Navy has a frigate bought second-hand from the USA where it was built in 1944, three fast missile craft, two fast gunboats bought from China, two fast attack boats that were once in Britain's Royal Navy, and 21 other craft, crewed by 2,600 officers and ratings.

The 3,500 personnel in the Air Force fly and maintain one squadron of Italian-built light jet fighters, one of Tiger fighters, 12 piston-engined trainer aircraft, two Hercules transports, 15 other fixed-wing machines and around 24 helicopters.

BUSINESS HOURS

Banks: Business hours are not standardised. Banks are *always* open Monday to Friday (including Ramadan) 0800-1130 but for additions to this core time see 'banking hours' on page *xx*

Shops: No set times; reckon on 0800-1200 and 1600-1900 in summer (1 July to mid-September, but even *that* varies) and 0830-1230, 1500-1800 in winter. Smaller shops open from 0600 and stay open at midday but by 2000 every one will have closed. There's always the exception: the Magazin Général in Mahdia is open until 2130.

Post Offices: The PTT controls the postal and telephone services, usually from the same building. Postal counters are open in summer 0800-1300 Monday to Saturday; in winter 0800-1200 and 1500-1800 Mon to Fri and 0800-1200 on Sat, but in Ramadan the hours are 0800-1500 Monday to Saturday.

Telephone offices are open 0800-2200 Monday to Friday.

Museums: Hours are 0900-1630 daily, possibly excluding Monday, from 1 April to 30 September; 0900-1200 and 1400-1730 for the remainder of the year.

ELECTRICITY

Electricity is usually at 220v but parts of Tunis are on 110v. Power sockets take plugs with two round pins so Britons will need a continental adapter.

FESTIVALS

Ramadan by day is a serious affair with abstinence from everything that makes life worth living, but after dark there is feasting and gaiety and it is the only time when there is genuine nightlife as opposed to the imported European version. Cafés and restaurants in the larger towns stay open past midnight as people stock up for the next day's abstinence. Then comes the feast of Aïd es Seghir at the end of Ramadan and life returns to normal.

Other festivals throughout the year and the country are designed to promote industry or tourism but they are nonetheless worth seeing. Here are some of them:

January: International Sahara Festival, Douz.

April: Orange Festival, Menzel Bou Zelfa (Cape Bon); Folklore Festival, Nefta, including camel wrestling; folklore and sports festival, Nabeul; the Tataouine games.

May: Drama Festival in the Roman theatre, Dougga; Music Festival, Sfax.

June: Hunting Festival, El Haouaria, with falcons caught in April; Cérès Festival, El Fahs; Andalusian music festival, Testour; El Jem Festival in the amphitheatre; Music festivals at Tozeur and Kasserine.

July: Aïn Draham Cultural Festival; Mining Festival, Metlaoui; Weaving Trade Festival, Ksar Hellal; Music and Art festivals, Béja and Médenine; Festival of the Sirenes, Kerkenah Is.

July-August: International games or concerts at Carthage, Hammamet and Tabarca; Folk singing and parades, Sousse; The Bizerte Festival; International Folklore Festival, Monastir; Ulysses Festival, Houmt Souk, with songs and dances of Jerba.

August: Festival of the Wheat, Béja; Election of 'Miss Jerba,' Houmt Souk; Religious Festival, Sidi Bou Saïd.

September: Wine Festival, Grombalia; Festival of the Evacuation, Bizerte.

November: Film Festival, Carthage; Date Harvest Festival, Kebili.

December: Oasis Festival, Tozeur, with camel wrestling and carnival; Oasis Festival at Douz.

Islamic calendar: Festival of Mouled (birth of Mahomet), Kairouan.

GAS

Bottogas, Agipgas and Primagas are available in 13kg cylinders which are of no use to tourists. Small cylinders of Camping Gaz are not available.

GOVERNMENT

France occupied Tunisia in 1883 and created a protectorate which gradually became a colony. Tunisians increased their objection to French domination of the economy and Habib Bourgiba, born 3 August 1903 in Monastir, founded in 1934 the Néo Destour, the 'New Constitution' party with independence as its aim; 30 years later he renamed it the Parti Socialiste Destourien.

In September 1955 France conceded internal self-government and on 20 March 1956 Tunisia gained its longed-for independence, with Bourgiba elected as its first prime minister by the Constitutional Assembly which convened on 20 May 1956.

On 25 July 1957 the chamber, now called the National Assembly, abolished the monarchy and deposed the hereditary sovereign, the Bey of Tunis, electing Bourgiba to the position of first president. He was re-elected on 8 November 1959 and on that same date in 1964, by which time his PSD had been declared the only legal political party. In May of that year the Government had seized all foreign-owned land but the people resisted moves towards collectivisation.

Bourgiba was returned unopposed on 2 November 1969 and again in 1974. On 18 March 1975 he was declared President for Life, ignoring unrest that was growing among students and labourers. In January 1978 the Union Générale des Travailleurs Tunisiens (UGTT, the general workers' union) led by Habib Achour, called a 24-hour general strike. Achour was imprisoned for a year then held under house arrest for two years before going back to lead the UGTT.

Since 1981 other political parties have been allowed to emerge and contest the 125 seats in the single-chamber National Assembly, but the opposition boycotted the election of 2 November 1986 and candidates of the Front National, an alliance of the PSD and the UGTT, were again returned unopposed.

This led in early 1987 to an explosion in the grounds of the Sahara Beach Hotel in Monastir, injuring a British tourist, and in November of that year 84-year-old Bourgiba's luck was reversed when his 51-year-old prime minister General Zine el Abinine Ben Ali deposed him with a medical certificate signed by seven doctors declaring Bourgiba was no longer fit to govern.

It's now a matter of waiting to see how long Bourgiba's name and statues dominate the towns; his portraits have already vanished from most public buildings.

HOLY DAY and REST DAY

It bears repeating that Friday is the Moslem holy day but due to the influence of colonialism Tunisia holds Sunday as the official day of rest.

Ramadan, the Islamic holy month, is governed by the lunar calendar and moves backwards 11 days each non-leap year relative to the Christian calendar, thus Ramadan starts on 8 April in 1989, 29 March in 1990, and 18 March in 1991.

INDUSTRIES

Tunisia is mainly an agricultural country but there are some surprising industrial ventures. Monastir is now well-known for its contribution to movie-making while Ksar Hellal, a few kilometres south-east, is the centre of a textile industry that makes denim for export to Europe and the USA where it's made into jeans.   The country's oil wells yielded 5½m tons of crude in 1986 from drillings near Sfax, Sbeïtla, and in the Grand Erg near the Algerian border. Most of it was piped to a terminal north of Gabès for export, or for shipment to Bizerte's refinery. Around 4,000,000,000 cubic metres of natural gas is extracted each year, with known reserves until the year 2020.

Five million tons of phosphates are dug each year from mines around Metlaoui and moved by rail, and there are lesser amounts of iron, lead and zinc ores.

Fifteen million hectares of land produce in an average year 1.4m tons of wheat, 700,000 tons of barley, 480,000 of olives and 420,000 of chili peppers. This hot and dry land also grows 230,000 tons of watermelons, 150,000 of potatoes, and the same amount of sugar beet which is refined at Béja. The yield of oranges is slightly less, and there are a mere 6,000 tons of dates.

Cape Bon specialises in growing citrus fruits, particularly tangerines, with olives in vast plantations around Sfax and Gabès, while the dates are concentrated in the main oases of Tozeur and Nefta.

There are 5.2m sheep, almost 1m goats, 620,000 cattle but only 180,000 camels. There are also 55,000 horses and 75,000 mules, and in a Moslem land where pork is tabu there are 4,000 pigs.

NEWSPAPERS

European newspapers are available in Tunis and the main tourist towns the day after publication. There are two Arabic and four French daily papers published from Tunis.

POLICE

The normal *police* wear blue-grey uniforms with leather belts and grey-white caps and their role is the same as police anywhere else. Those who put on white cuffs and caps are in the *police de circulation*, the traffic cops.

The *gendarmerie* wear khaki uniforms and white caps and are more concerned with state security. Both forces are armed with pistols in hip holsters.

In my experience the police are friendly and only once questioned me (detailed later) though I walked the streets with cameras around my neck and notebook in hand. I would unreservedly recommend you ask their help whenever it's needed.

POPULATION

Tunisia faces an uncontrollable population explosion. The 1975 census showed 5,572,193 people which had risen by 1,403,257 in just nine years; the 1985 estimate was 7,250,000 of whom 55% had yet to see their 20th birthday. The average density of population in 1985 was 44.4 per sq km — but half the land is uninhabitable.

The ten largest towns in 1984 (with figures in thousands) were Tunis (597); Sfax (232); Ariana, a suburb of Tunis (99); Bizerte (95); Jerba Island (92); Gabès (92); Sousse (84); Kairouan (72); Bardo (65) and La Goulette (61), both suburbs of Tunis.

Unemployment is high but the actual figure is a state secret.

POSTS AND TELEPHONES

The PTT, *Poste, Téléphone, Télégraph*, runs the postal and telephone service with an imposing building in each town. The postal side of the business is efficient and, at 300 mill for a letter to Europe (250 mill to France), is also cheap. Letters arrive within five or six days. Major hotels and some tobacconists — tabacs — also sell stamps.

International telephone calls must be made either through your hotel, which charges a premium, or from a special cubicle in the PTT. Using a silver payphone dial 00 for the international line, followed by your country code, the area code (less any initial zero), and the local number. Dialling tones are as in Britain and you get back any unspent coins, but the machine neither gives change nor accepts British 10p pieces, no matter that they look like dinar coins.

The *annuaire* (directory) covers the country in one volume, with some small communities having less than ten subscribers.

International codes vary slightly from one country to another; these apply in Tunisia:

Canada	1
Belgium	32
Denmark	45
Germany (West)	37
Netherlands	31
Norway	47
Sweden	46
Switzerland	41
UK	44
USA	1

PTT phone offices are usually open from 0800 to 2200 Monday to Friday, but there are the inevitable exceptions such as Médenine (0800-1230 Mon-Thurs and 0800-1300 Fri and Sat), and many tourist hotels are reluctant to allow non-guests to use the phone, particularly at weekends. There is no cheap rate.

PUBLIC HOLIDAYS

These are complicated as they involve two calendars. Those on the Gregorian calendar never vary as Easter, the most movable Christian feast, is not celebrated. Those marked with an asterisk (*) are in the Islamic calendar which moves backwards 11 days each year (except leap year), thus putting the Islamic New Year on 14 August 1988, 4 August 1989, 24 July 1990 and 13 July 1991. Dates so marked are true for 1989.

January	1	Gregorian New Year
March	20	Independence Day
	21	Youth Day
April	8*	Beginning of Ramadan
	9	Martyrs' Day
May	1	Labour Day
	8-9*	End of Ramadan (Aïd es Seghir)
July	15-16*	Feast of the Sacrifice (Aïd el Kebir)
	25	Republic Day
	4*	Islamic New Year (Ras El Am Hejri)
	13	Women's Day
October	14*	Birth of the Prophet (Mouled an-Nabi)

Five public holidays were dropped shortly after Habib Bourgiba's downfall, including his birthday (3 August), the anniversary of the founding of his Néo-Destour Party (3 September) and the evacuation of Bizerte (15 October). Youth Day was moved from 2 June to March.

PUBLIC LAVATORIES

There are very few public toilets in the country. Those at the main airports are smart and spotless but they're also the exception.

You will find toilets on all trains except the electric TGM from Tunis to La Marsa; they *are* on the short-run trains between Sousse and Monastir. Use the public conveniences in the larger bus and railway stations only in an emergency.

There are occasional unisex toilets in the towns but as they're never signposted you must rely on eye or nose to locate them; then the doors seldom lock and there is never any paper. The toilet in the Kasbah at Hammamet is unusual in having a cubicle for women, but with access through the men's urinal.

Official advice for any foreigner wanting a lavatory is to ask at a bar, restaurant or hotel, but this doesn't often work unless you're already a customer. The practical answer is to carry toilet paper at all times and to find a derelict building when nature calls.

RADIO and TELEVISION

French radio stations, particularly Radio Monte Carlo, give good reception in the north of Tunisia and the BBC World Service is available on 15.07 MHz or 19.91M.

Tunisia's own radio station has two national networks broadcasting news and current affairs in French and Arabic from 0600 to midnight, backed up by local stations in Sfax and Monastir.

There are two national television channels transmitting in colour from around 1800 to midnight; Chaîne 2 opens with the chimes of Big Ben and offers English lessons on Saturday. Italian television can be picked up in the north but reception is often poor...but there's always Algerian TV.

RESIDENCE and BUYING PROPERTY

Provided you can support yourself financially without taking up employment, there are no restrictions on becoming a permanent resident of Tunisia; state your case to the local gouvernorat (council) but don't expect to receive a work permit.

The only property which is likely interest European buyers is around the Cap Monastir Marina; if this is for you, transfer your money through recognised channels and you'll then be able to export it, with profits, when you sell. You can also expatriate any income from rents.

TELEPHONES — see 'Posts and Telephones'

TIME

Tunisia is GMT+1. The country adopts summer time, altering its clocks when the western Europeans — but not the British — alter theirs.

TOURIST OFFICES

The Office National du Tourism Tunisien has branches in all towns on the tourist circuit. In other places the local people have provided a Syndicat d'Initiative modelled on the French style, and in several towns you have both the ONTT and the SI.

WATER

Tap water is safe to drink anywhere in the country, but in the wetter north it is chlorinated, sometimes so much that it is unpalatable. South of Gafsa the water is perfect.

There are few street taps; if you plan to spend a day seeing the sights, drink as much as possible before setting out (but remember the toilet problem) and take a supply from the hotel unless you prefer to buy mineral waters. You may be able to fill up a bottle at railway, bus and some petrol stations, but not at mosques where the ablutions tap is seldom accessible.

WEATHER

In short, it's hot!

This table gives *average* temperatures in Celcius and Fahrenheit as an indication of what to expect:

	JAN	APR	JUL	OCT
TUNIS	11/52	16/61	26/79	20/69
HAMMAMET	11/52	16/61	25/77	21/70
SOUSSE	11/52	16/61	26/78	21/71
JERBA	12/54	18/65	27/80	23/74
TOZEUR	12/53	20/68	32/90	22/72

Concentrating on Monastir, this table shows *maximum* temperatures throughout the year, in degrees Celcius (first figure/) and the *average* daily sunshine hours (/second figure):

January	16/7	February	17/8	March	19/8
April	20/9	May	23/11	June	28/11
July	30/12	August	31/11	September	29/9
October	25/8	November	21/7	December	18/6

Sea temperatures vary little along the coast; these are the average figures for Hammamet in degrees Celcius:

January	14.5	February	14	March	13.5
April	15.5	May	18	June	20.5
July	23.5	August	25	September	23.5
October	21.5	November	19	December	15.5

WILDLIFE

The most important wildlife habitat in the country is Lake Ichkeul, on the north coast west of Menzel Bourgiba. Ichkeul is a freshwater lake in winter and spring, fed by rains in the mountains, but it becomes saline in summer and autumn as seawater drains back from the Bizerte basin to replace liquid lost by evaporation.

Alternating between 50 and 70 square miles (130 and 180 sq km), the lake is the world's only wetland recognised by three conservation societies and it is as vital to migratory birds as the Coto Doñana in Spain and the Camargue in France. Up to 150,000 birds overwinter here, including heron, egret and flamingo, teal and shoveller, pintail, redshank and godwit, coot and duck, stint and stilt. Its resident and breeding populations include the rare gallinule and, on the hills to the south, the lanner falcon and Egyptian vulture.

Elsewhere, birdwatchers can spot hoopoe in the olive groves, pelican,

Cap Blanc really is white

egret and flamingo on the shores of the Gulf of Gabès, and each autumn evening vast flocks of small birds coming in to roost in the trees lining streets in Sfax and other towns.

In the Atlas Mountains, which in Tunisia are hills, there are hyena, fox and jackal — and the wild boar is still persecuted by the huntsman.

Sadly, cats appear to be the most visible form of mammalian wildlife. In every town there is a population of feral cats which are the descendants of the strays of byegone generations. There's no need to warn you not to fuss them; they'll not let you get within yards.

WHAT YOU WON'T LIKE

Nowhere is perfect. My grumbles with Tunisia centred on beggars, almost always children and quite often well-dressed and obviously not in need. "Donne-moi un bonbon, un stylo, un dinar," is the wail and sometimes the child is astounded when he gets a sweet or a ball-point pen. But one poorly dresed boy in Carthage would not relent even with two stylos and I was relieved when he transferred his attentions to another tourist.

A man travelling alone will inevitably have a homosexual approach; I found that a slightly shocked refusal did the trick.

The Tunisians are friendly towards other people, but their attitude to wildlife and conservation is sorely behind the times, as you will observe from the many stray cats. Tunny are slaughtered off Cape Bon, migrating birds are shot or caught by falcons, and hunting is encouraged in the cork woods by Aïn Draham when most other African countries are banning the gun. There are sanctuaries for seals in the Galite Islands and for migrating wading birds at Lake Ichkeul, but there is scope for much more, particularly as Tunisia is on the central Mediterranean flyway.

THE PERSONAL TOUCH

Marriage...and the law.

IT WAS DUSK. I had been in Tunis city for half an hour, just long enough to find a hotel in the Medina, leave my luggage and set out on foot with cameras and flash, when two teenage girls walked beside me in the street.

"You take our photograph?" they asked in French.

"What would I do with it?"

They shrugged; it made sense. Then one touched me on the arm. "We're going to a wedding. Would you like to come?"

I was surprised. This was nothing like the conduct I had been led to expect from Moslem girls who were already addressing me in the familiar 'tu.' "Yes," I said. "I would. Whose wedding — yours?"

"A cousin. We're all going now to have our hair done — come with us and meet mother."

I followed them to a hairdressing salon and waited outside while they rushed in excitedly. Several moments later a stout middle-aged woman with strong European ancestry came to the door and asked me what I wanted. I gave her the story so far and said I'd go away if I was an embarrassment.

"No. You're welcome," she answered, and tried to repeat it in English. "The reception is at nine o'clock tonight (Monday) in the Salle de Mariages, Avenue de Madrid."

I promised to be there, with camera and flash, but I miscalculated the walking distance and arrived 20 minutes late. Daughters blushed slightly when they saw me but mother urged me to take a seat. I looked around at the community hall, taking in the 200 chairs, the elegant chandeliers, the five-piece band playing music midway between Western pop and Arab, and the elegant double throne where I presumed the newly-weds would soon be seated.

An hour passed. The seats gradually filled and people were standing around the walls, the men with glasses of soft drink from the bar in the outer hall.

I watched the women guests in particular. In this capital city only two paid any deference to Islamic custom by wearing simple veils, but they left their faces exposed. All the other women wore European-style dresses, liberally sprinkled with sequins. Several had off-one-shoulder costumes, one wore an off-both-shoulders dress, and a well-endowed matron had a very revealing neckline.

At half past ten the newlyweds arrived by car. The crowd clapped and whistled as the bride, in a white gown with off-the-face veil, walked beside her husband towards the twin thrones. The band was scarcely audible above the cheering as the couple took their seats and slipped their wedding rings off so they could put them on again for the benefit of the video camera.

By quarter to eleven I had managed to say farewell to my new friends,

Wedding in Tunis

and I set off on foot for my hotel in the Medina, all too aware of the valuable camera gear around my neck.

Was Tunis a violent city by night? I might soon know the answer. I walked past the Medina police station, paused to check my map, and strode on. Five minutes later, with my hotel barely 100 yards away, I heard footsteps behind me. Running footsteps.

I balled my fists ready and at the last moment put my back to the wall and faced my pursuers, two men in smart city suits.

"Police," one of them said, showing his warrant card. "Where are you going?"

When I'd shown them my passport, told they why I was in that spot with a camera, and named my hotel, they relaxed.

"Am I at much risk of being robbed?" I asked.

"The danger is there, as in any city. Go carefully, and don't walk the Medina so late at night on your own."

A few mornings later I was striding out towards the Tunis Nord bus station, one camera slung around my neck, when a burly man in his thirties flashed his police warrant card at me. "Photography not permitted around here," he told me and watched me put the camera away.

"Why not?" I wanted to know. "It is not illegal. And are there many plainclothes police in Tunisia?"

"Very few," he conceded. "This happens to be my patch; I'm looking for pickpockets, and a camera puts them on guard."

"Pickpockets? You get many?"

He nodded. "Around 20 a week, just in this little spot. They're mostly Iranians who've fled the Ayatollah and have run out of money. But where did you say you're going? Gare routière? I'll show you the way."

DISCOVER TUNISIA
THE TOURIST CIRCUIT:
CAP BON

Hammamet and the Cape.

HAMMAMET

Hammamet was the original showpiece resort of Tunisia and is now the biggest and most popular sunworshipping spot on the entire north African coast. Its hotels are among the smartest you will find between Tanger and Tel Aviv and the best of them, set in their own palm-studded grounds, offer every comfort you could wish for — or pay for.

It is a picturesque, well-kept and clean town of low-rise white buildings fronting onto a south-facing sun-trap beach protected by a small headland that's crowned by an ancient kasbah. But Hammamet is not typical Tunisia; it is a fragment of jet-set western culture set down on the coast of Africa, an island of near-naked Christians in an ocean of Moslem modesty — and it all began in the 1920s when the Rumanian millionaire Georges Sébastian asked the American architect Frank Lloyd Wright to build him the most luxurious house he could design, two km west of town at the head of the bay.

Sébastian's friends followed: André Gide, Paul Klee, Georges Bernados, and they brought their friends Flaubert, Maupassant, Oscar Wilde, Sacheverell Sitwell and even Winston Churchill. During the war the house had unwelcome lodgers when Reichsmarschall Rommel made it his headquarters, though he spent only three nights there.

With the return of peace Hammamet again became the playground of the western world, its newer visitors including François Sagan and Sophia Loren. The government bought Sébastian's house in 1959 and by 1964 had converted it into the International Cultural Centre, adding a theatre which is now the home of the Hammamet Festival of Art each July-August.

Pupput. The name Hammamet may remind you of the hammam or so-called Turkish bath, but the town takes its identity from the word for 'columns,' seen in earlier architecture. There is no connection at all between the original lemon-growing village of Hammamet and the ancient city of Pupput, whose ruins were discovered during the hotel building boom of the sixties; you can see some of those remains beside the Hotel Samira on the way out to Sousse, but the more interesting artefacts are in Tunis's Bardo Museum.

Hammamet has little to offer beyond the beach, the most obvious attraction being the 15th-cent Kasbah on 12th-cent foundations. It looks, and indeed it is, an impressive mass of stonework protecting the town centre, but all its historic associations, including its recent use as barracks for the Foreign Legion, have been swept clean to make way for a tourist souk. It's open 0800-2000 daily, for 500 mill.

The 15th-cent Grand Mosque, restored in 1972, has an interesting original minaret, and the old Mosque of Sidi Abdel Kader beside it is now a Koranic school.

Museum of the Ram. Part of the Kasbah houses the unusual Museum of the Ram, *le bélier*. The first room has three stuffed rams and plaster effigies showing rams in mythology, the third room, a long gallery, holds more plasters. The second explains that the collection was 17 years in the gathering but nowhere did I see an explanation: why a museum of rams at all?

Future plans. Abu Dhabi has agreed to provide between 40 and 50 million dinars to build a pleasure port and a further 3,000 hotel rooms in Hammamet by the end of 1989.

Verdict. The sheltered beach with its fine sand makes Hammamet ideal for young children. Teenagers are not so well catered for as they're too old for the organised sports and too young for most discos. The nightlife, if you choose the right hotel, can make it a perfect holiday spot for the late teens and twenties, but if you want to see the real Tunisia Hammamet will be a disappointment.

HOTELS: 4-star luxe: El Manar, 400b; Sinbad, 160r; **4-star:** Abou Nawas, 222r; Palm Beach 406b; Phénicia, 370r; Sheraton, 410b; **3-star:** Bel Azur, 578b; Continental, 178r; Dar Khayam, 230r; El Fell 410b; Fourati, 340r; Grand, 123r; Hammamet, 210r; Hammamet Beach, 514b; Kerkouane, 100b; Miramar, 158r; Le Président, 200r; Les Colombes, 486b; Les Orangers, 228r; Le Sultan, 252r; Nozha Beach, 172r; Paradis, 206r; Park Plage, 398b; Yasmina, 96r; **2-star:** Aladin 62r; Du Golfe, 120r; El Bousten, 424r; Garsaa, 60b; Le Pacha, 308b; Les Cyprès, 35r; Méditerranée, 448b; Olympia, 24r; Sahib, 210b; Saphir, 450b; Sultan, 252r; Tanfous, 225r; Tanit, 290r; **1-star:** Alya, 60b; Benilla, 64b; Hamilton House, 16r; Samaris, 17r.

APART HOTEL: Résidence Hammamet, 184r.

Budget-conscious independent travellers will find the cheaper hotels nearer the town centre, which is also more convenient for public transport. Package tourists opting for larger hotels may find themselves several kilometers from town, with taxis the only practical way to travel.

HOLIDAY VILLAGES: Baie de Soleil, 550b; Beau Rivage, 182r; Médina-Samira Club, 500r in bungalows; Omar Khayam, 242r.

CAMPING: Ideal Camping, near town centre; also try the Samaris Hotel for camping in the grounds.

RESTAURANTS: All the larger hotels have their own restaurants but there are several good places in the town centre; La Pergola, Les Trois Moutons, Le Berbère.

BUSES: SNT has 2 buses daily to and from Tunis; SRT has frequent serices to Nabeul; the bus station is on the beach beside the Kasbah.

LOUAGES: None. Nearest are at Nabeul.

RAIL: Station is inland at end of Ave Bourgiba; most services entail change at Bir Bou Rekba. See sample timetable.

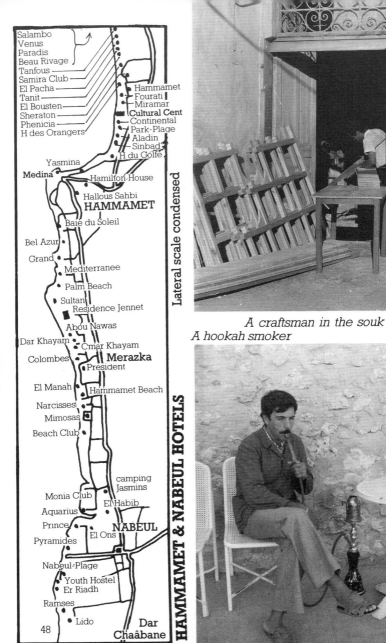

Salambo
Venus
Paradis
Beau Rivage
Tanfous
Samira Club
El Pacha
Tanit
El Bousten
Sheraton
Phenicia
H des Orangers

Hammamet
Fourati
Miramar
Cultural Cent
Continental
Park-Plage
Aladin
Sinbad
H du Golfe

Yasmina
Medina
Hamilton House

Hallous Sahbi
HAMMAMET

Baie du Soleil

Bel Azur
Grand
Mediterranee
Palm Beach
Sultan
Residence Jennet
Abou Nawas
Dar Khayam
Cmar Khayam
Colombes
Merazka
President
El Manah
Hammamet Beach
Narcisses
Mimosas
Beach Club

camping
Jasmins
Monia Club
El Habib
Aquarius
Prince
NABEUL
El Ons
Pyramides

Nabeul-Plage
Youth Hostel
Er Riadh
Ramses
Lido
Dar
Chaâbane

48

Lateral scale condensed

HAMMAMET & NABEUL HOTELS

A craftsman in the souk
A hookah smoker

MARKET DAY: Thursday.

FESTIVALS: International Festival of Art, and carnival, both end of July.

TOURIST OFFICE: SI: Ave de la République.

NABEUL

Nabeul is at the eastern end of the string of hotels running from the other side of Hammamet, but the town is completely different from its neighbour. Tourism is a thriving industry, but it's an extra to the traditional industries which have been practised for centuries.

In ancient times the town was second in importance to Carthage, and the Athenian statesman Thucydides, born around 450BC, spoke of an emporium at Neapolis. The town lost its importance during the third Punic War (149BC) after which Rome made it a satellite city. Eventually it became a colony, Colonia Julia Neapolis, from which comes its present name of Nabeul.

A Christian community was established here in the 3rd cent and survived with its Jewish neighbours until the arrival of Islam in the 7th cent, then Nabeul almost vanished from history until a mention in the 12th cent of the 'abandoned ruin of a great Roman city.' The only visible traces of this old city today are at the western end of town by the Jasmin Motel on Ave Habib Thameur.

Pottery. Neapolis may have died, but new Nabeul continues the Roman tradition of pottery-making, an industry which is taking full advantage of tourism. Traditional ware was glazed green or yellow with metallic oxides, and some artisans produced porous earthenware — chawat — suitable for plant containers, but the modern potter, using kaolin from the Khroumirie (the region around Aïn Draham) and French synthetic colours, makes a wide range of wares. Local clay is still used for the red bricks which are fired overnight in kilns on the edge of town.

Perfumes. The modern town has revitalised the other ancient crafts of masonry, perfume manufacture, embroidery and weaving. Much of the intricate stonework seen on buildings in north-east Tunisia was carved here or at the nearby village of Dar Chaâbane, featuring geometric patterns in deference to the Moslem abhorrence of carving images of living creatures. The perfumiers make good use of the orange and jasmine blossoms which add a fragrance to the air in spring, and the weavers in the nearby village of Beni Khiar use the local wool.

Happily, the ancient craft of making garum has now ceased. Garum, a sauce which the Romans put on meat, veg and even their fruit, was made from the guts of large fish and the complete bodies of small fish, salted, and left to mature in the sun.

The town has several modern attractions including the Archaeological Museum on Ave Bourgiba, which holds numerous artefacts from Neapolis to the coming of Islam. On the north of Ave Farhat Hached, behind the souk's arcades (restored in 1969) is the Bourgiba Mosque, restored in 1967 with the help of American members of the Peace Corps.

Market. The other attraction is the Friday market further along Ave Hached, now spoilt for the tourist by the presence of so many other tourists.

Nabeul also has an excellent beach and water sports, but the hotels and restaurants are gradually closing in.

HOTELS: 3-star: Aldiana Club, 220r; Er Riadh, 195r; Les Pyramides, 860b; Lido, 974b: Nabeul Plage, 278r; **2-star:** Aquarius Club, 297r; Ramses Club, 180r; **1-star:** Jasmins, 40r.

PENSIONS: There are several pensions springing up in the town centre, including: El Habib, 28b; Layali El Ouns, 58b; Les Hafsides, 16b; Les Oliviers, 30b; Les Roses, 18b; Monia Club 32b.

APART HOTEL: Résidence Les Pyramides, 258b.

HOLIDAY VILLAGES: Les Mimosas, 100b; Lido-Résidence, 256 bungalows; Maamoura Beach Club, 330r.

YOUTH HOSTEL: Beside Hotel Riadh; 56b.

CAMPING: Enquire at Jasmins Hotel.

BUSES: SNT has two buses daily to Tunis; SRT has frequent services to Hammamet; bus station on Ave Farhat Hached. Other bus services for Cap Bon area leave from separate bus station; see map.

LOUAGES: From back-alley near town centre.

RAIL: Two direct trains daily to Tunis and 9 to Hammamet; all other services change at Bir Bou Rekba.

MARKET: Friday.

FESTIVALS: Fête des Orangers, April; Summer Festival, August.

CAP BON VILLAGES

Nabeul is the best place to start if you're visiting Cap Bon by public transport. Windbreaks of prickly pear, known here as the figuier de Barbarie (Barbary fig), line the road protecting the fertile land from the saltpans along the coast to **Korba,** which was the old Curubis of Roman times. All that remain today are a few cisterns and part of the aqueduct, and the town of 32,000 people is better known for its Club Méditerranée, open from late May to September.

The fishing port of **Kelibia,** which is famed for its dry muscat wine, began life as the Phoenician Clupea. Destroyed by Scipio in 146BC and rebuilt, it was sacked three times by Spaniards between 1535 and 1547 in an attempt to put down the Barbary pirates. There's little evidence of this today, but you might appreciate the ruins of a large 4th-cent temple and Roman villa down by the port.

The port is one of Tunisia's best natural harbours and is a base for fishermen who land sardines and anchovies; nearby there's the national school of fishing, overshadowd like all else by the great walled fortress

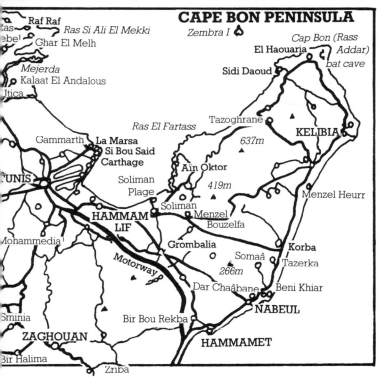

CAPE BON PENINSULA

standing on the hilltop behind.

Built in the 6th cent by the Byzantines, the fortress has been restored many times, the latest in 1978. In the part open to the public you can begin to appreciate the defensive works incorporated with each restoration, for this was the last stronghold of the Byzantines, and therefore of Christendom, against the advance of Islam; the Berbers later strengthened it in fear of reprisal raids from the Christians.

To the north of Kelibia lies **Kerkouane,** a town founded around 5th cent BC, abandoned at the end of the third Punic War and never reoccupied. Its existence was unknown until 1952 but, now excavated (and open daily except Monday), it reveals a small community of identical houses each with its own private bath, unlike the public baths the Romans preferred. A necropolis, discovered nearby in 1968, has yielded the largest wooden Punic statue yet found — that of a woman.

Cap Bon itself is dominated by the hump of **Jebel Sidi Aboid,** 393m high, from where you can see Sicily on a fine day. The cape is on an important bird migration route and is therefore ideal hunting territory for the resident falcons whose nests have been raided in early April for centuries; the young are trained to bring down partridge for the May festival and are then released...usually.

El Haouaria, lying to the west of the jebel, is noted for its two distinct caves. The Carthaginian quarries of **Ghar El Kebir** (Grand Cave) down on the shoreline produced hard building stone; the Romans added some barracks here in order — so the story goes — to keep the slave-miners under control, but there's no evidence to support the story that the caves later became a prison.

The cliffs here are jagged and waterworn, catching the fury of winter storms, making the seas a graveyard for shipping and a possible site for underwater archaeology some day.

The other cave is the **Grotte des Chauves-souris,** a vast cavern up on the mountainside where bats hang in their thousands. You may need a guide and you'll certainly need a good torch.

And if you come down to sea level again at Ras Addar, the northern tip of Cap Bon, you'll see on your left the sheltered white sands of **Rass Ed Dreck,** one of the most secluded and possibly the most scenic of beaches in Tunisia.

Twenty km to the north-west lies the gaunt **Ile de Zembra,** its vertical cliffs rising 432m from the sea. The only landing-place is at a small cleft on the south coast which gives access to the holiday village and sailing school which, incredibly, the Centre Nautique International has built here.

From late May to early July **Sidi Daoud** goes into the tunny-catching business. Fishermen fix the madrague, a vast net, off the Rass El Ahmer headland for the season, stretching from the surface to the sea bed 30m down and several miles wide. It funnels the migrating tuna into progressively smaller chambers ultimately leading to the final death chamber, a sturdy net cage at journey's end. When this is full, with fish up to 250kg, the fishermen put to sea early in the morning, haul the catch to the surface, then jump onto the seething mass for the matanza, the ritual slaughter with knives and cudgels.

Until recently tourists could get written authority to go out in accompanying boats and watch the carnage, but the Office National des Pêches is having second thoughts on the matter.

This north coast of the Cap Bon peninsula is much more scenic than the flat south side, and the road soon winds around the base of a rugged hill rising to 602m at Jebel Sidi Abd Er Rahmane several miles inland. At the tiny village of Bir Meroua a 6km side track leads off to the spectacular but utterly isolated beach of **Marsa Ben Ramdam,** guarded by an old fort.

The more interesting and newer road from Bir Meroua swings seaward around the spectacular crags of Jebel Korbous (419m), but this is not the route taken by public transport. A few kilometers along at **Aïn Atrous** — Billy-goat's Spring — there's a rock outcrop close to the sea with curative and purging waters gushing from its base at a constant 50°C.

This is the first of several such thermal springs; 2km along the road is **Aïn Sebia**, the Spring of the Virgin, whose waters are reputed to taste like diluted spinach juice. In nearby **Korbous** is **Aïn Chefa** with the reputation of being able to cure rheumatism and stomach upsets, probably even those resulting from a visit to Aïn Sebia.

Aïn Araga, the 'Spring That Makes You Sweat,' is in an unlit subteranean tepidarium — call it a Turkish bath — that has been in use since Roman times. It's open to men in the mornings, women in the afternoons, and is claimed to cure obesity, arthritis and sterility, although infertile women

The capitol at Dougga (ONTT)

have long been seeking an alternative remedy by sliding down the highly-polished Zerziha Rock 'in an appropriate posture.'

The white buildings of Korbous at the bottom of its narrow ravine mark the site of Aquae Calidae Carpitanae, where wealthy Romans from Carthage came by boat to sample the healing waters. The outside world forgot the village for generations until in the 19th cent Ahmed Bey, the monarch of Tunisia, built a small pavilion high up the slope near the Zerziha Rock. In 1901 the pavilion became a thermal clinic using the 55°C waters of Aïn El Kebira, the 'Great Spring.'

The French architect Lecore Carpentier who designed modern Korbous built himself a villa in an even more precarious site than the bey's pavilion but with the coming of the republic this has become a presidential palace, though little used because Bourgiba preferred Monastir.

The last important thermal spring is at **Aïn Oktor** to the south of Korbous. Beside an expensive hotel catering for people taking the cure stands an ugly building where you can sample the Oktor waters free — or you can go to the nearby workshop and buy one of the 10,000 bottles filled each year with Aïn Oktor water from any of its eight local springs.

For years **Sidi Raïs** has been a forgotten resort of houses on stilts. In the early 80s developers looked at the possibility of building a vast hotel complex here with a suggested 12,000 beds. The project is now likely to begin in the early 1990s but to help with publicity the local stretch of beach has already been renamed the Tunisian Costa del Sol, the Côte du Soleil.

The last town on the cape is a strange place. **Soliman** was founded around 1600 by a Turk called Suleiman; it was seized in the 17th cent by Spaniards from Andalucía under whom it prospered for 200 years until hit by bubonic plague which reduced its population from 20,000 to 4,000. It was blitzed in 1943 but has now increased its numbers to 15,000 and gone in for the production of olives and other fruit.

Soliman's main mosque is also strange; built in the 17th cent by the supposedly Christian Spaniards, its square minaret (signifying it serves the mainstream Malekite sect of Islam) is topped by an unusual roof of semicircular tiles. The town's other mosque, completely rebuilt after the 1943 bombardment, has the octagonal minarets of the Hanefite sect, descendants of Turkish settlers. Both sects belong to the Sunni faction, not the Shi'ite prevalent in Iran.

A side roads leads to Soliman Plage which has two hotels and a good beach but little else of interest.

The village of **Grombalia** on the main Tunis highway is the centre of the Tunisian wine industry and in Sepember comes to life with the Fête des Vendages, the Festival of the Grape Harvest, which has been attracting visitors since 1956.

HOTELS: El Haouaria: unclass Épervier ('Sparrowhawk'), 22b; **Kelibia:** 1-star Florida, 13r; unclass El Nassim, 30r; **Korbous:** 3-star Aïn Oktor, 27r; Les Sources; 2-star La Clinique, 28r; **Menzel Temime:** 1-star Temime, 88b; **Soliman:** 1-star Sol y Mar, 200r; El Andalous, 135r, both on Soliman Plage; unclass Chiraz, 16r.

HOLIDAY VILLAGES: Kelibia: Mamounia, 86r; El Mansourah, 232b; **Korba:** Club Méditerranée.

YOUTH HOSTELS: Kelibia, 40b; Menzel Temime, 50b.

CAMPING: By El Haouraria beach.

MARKETS: Sunday, Korba; Monday, Kelibia; Tuesday, Menzel Temime.

FESTIVALS: Matanza, Sidi Daïd, May-July; Festival of the Vine, Grombalia, September.

BUSES: Korbous: 2 daily to Tunis.

CAP AFRIQUE

Monastir, Sousse, Mahdia, El Jem, Kairouan, Sfax.

MONASTIR

The tourist part of Monastir is the smartest, cleanest, newest and brightest town in Tunisia, though standards drop appreciably on the outer fringes. This facelift is due solely to the fact that Habib Bourgiba was born there, and during his presidency his birthday of 3 August was celebrated in the town.

Monastir has been of strategic importance throughout its history; there was a Punic settlement on the headland, Caesar began his conquest of Ifriqya (Africa) here, and the caliphs of Islam fortified the town in the 8th cent with the fine Ribat. When Kairouan went into spiritual decline Monastir briefly took its place, and the legend grew that to stay three days in Monastir granted one the right to enter Paradise — in fact, one of the Gates of Paradise was supposed to be right here.   But it took 20th-cent presidential pride and power to undertake the rebuilding of the town, both inside and outside the defensive walls. As a result, the medina has lost virtually all its character along with its history. The planners have not fallen into the trap of creating a modern town of stainless steel and concrete but the best you can say is that it is pseudo-Tunisian and will be alright in a hundred years.

Outside the walls and towards the corniche, Monastir has a unique mix of unspoiled history in its Ribat and Great Mosque, of smart hotels that could be anywhere — and the amazing spectacle of the Bourgiba family mausoleum and a giant open-air film set.

Film industry. The southern wall of the Ribat is now almost permanently incorporated into a set which specialises in films with a Biblical connection. Immediately to the south is a metal building large enough to be the hangar for an airship, with the space between converted into a quarter of ancient Rome. A hundred yards away is a reconstruction of Jerusalem — though these locations are liable to change their identity with the demands of the film industry.

In 1976 Zeffirelli came here to shoot *The Life of Christ*, followed by the Monty Python team with *The Life of Brian*. In 1983 American television built Jerusalem and Rome for *AD: The Revolution of Love* and when I was there the carpenters were completing a year's work ready for three days' shooting of *AD: Anno Domini* for International Films. Filming is usually done in the winter but a policeman is on duty year-round to discourage the passing tourist from using his own camera on set.

Ribat. The Ribat, begun in 796 by Harthama Ben Ayan, has had so many restorations over the centuries that only the masonry of the north, east and west corners is original. Most of the southern side is 9th-cent with the remaining walls 11th-cent, except for large sections replaced in the 18th and 19th cents. The inner oratory, from the 16th and 17th cents, which separates the men's ribat from the women's, became an Islamic museum in 1957 and holds a small but impressive collection of ancient manuscripts and toilet articles from most of the caliphates who have ruled north Africa since the Islamic conquest.

Bourgiba Mausoleum. From the top of the Ribat's tower there is an excellent view of the town and coast, but the most impressive feature is the

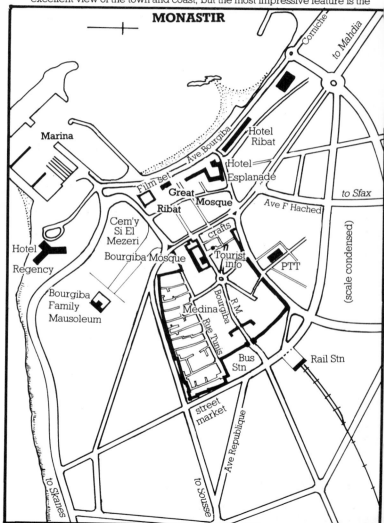

Bourgiba family mausoleum at the end of its 250-metre drive through the Cemetery of Sidi El Mezeri. The mausoleum, with a dome that really is covered with gold leaf, was begun in 1963 and improved in 1978, and included a small marabout that was already on site. Entry is forbidden but there are no restrictions on photography as our cover picture shows.

Princess Mona? At the gate of the El Mezeri Cemetery, named from a 12th-cent imam, an Arabic inscription attributed to Mezeri mentions a princess Mona. Some people believe Monastir takes its name from her rather than being a corruption of the Punic *Rous Penna.*

Bourgiba Family Mosque. The family mosque, which sits at the eastern end of the medina, was also begun in 1963, taking five years to complete. It is truly impressive, not only for its size — the prayer chamber can hold 1,000 people — but also for its immaculate construction using the best materials available. As with all but a select few mosques, only the courtyard is open to visitors, with no fee for entry but with a donation requested as you come out.

Great Mosque. The 9th-century Great Mosque by the Ribat is by comparison great only in its formidable masonry.

Presidential Palace. Habib Bourgiba, the local boy who made it to the top, built his principal presidential palace 4km west of town on the headland of Skanès; while the palace is understandably off limits it is possible to visit the gardens which extend along the coast for almost 2km, overlapping the end of the airport. Ask for written authority at the tourist office.

Marina. Monastir's Port de Plaisance — Pleasure Port — is the smartest marina in the country and in keeping with the town's image. The enclosed basin can hold 400 yachts and within the complex are a score of small apartment blocks, a cinema, restaurants and a souk. In 1987 a week's rental for a suite in the aparthotel began at 97TD, or you could buy a 50-year lease of a two-to four-room apartment for 40,000TD. Mooring fees for a 10m yacht were 400TD a year, or 8,000TD for a 50-year lease. The new Regency Monastir Hotel overlooks the marina.

The jetty which forms the main breakwater for the marina also gives access to the former Ile de Sidi El Gadamsi, once the base for tunny fishing.

Verdict. There is much more to see in Monastir than in Hammamet, but not as much to do. The beach is good though not sheltered, and gives the impression of being separate from the town. The town is attractive but, like a large film set, isn't quite real. Good rail access to Sousse for seeing the *real* Tunisia.

HOTELS: 4-star luxe: Regency Monastir, 250r; **4-star:** El Habib, 500b; Hyatt Regency, 384b; Jockey-Club (Dkhila Club), 200r; Kuriat Palace, 500b; Novotel Sidi Mansour, 133r; Robinson Club, 628b; Skanès El Hana, 250r; Skanès Palace International, 150r; **3-star:** Abou Nawas; Esplanade, 130r; Ruspina, 166r; Sahara Beach, 1,036r; Sun Rise, 416b; Tropicana Club, 500b; **2-star:** Houda, 350b; Les Palmiers, 64r; Rivage, 410b; Sangho Farah, 324b; Skanès Rivage, 196r; Tanit, 252r; **1-star:** Yasmin, 23b; **unclass:** Mourabou.

APART HOTEL: Marina, Cap Monastir, 198b.

HOLIDAY VILLAGES: Club Méditerranée, 570b; El Chems (exclusive to a French organisation).

YOUTH HOSTEL: Near bus station, 64b.

RESTAURANTS: Le Central, Le Grill, La Marina, La Pizzeria and Le Sinbad are all smart restaurants on the marina, with prices to match the setting. Le Rempart is on Ave Bourgiba and Hannibal is in the artisan quarter near the Bourgiba Mosque; there is little else.

MARKET: Street market at west corner of medina.

BUSES: Société du Transport du Sahel (STS) runs daily services to Tunis (0445 depart), to Sfax (0500, 0600, 1100), several to Sousse, and a town service every 20 min. Bus station is by Bab El Gharbi *but it's easier to take the train to Sousse and travel from there.*

RAIL: 15 trains daily to Sousse; 4 to Mahdia.

FESTIVALS: International Theatre Festival, April; Trade fair, International Folklore Festival, both in August.

TOURIST OFFICE: ONT: Rue de l'Independance near Bourgiba Mosque.

SOUSSE

The Place Farhat Hached is the unrivalled centre of Sousse from where you can see most points of interest; to the north-west the PTT (letters only), to the north the tourist office at the end of Ave Bourgiba which leads to the smart restaurants and the beach; to the east the port from where you can cruise on a fishing boat; to the south-east and a mere stone's throw away is one of the bus stations; and to the south-west there are the great walls of the medina with louage pick-up points at their base. And inside you might glimpse the Ribat and the Great Mosque.

Hannibal's elephants. The Phoenicians founded a city state here in the 9th cent BC though nothing is known of it today, not even its name. In the 6th cent BC the city came under Carthaginian influence and was dragged into the Punic Wars. Agathocles, the 'Tyrant of Syracuse' and king of Sicily from 307BC, sacked this anonymous city, and in 219BC Hannibal planned his attack on Rome from here.

Hannibal's journey over the Alps with his 37 elephants is part of classic history, and in defeat he returned to the city which we can now call Hadrumetum. Hadrumetum and Carthage supported Rome in the Third Punic War and as a reward each community was granted the status of a free city.

Pompey. But Hadrumetum made the wrong choice in the Roman civil war and backed Pompey against Caesar. Trajan demoted the city to colonial status where it slumbered until Diocletian made it the capital of the new north African state of Byzacenia.

The Vandals briefly conquered Ifriqya and renamed Hadrumetum Hunericopolis though there were no Huns in the city; the reconquering Byzantines gave it the name of Justinianopolis which the later Arab invaders abbreviated to Susa, and that's the name by which it's still known in Arabic.

The Islamic conquerors sailed from Susa in 827 to attack Sicily, the Normans seized the port in the 12th cent, the Spaniards of Andalucía took it

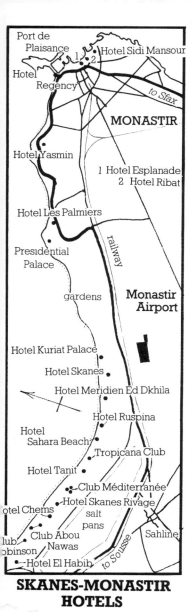

Left map:

Port de Plaisance

Hotel Sidi Mansour

1
2

Hotel Regency

to Sfax

MONASTIR

Hotel Yasmin

1 Hotel Esplanade
2 Hotel Ribat

Hotel Les Palmiers

railway

Presidential Palace

gardens

Monastir Airport

Hotel Kuriat Palace

Hotel Skanes

Hotel Meridien Ed Dkhila

Hotel Ruspina

Hotel Sahara Beach

Tropicana Club

Hotel Tanit

Club Méditerranée

Hotel Skanes Rivage

Hotel Chems

salt pans

Club Abou Nawas

Sahline

Club Robinson

to Sousse

Hotel El Habib

SKANES-MONASTIR HOTELS

Right map:

Selima Club

Club El Kantaoui

El Mouradi

Abou Sofiane

Diar El Andalous

golf links

Green Park Hotel

Marhaba International Beach Club

El Kanta

Les Maisons de la Mer

Port El Kantaoui

Mariem

Bulla Regia

Hannibal Palace

School for hoteliers

Hasdrubal

Alyssa

Salem

Shérazade

Hill Diar

El Ksar

Marhaba Beach (Tour Kalalaf)

Marhaba

La Sofra

Marhaba Club

Marabout

Jawhara

Riadh

SOUSSE

SOUSSE-PORT EL KANTAOUI HOTELS

59

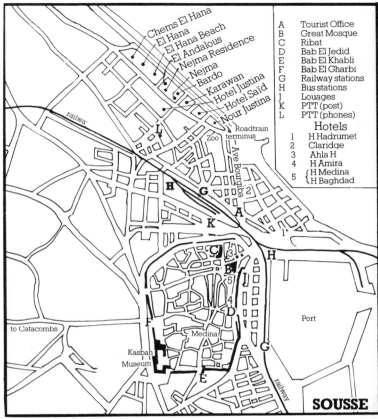

Chems El Hana
El Hana
El Hana Beach
El Andalous
Nejma Residence
Nejma
Bardo
Karawan
Hotel Justina
Hotel Said
Nour Justina

railwa

Roadtrain
Zoo   terminus

Ave Bourgiba

railway

Kasbah
Museum

to Catacombs

Medina

Port

SOUSSE

A	Tourist Office
B	Great Mosque
C	Ribat
D	Bab El Jedid
E	Bab El Khabli
F	Bab El Gharbi
G	Railway stations
H	Bus stations
J	Louages
K	PTT (post)
L	PTT (phones)

Hotels

1	H Hadrumet
2	Claridge
3	Ahla H
4	H Amira
5	{ H Medina
	{ H Baghdad

in the 16th cent, and the French bombarded it in the 18th cent before becoming its colonial masters.

Modern Sousse. Modern Sousse, the so-called 'pearl of the Sahel,' is an industrial city specialising in food processing, textiles, and assembling motor vehicles, but it has managed to absorb an astonishing growth in tourism from 200 beds in 1956 to around 17,000 in 1987.

Medina. The medina is a very well preserved medieval city that has survived all attacks, including the tourist invasion, architecturally unscathed, and the little shops which sell tourist goods are comfortably scattered among those dealing in spices, fruits or meat — though it can be a bit disconcerting to see a complete cow-head hanging on a shop front.

Great Mosque. The Great Mosque is perhaps the most impressive feature, standing sentinel just inside the medina gates. Built like a fortress in 851, it has recently been faithfully restored to its 11th century appearance and is one of the few mosques the visitor can enter without first seeking permission; but the prayer chamber is still out of bounds. Tickets are available at a blue door near the Ahla Hotel opposite, from 0900 to 1400 daily except Friday, though these hours frequently change.

All mosques look plain and empty in comparison with churches and this one is among the emptiest, but we must remember that the Moslems use their mosques exclusively for prayer.

Ribat. Across the square stands the Ribat, built at the same time and with the same purpose, the defence of the medina's main entrance against marauding Christians. Since the growth of tourism all of Sousse has been cleaned, and the removal of tons of earth from around the Ribat walls, the accumulation of centuries, has emphasised the building's sturdy feaures. It is of necessity a gaunt place around 30m square, and is acknowledged to be the best example of its type in north Africa.

Inside, visitors can see something of the cells in which the marabouts lived in periods of peace, while the battlemented parapet with its lookout tower shows it was also a formidable fortress. The first-floor prayer hall on the south wall, not open to the public, is claimed to be the oldest surviving mosque in north Africa still in its original form.

Souks. The medina's main streets form a rough coss, the north arm being the Rue d'Angleterre. At the street's southern end, in the middle of the medina, is the Kalaout El Koubba, a Moorish café of the 10th cent which should by now have become the Museum of Traditional Arts.

Bou Ftata. From the Kalaout the souks lead south and west; south also takes us to two small mosques of which the further one, the Mosque of Bou Ftata, was built between 838 and 841 and has cufic Arabic inscriptions — highly stylised writing which originated in Kufa, Iran. The flamboyant script splashed with vowels which is more often seen in mosques is the 10th cent cursive style which totally replaced cufic by the 13th cent.

Museum and Kasbah. In the south-west corner of the medina, with access from outside the walls, is the museum, occupying part of the Kasbah. This museum is worth visiting for its outstanding exhibits of mosaics occupying several rooms; a highly intricate work showing Neptune in his underwater kingdom is among the best of its kind in the world.

The Kasbah, built at the highest corner of the medina walls, offers a good panorama of the city from its Khalef Tower though for a more intimate view you could climb the walls by the Great Mosque and look down on the Place des Martyrs.

Budget hotels. Sousse's medina, like all other medinas in Tunisia, is where to find the cheapest hotels. The standard is not three-star but they are all clean.

Railway. Outside the medina, Sousse is new, much of it having been rebuilt since the North African War. It is therefore surprising to see the railway carving its way through the city as if it were an afterthought, and stopping all traffic on the Place Hached many times a day. The stations are along the Ave Ayachi and by the Bab El Jedid, the latter having a separate platform for the Metro trains to Monastir.

Zoo. Sousse has few other attractions. The tiny zoo at the southern end of the Route de Corniche (entry 100 mill) is more like a smart botanic garden with a few animals as residents. The Catholic church of St Felix, backing onto the Rue Constantine in the north of the city, has plaster reliefs of the stations of the cross as its main feature.

Catacombs. The Christian catacombs of Hermes, Severus and the Good

On the beach at Sousse

Shepherd are unusual for north Africa, but are difficult to visit. There are 15,000 tombs from the 3rd and 4th cents in 240 galleries along 5km of tunnels, but less than half of them are open to view and then normally only to organised parties or to archaeologists. Ask for further information at the museum and if you're accepted, don't forget to take a good torch.

The catacombs were discovered in 1888 and already a legend has grown, claiming that a tunnel leads from here to the great amphitheatre of El Jem, for the recovery of Christians slaughtered in contests with gladiators.

Market. The Sunday morning camel market, occupying a three-acre site at a junction 3km along the road to Sfax, has become a popular attraction, with tourists greatly outnumbering the camels.

Port El Kantaoui. A smart little Toytown train runs from the north end of Ave Bourgiba to Port El Kantaoui serving all the tourist hotels along the route. The fare of 2TD is a little high, but you're paying for the novelty. Port El Kantaoui itself was built in 1971 purely for the tourist trade; the smart

The Toytown Train to Port El Kantaoui

marina holds 300 yachts and the community offers a wide range of sports including sailing, diving, tennis, horse riding and golf on the 27-hole links.

Verdict. Sousse outshines all other resorts for diversity of interest. The beach is excellent save for the blemish of a waste discharge near town, though it is not as sheltered as the Hammamet beach. The tourist hotels are bigger and brasher than elsewhere but if you want to travel independently there are several adequate and much cheaper ones in the medina. Sousse has the best night life in Tunisia, but that doesn't say much.

The city itself has much of interest and there are good connections by train to Monastir, by bus to Tunis and by louage to Kairouan. For a holiday that gives you something of everything, Sousse is unbeatable.

HOTELS: 5-star: Diar El Andalous, 300r; Hannibal Palace, 235r; **4-star:** Asdrubal, 472b; El Hana, 131r; El Kanta, 255r; Marhaba Beach, 244r; **3-star:** Abu Sofiane, 350b; Bulla Regia, 104b; El Hana Beach, 633r; El Ksar, 240r; El Mouradi, 242r; Farès, 73r; Hadrumete, 36r; Hill Diar, 194r; Marabout, 206r; Marhaba, 474r; Marhaba Club, 205r; Nour Justinia, 172b; Saïd, 100b; Scheherezade, 208r; Sousse Palace, 240r; Tour Khalef, 505r; **2-star:** Alyssa, 340r; Boujaafar, 57r; Du Parc, 64b; El Kaiser, 94b; En Nacim, 25r; Hadrumete, 70b; Jawhara, 260r; Justinia, 132r; Karawan, 120r; La Sofra, 31 bungalows; Riadh, 70r; Salem, 200r; Salima Club, 594b; **1-star:** Ahla, 24r; Amira, 12r; Claridge, 28r; Essaada, 105b; La Corniche, 25r; Medina, 100b; Mestiri; Zouhour.

At Chott Myriem, between Port El Kantaoui and Herlga: **3-star:** Open Club, with vast range of activites, 315r; **2-star:** Tergui Club, 442r mostly in bungalows.

HOLIDAY VILLAGE: Club El Kantaoui, 325r.

APART HOTELS: Africa Beach, 32b; Diar El Andalous; Fares, 180b; Les Maisons de la Mer, 318 studios; Okba, 100b; Residence Nejma, 127 studios; Samara, 614b; Soussana, 96b.

YOUTH HOSTEL: Blv Taïeb Mehri, 130b.

CAMPING: Between hotels Marhaba and Marabout; ask at either.

RESTAURANTS: Tip-Top on Route de la Corniche is top in star rating as well as name. Others on this road include L'Albatros, L'Ambassadeur, L'Escargot, Le Kandy, Le Marrakech and Le Pacha; their star ratings vary but you can judge by outside appearances.

Other restaurants of note are on the Ave Bourgiba or the better boulevards in the new city, and there are several at Port El Kantaoui. For budget eating try near the telephone office (see below).

POST AND PHONES: The main PTT building at the end of Ave de la République is for postal business; international phones are in a separate office near St Felix Church; go north along Ave Ayachi, cross Ave Victor Hugo bearing right to small sidestreet leading north.

BUSES: There are several bus stations, the main one is on Ave Leopold

Senghor near St Felix Church but on the other side of the tracks. The more convenient bus station is by the port, but its schedule is different.

LOUAGES By the main medina gate for destinations north; Ave Mohammed Ali, by medina walls to south, for destinations south.

RAIL From Bab El Jedid, Metro to Monastir and Mahdia; see timetable on page 23. Good main line services to Tunis and south to Sfax and beyond.

NIGHT CLUB: Topkapi, on Ave Bourgiba.

TOUR OPERATORS (EXCURSIONS) On Route de la Corniche: Abou Nawas Travel, Atlas Voyages, Car Tours, Hammamet Travel Service, Star Tours, Tunisian Travel Service. One Ave Bourgiba: Carthage Tours, Hassen Travel Co, Transtours, Travel Sousse Express. Elsewhere: Chams Tours, Rue Ali Belhaouane; STATT, Ave Mohammed V; Tourafric, Rue Khaled Ibn Walid; Tunisie Tourisme, Port El Kantaoui; Medina Tours, Ave Med Ali.

FESTVALS Regional Festival of Pop Art, mid-March; festival of Baba Aoussou (folk dances), national fair, El Kantaoui festival, all in July.

TOURIST OFFICES SI, Place Farhat Hached; ONT, Ave Habib Bourgiba.

MAHDIA

Obaïd Allah declared himself to be a direct descendant of Mohamet through the Prophet's daughter Fatima. He therefore appointed himself the Saviour, El Mahdi, and the founder and leader of the Fatimite sect of Islam — in today's term, the Shi'ites. In 910 he defeated the moderate Aghlabid dynasty, today's Sunnis, and proclaimed himself caliph. He abandoned Kairouan and chose an isolated headland for his new capital, Mahdia.

The site was ideal and as easy to defend as the Rock of Gibraltar. The Mahdi personally laid the first stone for the town's wall which crossed the peninsula at its narrowest point; from that first stone laid in 916 the wall grew to a fortification 10m thick with a single gate in the middle guarded by two towers.

Inside, the Mahdi added the Great Mosque, a small port, and a palace. He condescended to allow a few merchants to have their warehouses in his city but compelled them to live outside the walls, saying they could have their wares by day and their wives by night.

Cairo. From the outset the Mahdi had little interest in his native land, still called Ifriqya, and he soon led the religious conquest east to Egypt where his followers built the new city of El Kahira — 'the Victorious,' known today as Cairo — as the home of the Fatimites.

In 947 Abu Yazid of Tozeur, known in history as 'the man on a donkey,' unsuccessfully besieged Mahdia for seven months, after which the third Fatimid caliph of Ifriqya, Abu Tahar Ismaïl, moved his capital from Mahdia back to Kairouan, leaving the remaining inhabitants on the peninsula to become fishermen, merchants and ultimately pirates.

The Fatimite fetish faded in Kairouan and the people renewed their allegiance with the Sunni Caliph of Baghdad, slaughtering some of the remaining Fatimites so brutally that the Egyptians decided on revenge. In 1057, shortly before the Norman Conquest of Britain, they sent a troublesome people, the nomadic Hilalians, to wreak vengeance on Ifriqya; the Hilalans terrorised the countryside, shattered trade and communications routes, and destroyed the last vestiges of a central government inherited from the Romans.

Norman Conquest. Ifriqya was defenceless. The Christians soon realised it and in 1148 the Normans, who had already followed their success in Britain by seizing southern Italy, Sicily and Malta, turned on Tunisia, capturing Mahdia and burning the villages outside its walls.

Roger II of Sicily held Mahdia for the Normans until 1160 when the Muwahid Caliphate regained control for Islam and Mahdia began its period of greatest prosperity as a trading port. The French and Genoese returned in 1390 with English help and besieged the peninsula for months, but it took the Turkish pirate Dragut, known in his own land as Turgut Reis, to capture Mahdia, which he did in 1549. Already an old man, he went on to take Tripoli in 1551 and he died at the Siege of Malta in 1565.

Spanish. Meanwhile, Carlos V of Spain, the Holy Roman Emperor, seized Mahdia in 1550 by direct assault from the sea and held it for four years. They turned the great mosque into a church and buried their dead in its floor, then before pulling out they exhumed their compatriots, smashed the mosque, and completely destroyed the city walls.

Dark Tunnel. The caliphs used the Spanish rubble to build one of the most impressive town gates in the world, the Skifka El Khala, the 'Dark Tunnel,' around 30m long and divided into seven sections each of which could be sealed off by dropping a huge portcullis weighing eight tons. The grilles have long gone and the Skifka is now a souk, but the Dark Tunnel is still among the most formidable town defences you're likely to see. A staircase leads from the rear of the adjacent town hall and up the south wall of the Skifka for an impressive view over the town.

Mahdia today. The old town of Mahdia is still an impressive sight with narrow alleys running the length of the peninsula to the open headland of Cap Afrique, covered by a vast Moslem cemetery used from the 10th to the 16th cents and reaching to the lighthouse at the tip of the headland. On the southern flank local fishermen still use the 10th cent Fatimite harbour whose entrance was originally guarded by an arch similar to the Colossus of Rhodes, and by a chain drawn tight at water level.

Weaving. The central alley of the old town, named Rue Oubad Allah El Mahdi from its founder, leads from the Skifka to the central square, Place Kadi Noamene, passing the Syndicat d'Initiative which has very little information to offer, and the silk museum, which is closed for an indefinite period.

Silk weaving had been one of the town's industries since 11th cent Jews brought the skills from Libya, but the invention of Nylon — developed in New York and London, hence its name — destroyed the market. The backstreet looms now weave wool into blankets and other household goods.

Great Mosque. The Great Mosque stands on the southern side of the Place Kadi Noamene, but the impressive structure you see was built between 1961 and '65 as an exact copy of the Mahdi's original of 921. A thousand years ago the builders had sufficient skills to extend the mosque

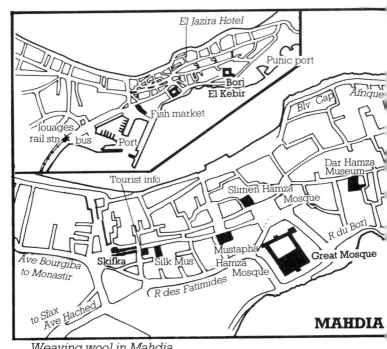

MAHDIA

Weaving wool in Mahdia

foundations a few metres out to sea, with two of its walls also serving as sea defences.

The mosque has seen some bloody history, most notably in 1016 when the returning Sunnis massacred the remaining Fatimite population within these walls, an act which prompted the Hilalian retribution. The name Fatima and its male version Fathi, by the way, are Arabic for 'faithful,' a strange transposition of the English word 'faith.'

Borj. Between the Great Mosque and the Fatimite port stands the gaunt fortress of Borj El Kebir, the 'Great Castle,' founded in 1595 by the Turk Abu Abdallah Mohammed Pasha. A legend claims that a tunnel runs from this fort to the catacombs at Sousse and so connects with the amphitheatre at El Jem, but the Mahdia legend embellishes the Sousse story by claiming that elephants trod this tunnel carrying building stone for the Roman masons. In truth the Romans were never at Mahdia though there were elephants aplenty.

The new town. Beyond the Skifka, Mahdia is much like any other Tunisian town. The new fishing port is the fourth largest in the country and beside it is a large open space which serves as the bus and louage station; the railway came in 1985 and its station is also conveniently sited here. On the north side of town the Ave Bourgiba has a bank, the PTT, the Grand Hotel, the Magazin Général — and a barber who also performs circumcisions. The road eventually leads to the beach and three tourist hotels.

HOTELS: 3-star: **Club Cap Mahdia, 506b; El Mahdi, 145r; 1-star:** Sables d'Or, 202b.
Town centre unclassified hotels are El Jazira (24b) which has a welcome feminine touch; Grand, 36r; Rand, 20b.

RESTAURANTS: All in the old town and all specialising in fish: Le Corsaire, Lido, Medina.

BUSES and LOUAGES: One SNT bus a day each way on the coast run to Sousse and to Sfax. There is a much better louage service to nearby towns.

RAIL: Five daily to Sousse and two to Tunis, with corresponding return trains.

MARKET: Friday.

TOURIST OFFICE: SI, on the main street near the Skifka.

THE CAP AFRIQUE AREA

Ksour Essaf, 'Castle of the Sparrowhawk,' grew in the 16th cent around the tombs of two Moroccan marabouts. From here a road leads to **Rass Salakta,** site of the Roman settlement of Sullecthum founded around 46BC. North of the little harbour are a Roman necropolis and an archaeological museum of which the main exhibit is a mosaic lion from the villa of a Roman named Leontius. And to the south, around 2km away, are the Christian Catacombs of Arch Zara and a nearby ancient cistern.

Ksar Hellal is the centre of a thriving industry making denim for export to jeans manufacturers in Europe and the United States. Denim was originally made in France as its name, *de Nîmes*, recalls. Hellal is also the town where in March 1934 Habib Bourgiba created the Néo Destour Party from the ashes of the 1920s Destour.

Itinerant Jews gave **Moknine** its reputation as a manufacturer of jewellery, but the town is now known for the production of chawat, the porous earthenware also found at Nabeul. The local Museum of Art and Popular Crafts, located in the former Mosque of Sidi Babana, shows samples of the town's wares plus a display of coins from the Roman to the Ottoman periods.

You'll need your own transport to visit **Thapsus,** the city founded by the Phoenicians and where Caesar's legions defeated Pompey's forces in 46BC. The only remains are of the port, now partly submerged.

Hergla is on the site of the Roman Horraca Caelia and a 6th cent Bysantine fort which the invading Arabs razed, killing all the occupants. The villagers now grow esparto grass, the fibres being retted (soaked) out to make filters for cleaning olive oil.

MARKETS: Monday, Moknine; Friday, Ksour Essaf and Jemmal, where you may find camels on sale.

EL JEM

El Jem is an enigma. The town itself is a market for local farm produce, with no tourist office, a poor shopping centre, a mediocre bus service and one modest hotel. Yet it has the best preserved Roman amphiheatre in the world, more impressive than the one in Rome though slightly smaller.

This huge edifice is visible for miles in every direction across the flat and semi-arid landscape and totally overshadows the town, yet it has so far escaped commercial exploitation of any kind.

Amphitheatre. The oval amphitheatre or coliseum is 149m long by 124m wide and stands 36m high. Building began around the end of the 2nd cent AD and tailed off around 230 before the work was completed. The structure could hold between 30,000 and 35,000 people, which was the entire population of the city of Thysdrus, though there are a mere 12,000 people in today's El Jem.

The enormity of the coliseum is impressive in the extreme, mainly because there is nothing else for miles to detract from its size, and this despite the disastrous explosion of 1695 when Mohammed Bey destroyed the north side to drive out the supporters of his rival for the throne, Ali Bey. The townspeople benefited from the incident by having a lifetime's supply of ready-quarried building stone at hand.

Bare bones. When Mohammed Bey laid bare the bones of this vast building he inadvertently added to its appeal, for it's now possible to study exactly how the Romans designed the place, and V-slots in each block show how it was lifted into position with giant tongs. The coliseum may be partly ruined, but one can still climb 99 steps on the south side and so reach fourth floor level some 27m above ground. In the centre of the arena another 16 steps lead down to the tunnel which gave access to the cells where unarmed humans were held before being thrown to the lions on centre stage.

Grim history. When you come to El Jem, stand for a few moments in this gloomy passage, discovered as recently as 1904, and picture the coliseum as it might have been 1,700 years ago when human and animal life was cheap. Prisoners of war, slaves, bankrupts, criminals, Chrstians — they were all considered fair game to be cast into the arena and there fight to the death against a gladiator armed with sword and trident. Worse still was when humans were matched with lions and were literally torn limb from limb while still alive. There is a record of a young woman who was dismembered in this way three days after she gave birth down in those dungeons.

Thysdrus. Thysdrus was first mentioned in the annals of the Punic Wars in the 3rd cent BC, but it became an important town only in the 1st cent AD with the development of an overland trade route and the production of olive oil here for the Roman market. Fortunes were made, villas built, and eventually work began on this vast amphitheatre.

Maximinus. This was not enough for the ambitious Thysdrusians. In 238, before the coliseum was completed, the city denounced Emperor Gaius Julius Maximinus for his tyranny and his high taxes, and they killed the local tax collectors. They then proclaimed the 80-year-old Proconsul of Ifriqya, Gordian, as Emperor of all Rome. Carthage supported Gordian and when the Senate in Rome officially approved the choice, Thysdrus bathed in glory as the kingmaker.

Only Gordian was unhappy, for he didn't want the imperial burden and he committed suicide.

El Jem's vast amphitheatre

Restoration work closes the amphitheatre on occasions but it's normally open at standard museum hours every day, with the 1TD entrance fee going to the Association de Sauvegarde de la Ville d'El Jem. By the way, the town is often called El Djem which was how the name was spelled before the language reform of 1971.

Museum. The museum (open daily except Mondays) at the edge of town on the road to Sfax, holds an impressive display of mosaics from ancient Thysdrus, the masterpiece being a finely preserved work showing two lions killing a wild boar — even in their leisure the Romans could not escape their morbid interest in cruelty. The ticket which allows you into the museum also admits you to the open area beyond where excavations are steadily progressing, unearthing yet more mosaics among the foundations of the Roman community. There is also evidence of an earlier and smaller amphitheatre.

HOTEL: 1-star Relais Julius, 30b.

BUSES and LOUAGES: Bus connections south and north along the main road; could be a better service. Louages start from the new bypass and supplement the buses' destinations.

RAIL: Reasonable services north and south, but not all trains stop here. See timetable.

MARKET: Sunday.

FESTIVAL: Festival of El Jem with traditional dancing in the amphitheatre in June.

KAIROUAN

There's usually some geographical reason why a town is built on a certain spot. Kairouan, the holiest city in Islam after Mecca, Medina and Jerusalem, is an exception. In the Year of the Hegira 50, or 670 in the Christian calendar, Oqba Ben Nafii was leading the third wave of Arab invaders into Ifriqya. Somewhere along the route of the camel caravan — karawan in phonetic Arabic — he called an overnight halt for his army. He kicked the dust and found, believe it if you will, a golden chalice he had lost in Mecca some years earlier. His greyhound Barrouta then scratched in this open, dry and featureless plain and revealed a spring ready to gush forth. Oqba recognised the work of Allah and declared that this was the holiest place in Ifriqya and must be the site for his new capital.

The location also had some strategic advantages. It was far enough from the coast to deter Byzantine raiders, far enough from the mountains to deter Berbers, and no advancing army of any colour could hide on this treeless plain.

But Kosaila, ruler of the Christian Berber tribe of Auraba, came down from the hills in 682 and scored his first victory over these newcomers. Around 688 the Auraba seized Kairouan, but Kosaila was killed in the battle.

The Arabs came back in force under Hassan Ben En-Nooman, recaptured Kairouan and confirmed it as their choice of capital. Under the

Aghlabid Emirate of the 9th cent, Kairouan grew to become the most important city between Fez and the Nile, with palaces and other buildings appropriate to its status.

Obaïd Allah changed all this when he became the Mahdi and deposed the Aghlabids. His new Fatimite cult called for a new capital and he chose Mahdia (q.v.) although his successors moved back to Kairouan. The Hilalian revenge, sent from Egypt, thus threw its strength against Kairouan which capitulated in November 1067 after a siege of several years.

Ifriqya was shattered and fell victim to raids from Normans, Genoese and Spaniards, and when it was once again in a position to have a capital, Tunis was the natural choice. But Kairouan retained its status as the holiest Islamic city in Africa, and tradition has long held that seven pilgrimages to Kairouan equal one to Mecca.

So venerated was Kairouan that before the French arrived in 1881, Christians could enter the city only with written authority from the bey, and Jews dare not come within sight of the walls.

Kairouan today. Your first call in Kairouan should be at the Syndicat d'Initiative in the smart Moorish-style building opposite the city's main gate, the Bab Chouhada; I found the opening hours to be 0800-1330 and 1500-1700 though the fountain courtyard, well worth a visit for its own sake, is open from 0730-1745 daily.

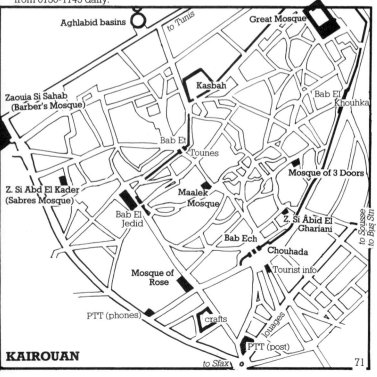

KAIROUAN

71

Tickets. Here you can buy your single composite ticket which grants access to the Great Mosque, the Aghlabid Basins, the Zaouia (or zawiya, a small mosque) of Sidi Amor Abbada and the Zaouia of Sidi Abd El Ghariani. Admission is strictly by ticket which is valid for one day, but you can arrange for it to be postdated. It is possible to visit all the sites within the day on foot, but for comfort you might consider taking a taxi to the Great Mosque and the basins and walking from there.

Great Mosque. *Open 0800-1230, 1630-1730 in winter; 0800-1230, 1445-1630 in summer, but closed on Friday afternoons.* Oqba Ben Nafii began building the Great Mosque, now also known as the Mosque of Sidi Oqba, in 670, the first mosque to be built west of the Nile. Kosaila's Berbers destroyed it in 688 and Hasan Ben En-Nooman began the first replacement in 695. The governor Yazid Ben Hatim enlarged it in 774, and in 836 the Emir Ziyadet Allah demolished it and built yet again, resulting in essence in the mosque we see today, though there were further alterations in 862 and 875.

It truly deserves the title of Great Mosque, for its trapezoid shape is 135m long by 80m wide, and 50 stone columns surrounding the courtyard support the porticos built in the 9th cent. The courtyard, 68m by 53m at its greatest, has two large cisterns in the centre to catch some of the meagre 300mm of rain which falls here in an average year; the water has been hauled up for centuries by leather buckets, their ropes cutting deep grooves in the stone rim.

The walls of Kairouan   *Zaouia of Sidi Abid El Ghariani*

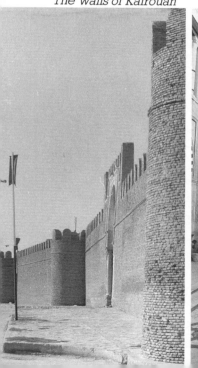

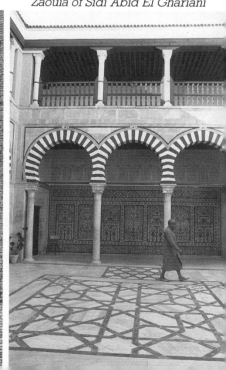

The 35m high tapering minaret on the north side may date from around 836 though some authorities place it a century earlier and claim it may be the world's oldest Islamic minaret. It is slightly offset from the remainder of the mosque which was built at a different time — earlier or later, according to your school of thought.

Prayer chamber. Cedar doors on the southern side of the court lead into the prayer chamber which has 17 naves and many columns of marble and porphyry supporting its expansive roof; legend claims that it is impossible to count the columns without the risk of being struck blind, but in fact the mosque has 600, large and small. The prayer chamber in its entirety is off-limits to non-Moslems as a result of the 1972 law, yet during the French Protectorate of 1881 to 1965 this was the only mosque in Tunisia that was open to non-Moslems as its courtyard had — and still has, for that matter — been irredeemably desecrated by a cavalry regiment which sought refuge from the plague then rampant in the city.

Entry to the mosque is through the single door on the west side, but the ornate Lalla Rihana Gate on the east wall is worth a brief visit. Built in 1924 and opening directly into the prayer chamber, it is named from a holy woman who is buried nearby.

Aghlabid Basins. The Aghlabid Basins off the main Tunis road may be something of a disappointment as they are merely two large open cisterns. The larger, 128m in diameter, has a small stone island in the centre on which the Aghlabid emirs used to relax, surrounded by fresh water in the semi-desert. A subterranean passage connects with the smaller basin, 37.4m in diameter. Both received their water by aqueduct from Jebel Cherichira (462m), 36km to the south-west.

The basins have been restored and are now full of a greenish water, with a second large basin a little to the east in a poor state of repair.

Zaouia of Sidi Saheb. The zaouia of Sidi Saheb is also known as the Mosque of the Barber. Abu Zama El Belaoui, who died in Kairouan when the city was in its infancy, was a companion of the Prophet and carried three of the hairs from Mahomet's beard — one under his tongue, one next to his heart, and the other on his right arm — so giving rise to the somewhat scathing Christian name of The Barber.

Nothing remains above ground of the original zaouia, and the building we see is mainly from 1629, the work of Hammouda who was bey from 1613 to 1631, but there have been several restorations, some as recently as the 19th cent.

The First Court leads through a darkened room to the Patio of the Medersa, a beautiful little enclosed area which gives access to the Second Court and the prayer chamber — though not to non-Moslems.

Moslems seldom inter their venerated dead inside a mosque, but this zaouia holds the remains of Sidi Saheb and of Sidi Shrif Bin Hindu, architect of the Great Mosque. Mosques have fewer plaques than do churches but there is one here erected by Abu Abd Allah Mohammed Pasha, 'lord of the throne and of the city of Tunis, son of the magnanimous fire king.' Another, off-bounds, urges, also in Arabic: 'Pilgrim, do not forget that here lies a companion of the Prophet of God.'

Barbers throughout Tunisia practise circumcision as a sideline to their normal business. Perhaps that is why the Mosque of the Barber is also the setting for a mass circumcision on Mahomet's birthday, which is a festival in this holy city.

The wealthier fathers organise the event, with the children wearing their best clothes and riding on horseback to the accompaniment of trumpets and tambourines. Each boy is taken to the sanctuary, a small chamber leading off the Second Court, and at the instant of the first cut his father throws a jar of sweets on the ground to distract the lad and muffle any cries of pain: his friends enjoy the rewards. Later, the boys go back to town in procession with the barber leading the way.

Zaouia de Sidi Abid El Ghariani. The little mosque of Sidi Abid El Ghariani, the fourth place mentioned on your ticket, is a truly small mosque on the south side of the Rue Sidi Gueriani — same name but different spelling — inside the medina's main gate.

The mosque was built in the 14th cent but commemorates a holy man who died around 1402 and whose remains are in a filigree-decorated tomb in a gallery on the left of the tiny but impressive court. Indeed, everything about this mosque is impressive except its size, showing that the recent restoration was done to good effect. The mosque is now the home of the Association de Sauvegarde de la Médina de Kairouan and holds a tiny museum of Arabic coufic calligraphy as shown on tombs from the 9th to 11th cents.

Mosque of Three Doors. Your tourist ticket has done its work but there are still several other sights awaiting you in Kairouan. The Jama Tleta Bibane, the Mosque of the Three Doors in the street of the same name (but in French), was the work of Mohammed Ben Kairouan El Maafiri, born in Córdoba, Spain. Restoration is due to start soon on this mosque begun in 866 but dismantled stone by stone and rebuilt, with a minaret, in 1440; the cursive inscriptions on the façade date from this era but the coufic carvings are originals, showing how Arabic script has altered.

Mosque of the Sabres. The Mosque of Sidi Amor Abbada, better known as the Mosque of the Sabres, is near the Mosque of the Barber. Amor Abbada was a man of several skills; a blacksmith, a marabout, and a dervish — member of that Turkish dancing sect which Kemal Atatürk banned. In 1860 he built the five-domed mosque; he died in 1871 and his body lies in its tomb within the mosque, guarded by several large sabres which he had wrought.

According to foklore, Idi Amor persuaded the bey to send to Kairouan the anchors which Noah had used on the Ark at the summit of Mount Ararat, 'in order that Kairouan should forever be anchored to Tunisia and to the bey.' The four anchors, which weigh about a ton apiece, are now on the premises of the Mosque of the Barber.

Bab Chouhada. The main gate to the medina, Bab Chouhada or Martyrs' Gate, was attributed to leatherworkers as Bab Jalladin, until 1952. Work began on the walls in 761, with the ramparts added from 1052. Hussein Ben Ali restored them between 1706 and 1712 and they have received further attention in recent years to repair the damage done by Rommel's Afrika Korps which urgently needed stone for an airstrip.

Bir Barrouta. Water has always been scarce in Kairouan so it's not particularly surprising to find a water pump in the centre of the medina. Bir Barrouta, the Well of Barrouta, a short distance from Bab Chouhada, is reputedly the source of fresh water that Oqba's dog Barrouta discovered on that first bivouac along the caravan route in 670.

The wellhouse is 18th cent, since restored, but the driving force is certainly primeval — a blindfolded camel which spends its day walking a circle turning a large horizontally-mounted wheel which drives a vertical wheel which scoops up water from around five metres deep. This ancient device is called a noria and is the subject of two ancient beliefs: that this well has an underground link with Bir Zem-Zem, the sacred well of Mecca; and that he who drinks from it is assured of a return, some day, to Kairouan. Dare one suggest the camel ought to drink elsewhere?

Carpets. You will not spend more than a few hours in Kairouan without being asked to buy a carpet, product of the city's main industry for centuries. All are hand-made from wool and, as in Turkey, there are two basic techniques involved: weaving and knotting.

Woven carpets, mergoum, are of Berber origin and are basic to their nomadic life, providing tent roof and floor, clothing, bedding, and wraps for their other worldly goods. You will see Berber women in the south of Tunisia dressed in this type of material.

Knotted carpets are by far the more traditional and were originally made only as prayer mats so the ritually-cleansed Moslem would not soil himself when he bowed his head in prayer. The design has a religious motif, springing from the diamond-shaped lantern in the Great Mosque here in Kairouan, and the most intricate carpet, needing up to 150,000 knots per square metre, calls for weeks of painstaking work. Traditionally a young woman would present her first-woven mat to the Mosque of the Barbers, which explains why there are so many, even out on the floor of the First Court.

Industry. Kairouan's abysmal location has ruined any chance of trying to develop agriculture, yet three-quarters of the people derive their living from the land which provides employment for five months in the year at best, the exceptions being the shepherds who tend the flocks that produce the wool for all those carpets. Several small barrages now protect the city from the ravages of flash floods and provide a little water for irrigation, but the majority of the work force must find a living where it can, which explains the number of wandering carpet sellers and tourist guides.

The small craft workshops are expanding but the birthrate outstrips them, and the only other major source of income is the local cigarette factory. Where else but in Kairouan — Karawan — would you expect to find Caravanes made?

Raqada. On the southern fringe of Kairouan lie the insignificant remains of the royal palace of the Fatimite caliph Sabra Mansourya, who moved his court back to the city after quitting Mahdia.

Seven kilometres further south is Raqada (Reqqada, the 'Sleeping One'), a royal city founded here in 876 by the Aghlabid emir Ibrahim II because he couldn't get night's full sleep in Kairouan. A thousand years ago it had at least three elegant palaces within its city walls but war and weather have done their damage. Raqada is best remembered as the city where the Mahdi came to prominence and from where he went to found his new power base of Mahdia, but trial digs in 1960 revealed another side to its history with the discovery of a Roman cemetery used from the 1st to the 4th cents.

Islamic Museum. A few hundred metres from Raqada stands the National Museum of Islamic Art (closed on Mondays) in a building originally planned as a palace for former president Bourgiba but converted a year or so before his enforced retirement.

The museum concentrates on local exhibits and gives pride of place to a collection of gold and silver coins found at the Sabra Mansourya site; among them are a few coins of Abu Yazid, the man who came on a donkey from Tozeur to lay siege to Mahdia in 947.

Verdict. Kairouan is not a resort, but a day or two spent here could be among the most memorable part of your visit to Tunisia; you should certainly see the city even if only on a short excursion. There are several good hotels but for the experience of sleeping in the medina (assuming you're otherwise at a tourist hotel) I recommend the unclassified and cheap Marhala at 35, Souk El Belaghija (tel 07.20736), recently converted from a rambling old hostel. It's full of character and has good views from its roof.

Most normal town activity is condensed into the small area around the Place de l'Independance where you can find banks, the Magazin Général, restaurants, the Syndicat d'Initiative, louage stands and, to the east, the bus station.

HOTELS: 4-star: Continental, 352b; **3-star:** Aghlabites, 64r; Splendid, 43r; **2-star:** Tunisia, 35r; **unclass:** Barrouta; Du Bonheur; El Menema; Marhala, 69b; Sabra, 56b; Salama. (A **hammam** is beside the Hotel Sabra.)

YOUTH HOSTEL: By Aghlabites Hotel, 10b.

RESTAURANTS: Dar Es Salaam, Ave de Fès, is the smartest. Try also those in the Ave de la République, the Barrouta (by hotel of same name in the medina), and the Neptune in Rue Habib Thameur. *Makhroud,* a Kairouan speciality, is a pleasant sweet dish sold in the souks: try some.

BUSES: Eight buses daily to Tunis, three each to Sousse and Zaghouan, two to Gabès, one each to Gafsa, Tozeur and Nefta. Bus station: turn right at north end of Ave de la République.

LOUAGE: Good services; louages start from Ave de la République and Ave Habib Thameur.

RAIL: Good connections; see timeable.

PTT: Post office is at main roundabout at south end of Ave de la République (formerly Rue Farhat Hached); Phones office wih one international kiosk is on main west bypass (Ave Zama El Balaoui, formerly Ave de la République) near Office National de l'Artisanat.

CRAFTS: For carpets and other crafts consult the Office National de l'Arisanat, Ave Ali Zouaoui.

MARKET: Monday.

FESTIVALS: Muled, the Prophet's birthday; Summer Festival in July.

TOURIST OFFICE: SI; Ave Bourgiba.

SFAX

Sfax is not a tourist resort but as the second city of Tunisia, and more compact than Tunis, it is well worth a visit. The city is heavily industrialised yet without the smoking chimneys or grinding factories: it processes the animal, vegetable and mineral resources of its region and as a result is known as the Capital of the South.

Olive oil. You can't fail to miss the olive plantations around Sfax. More than 6,000,000 trees, all planted since 1800, line the roads from Mahrès in the south to the fringes of the semi-desert around El Jem in the north, and occupy 70% of the cultivated land in the region.

An average harvest yields 50,000 tons of olive oil but in the good seasons, which seem to come every third year, the output can reach 80,000 tons. Mechanisation is slowly coming to olive picking, but as it calls for trees to be planted in a set pattern progress will be slow. In the meantime around 30,000 pickers gather the crop from late November by beating the trees with sticks and collecting the fruit that falls onto plastic sheets laid on the ground.

Another 10,000 workers in the scores of small oil mills around Sfax press the fruit, the first extraction making the top quality olive oil used mainly in cooking, the second pressing, the 'grignons,' often with the help of solvents, yielding lower-quality oil for soap-making, with the residual cake going for cattle food or fertilizer.

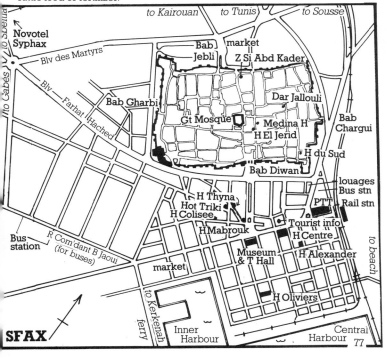

Other industries. Sfax is a busy fishing port, so naturally there is also an industry canning tuna and other fish in olive oil. And as Sfax has the country's busiest port, the finished product is shipped direct from here.

The port handles much of the phosphate mined at Metlaoui in the west, but several factories convert it into superphosphate before shipment. And a quarter of a million tons of sea salt is shipped to Europe every year from the pans to the south of town: you may notice flamingoes feeding there.

Cuttle-fish. Among the more unusual exports recently has been around 40 tons a year of cuttlefish shell, which when crushed is added to rice to prevent it forming a solid mass when cooked; it's also used for polishing hardwoods.

Grape and grain. If 70% of the farmland is devoted to olives, the remainder grows top fruit, mostly almonds but also sizeable quantities of apples, peaches, apricots and figs, and some quality grapes. Esparto grass from the Kerkenah Isles is woven into a variety of goods, or processed to yield cellulose and raw fibres. There isn't much cereal grown this far south as the rainfall is so unpredictable, but Sfax is the centre of a small perfume industry using blossoms which you would normally expect to find in the well-watered areas.

Sponges. And from November to March, sponge-fishermen reap their own harvest. Traditionally, divers have gone down to 30m (almost 100 feet) with nothing more than a lungful of air and a rock in each hand, but grappling-hooks began to replace them recently until it was realised how wasteful this system is, losing many of the mature sponges and damaging the young ones. Divers are now back in business, wearing breathing gear but restricting themselves to four or five descents in a working day.

Sfax in history. The Romans knew the town as Taparura, but its modern name derives from the Arabic *fakous*, a cucumber once grown here. Sfax has always prospered and its people have consequently felt a little bit superior to the remainder of their countrymen. It was the only city to hold out against the Hilalian onslaught, and from 1095 to 1099 it was independent.

It fell to Roger of Sicily in 1148, returning to the Islamic fold in 1159, but in 1864 it supported the revolt of Ali Ben Ghedahem against the Bey of Tunis. In 1881 it resisted the French takeover until a naval squadron bombarded the town and made its people think otherwise; it was badly bombed in January 1943 with much of the new city built on the ruins, and in 1947 it led the 5th of August revolt against the French, commemorated in the name of the Boulevard des Martyrs.

Hedi Chaker Sfax is the birthplace of Hedi Chaker, a member of the Destour and president at a secret meeting held on 18 January 1952. Chaker was assassinated by the *Main Rouge,* 'Red Hand,' in September 1953 and is now commemorated in the name of many streets around the country, including one in Sfax's new town.

The people of Sfax have such political and economic power that the Government must listen to them much as the President of the USA must pay attention to the Jewish vote: in fact, the people of Sfax are enviously called the Jews of Tunisia, strange praise in a Moslem land. Indeed, this was the only large town in the country in which I never saw a beggar, not even a well-dressed boy touting for the odd dinar. Economically, there is no need in such a prosperous city — but there aren't many tourists either.

The Medina. The relative absence of tourists means that in Sfax you can appreciate an unspoiled medina: it is a sad testimony that tourists of necessity ruin the very things they come to see. The small shops offer clothing, leather goods, perfumes, pastry, and genuine craftware, but there's not one specialising in souvenirs. Nor is there much fruit and veg; that's in the modern market to the north of Bab Jebli.

Despite the attacks by cannon, naval guns, and aircraft, the medina walls are among the best in Tunisia, albeit heavily restored in places. Bab Diwan, the main gate, was built in 1306 and repaired in 1619, 1646, 1748, and again after the Second World War.

Deep in the medina, the **Dar Jallouli** Museum of Arts and Popular Traditions, in a smart house built in 1728, recreates living conditions from the 18th cent to the present, with the three-storey building being the main exhibit. The dining room holds a pipe for smoking hashish, the kitchen has the equipment necessary for making perfumes at home, and on the first floor is a display of wedding dresses.

Marriage traditions. A marriage ceremony in Sfax, as elsewhere, traditionally lasted for seven days, with the bride leaving her father's house on the fourth day to move in with her new husband; on the sixth she would jump over a bowl of fish, a symbol of affluence and fertility. The museum does its best to portray these and other traditions which have almost faded into history.

The top floor has a wide range of Arab script, including painting on glass, another of the ancient crafts practised in Sfax.

Great Mosque. The Great Mosque, begun in 849 by one Ali Ben Salem El Jebiniani, was rebuilt by the Fatimites in the 11th cent and further altered during the Ottoman dominion of Tunisia. Its unusual minaret looks like three squat towers one atop another, and on the mosque's eastern wall there is a Byzantine panel with a Greek inscription and two peacocks beneath it. In view of the Islam distaste for carvings of living creatures it's a wonder this wasn't either plastered over or cut away, particularly with the Turkish involvement: when the Turks conquered Constantinople they plastered over every sculpting inside every church.

Hotel Sfax Centre and the Syndicat d'Initiative

Evil eye. If you're staying in Sfax, may I recommend the little Hotel El Jerid off the Route de la Grand Mosqée just inside the Bab Diwan? It's a spotlessly clean, new hotel with washbasins in every room, but its main attraction is that it's built inside the Souk El Jerid, with access through a clothing shop. The original souk on this site specialised in dead chameleons which were supposed to ward off the evil eye.

Westminster chimes. In the new part of town, the Archaeological Museum stands out because of its unusual architecture. On the corner of avenues Habib Bourgiba and Hedi Chaker, named from the local boy, this building in eyecatching pink with a tall clocktower on the left — *that's* a rarity in Tunisia! — and a silver dome in the middle could be anything. Mosque? Palace? Hotel de ville? There's no Latin inscription by the gate or near the door to tell you its ground floor is the museum of archaeology and its first floor is indeed the town hall.

This is the only chiming clock I noticed in Tunisia, and its Westminster chimes, imitating Big Ben, sounded blissfully out of place. They weren't quite so welcome at three in the morning when the city lay otherwise silent.

Museum. The museum specialises in mosaics and is a rival in miniature to the Bardo. If you're interested you will spend an hour or more inside (but not on Mondays); if you're not, it's worth noting that the best exhibit is of Daniel praying in the lions' den.

Sfax has almost no beach; the sand that was dumped after the Second World War has been taken away by the sea. The nearest good beach is at Sidi Mansour, 12km north.

HOTELS: 4-star: Centre, 260b; Novotel Syphax, 254b; **3-star:** Les Oliviers, 120b; **2-star:** Colisée, 100r; Mabrouk, 78b; Mondial, 43r; Thyna, 27r; **1-star:** Alexander, 72b; Triki, 26r; **unclass:** Besbes, 38b; El Habib, 53b; El Jerid, 20b; Ennaim, 82b; Essaada, 43b; Jamaica, 45b; Le Maghreb, 24b; Medina, 32b; Paix, 44b.

YOUTH HOSTEL: to the west of town by the stadium, 133b.

BUSES: There are two bus stations. The bigger one is to the west of the new town (see map) and the smaller is in front of the railway station. Buses serve all major towns.

LOUAGES: The louage stand is opposite the PTT.

RAIL: Coastal services; see the timetable.

POST and TELEPHONE: By the louage stand, of course — near the railway station. Post and telephone services from different parts of the same building.

FESTIVALS: January: Festival of Aghareb, 23km south, with horse racing and folk dancing. May: regional music festival. September: Moussem, the religious festival of and at Sidi Mansour at the saint's tomb.

TOURIST OFFICE: SI; in kiosk in the centre of Place de l'Independance.

THE ISLANDS

Kerkenah and Jerba.
THE KERKENAH ISLANDS

A few days on the Kerkenah Islands is the closest most of us will ever come to living the life of Robinson Crusoe. The isles are a breath of tropical paradise dropped by accident in the Mediterranean; if Kerkenah had a bit more tide and the palms grew coconuts instead of dates, you could easily imagine you were in the south Pacific.

There is very little to do on Kerkenah. That makes life difficult for the 15,000 islanders as the youngsters drift away to the mainland for work, but for the tourist it creates a true lotus-eater's paradise for the charm of Kerkenah lies in its isolation and its laid-back lifestyle with half the day's work done by the time you've ambled to the beach. But in deference to today's hectic lifestyle, the bigger hotels provide activities for those who must have them.

Desert isles. The two main islands are Gharbi, 'Western,' also known as Melita from its only village, and Chergui, 'Eastern,' which has the optional name of Grande Kerkenah; they are linked by a 600m causeway built by the Romans. Gremdi, Sefnou and Roumedia (Er Roumadia) are the only other isles big enough to have names but others come and go depending on the tide.

Life in Kerkenah is two-dimensional. The land — sand would be a better description — never rises more than 10 feet above sea level, and the surrounding waters are so shallow you feel you might wade back to the mainland. The slightly anaemic-looking palms, with a scattering of olives, almonds and figs, grow almost everywhere except in the bitterest of salt pans, for there is no fresh water on the islands.

Fishing. The Kerkennians weave palm fronds into thin mats, almost as thin as screens, which they fix in the shallow sea on struts of palm timber. The screens are either arranged vertically, making compartments in the sea, or supported flat at the surface.

The fishermen, armed only with sticks or thin planks, beat the warm water and send the terrified fish, usually mullet, leaping into the compartments or onto the platforms from where they're easily collected. They call this unusual method of fishing *la sautade,*, the leaping, but its contribution to the national fishing economy is, like everything on Kerkenah, minuscule.

The entire economy of the islands is so fragile that a company, the Société de Mise en Valeur des Iles Kerkenah, SOMVIK, is charged with exploiting their potential, which means promoting tourism.

SOMVIK. SOMVIK has rightly decided to capitalise on the Robinson Crusoe image which makes Kerkenah so attractive to the lotus-eating visitor, so five of the six hotels are clustered in one small group on Chergui allowing you the choice of enjoying your solitude in the company of several hundred other visitors, or truly escaping from the madding crowd by bus, on foot, or by hiring a cycle from the holiday village. The sixth hotel is in the small village of Remla — but if you really want to go it alone on a desert island, Kerkenah is the ideal place for a camping holiday as long as you're within reach of water.

Hached and Bourgiba. Throughout Tunisia, hotel names give an indication of the region's history, and the Hotel Farhat recalls that Farhat Hached, whose name graces so many roads, was born at Ouled Kacem on Grande Kerkenah. He founded the Union Général Tunisien du Travail, the UGTT or General Workers' Union, in Sfax in 1945, saw it become the main force in Bourgiba's Néo-Destour, and was assassinated by counterterrorists in December 1952. The road through Ech Chergui leads to the northern headland and a small Bourgiba Museum which treasures some of the reminders of the ex-president's escape from French custody, also in 1945, and his escape into Libyan exile through these isles.

Ech Chergui is also noted for its carpets and you may be able to see weavers at work near the school.

Two ruined fortresses constitute the islands' other curiosities. The Borj Hassar (or Hissar or Hsar), 2km along the track from the hotels, is a Spanish castle built on what serves as a hill in these flat isles, and the Turkish Tower is on the north shore of Gharbi.

Kerkenah in history. The Greeks were the first people known to have visited these islands which they called Kyronnis; the Carthaginians were frequent callers, followed by the Romans who renamed them Cercina. Hannibal took brief refuge here in 195BC after the Roman emperor Scipio defeated him at Zama (El Jamaa, near Makthar), but after the Arab conquest the islands were too vulnerable to Christian reprisal attack and were abandoned until the 18th cent.

Verdict. Don't come to Kerkenah for a long stay if you're the active type; its charm is that there's nothing to do and all the time in the world in which to do it, though there are the inevitable activities at the larger hotels. Depending on your outlook on life, Kerkenah could be the nearest thing to Paradise — or to Hell on earth.

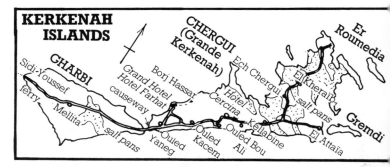

HOTELS: 2-star: Farhat (tel 04.81.536, 04.81.042; telex 40.837) 308b. Swimming, bar, boutique, night-club, money change. Lively atmosphere. The hotel was opened in 1975 as a collection of single-storey annexes around the multi-purpose reception-restaurant-bar. *Shares horse-riding and tennis facilities with its neighbour,* the Grand (tel 04.81.266, 04.812.565; telex 40.846) 225b. Swimming, mini-golf, bar, boutique, night-club, hairdresser, money change. Main hotel block with three smaller annexes up to thee storeys.

Unclassified: Cercina (04.81.228) 70b in bungalows; El Kastil (04.81.212) 22b in bungalows.

The above hotels are all at Plage Sidi Frej.

El Jazira (04.81.221) in Remla village; 34b.

HOLIDAY VILLAGE: Residence Club Sogetel (04.81.221), Plage Sidi Frej. 380b in 2-bed bungalows grouped around toilet blocks. Swimming, tennis, riding, cycle hire, bar, night-club.

BUS: A bus trundles along the only road from the ferry to Remla. No louages.

FERRY: see page 28.

FESTIVAL: Festival of the Sirenes; mock weddings in local costume, folk dancing, fishing contests, etc. July into August.

JERBA

Or is Jerba the lotus-eater's paradise? This picturesque island 30km wide by 28km north to south, had enough hotel beds in 1987 to take in more than 15,000 visitors, with plans to accommodate another 8,000, almost all of whom come for the sun, the sand and the sea, the diet of the modern lotus-eater. The expression has more significance for Jerba as it's quite possible that Ulysses called here on his return from Troy and saw the islanders sipping the nectar-like juice which gave them oblivion.

Or he may not. Mallorca, Menorca and Gozo (Malta) all claim to be the original island paradise and all have legitimate claim. It would help if we knew what the legendary lotus may have been — was it perhaps lâghmi, the juice of the Jerban date palm which makes quite a potent cocktail?

Meninx. The Phoenicians, Carthaginians and Romans certainly came here, all calling the island Meninx from its main settlement which is now the hamlet of El Kantara. The Romans knew the present island capital, Houmt Souk (Houmet Es Souk means the 'market quarter'), as Girba, from which the name Jerba derives.

Meninx, or Girba, was important in Roman times if only because the emperors Gallus and Volusianus, father and son, were born here.

The Vandals seized Carthage in 429 and quickly consolidated their hold on much of the Barbary Coast, leaving not a trace of their hundred years' stay when the Eastern Roman emperor Justinian, dedicating himself to the reconquest of the west, sent his general Belisarius into Ifriqya in 535. Within 30 years Byzantium had reached what is now Cape St Vincent in Portugal.

Jews. Meantime, in 586BC away in the Holy Land, King Nebuchadnezzar of Babylon destroyed the Temple of Solomon in Jerusalem and so set in train another exodus of Jews, many of whom settled at Hara Kbira, 'Great Ghetto,' now the village of Es Souani just outside Houmt Souk, and at Hara Seghira, 'Small Ghetto,' now Er Riadh. They lived in total harmony with the Christian Berbers and their new Byzantine overlords.

Byzantium could not withstand the furious onslaught of Islam in the 7th cent and the Berbers gave up Christianity with some reluctance. Two centuries later when the Fatimite sect was emerging, the Berbers under their leader Abu Yazid, that man on a donkey, rose in short-lived revolt against this latest attempt to alter their faith.

Kharijites. The Berbers of Jerba were the only people who held on to the Aghlabite version of Islam when the remainder of the country succumbed to Fatimism, and they came to be known as the Kharijites — the Departers or Deviants, which they still are today. And the Jerban Jews never did renounce their faith.

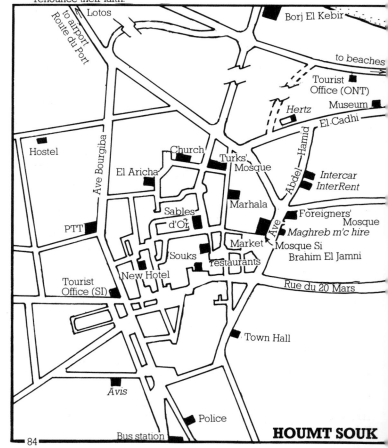

The Hilalians left them almost unscathed but between 1510 and 1560 when the Spanish and the Turks struggled for control of Jerba, the people were caught in the crossfire.

Yet another race of people appeared on the island in the 19th cent with the arrival of black Sudanese workers, a mixture of freed slaves and unwilling migrants. Even now they speak their own dialect of Arabic and perform their juju dances with origins in darkest Africa.

In this century the trend has been towards migration from Jerba as machine-woven cloth undermined the economy of the island's hand weavers. Many of the Berbers moved to the mainland or to Europe and seemed so attracted to shopkeeping that the word Jerban has come to mean a storekeeper throughout the country.

After the creation of Israel and particularly after the Six-day War, many Jerban Jews have made that one-way journey to their own Promised Land. Other Jews who hold Tunisian passports have travelled to Israel and back for business or pleasure, going via France and not having their passports stamped on the second leg of the journey.

Fruit, fish and furnaces. The Jerbans are unique for a Mediterranean people in not building their houses in tight defensive clusters. Instead, as if defying the raiders, they spread themselves out, each family living on its smallholding and so preserving its privacy and independence. As a result the villages are small — even Houmt Souk has only 16,000 people out of the total island population of 75,000 — and the east-central irrigated part of the island, between El May and Midoun, is a patchwork of green orchards and market gardens amid the dryer landsacape.

Around 1,200,000 palms dot the desert isle, but producing poor quality dates. The juice that goes to make lâghmi is extracted from the trees least likely to fruit, as this great loss of sap, either from a deep gash in the bark or from the base of a leaf stem, can prove fatal.

There are some 700,000 olives, a few of them planted by the Romans 2,000 years ago, but their average yield of 13kg per tree is low by Tunisian standards. When you learn that the old-style hand-operated press takes a day's work to produce a litre of olive oil, the economics are obvious. Only the cultivated apple, almond, citrus and pomegranate trees of the fertile belt compensate by cropping well.

And fishermen still put to sea in felucca-like vessels with flexible masts supporting lateen sails, much like their forefathers of fifty generations ago.

Pottery has been a Jerban craft for centuries, using the red clay of Guellala on the southern coast. The Phoenicians probably introduced the potter's skill to this community which they called Haribus, but the modern craftsman has mostly forsaken the traditional amphora or water pot to concentrate on high-profit articles for the tourist trade.

Weaving is another important local industry, despite the competition of the machine-powered looms of the Far East, with the women using wool from the island's 12,000 sheep to make their blankets and clothing. You may occasionally see women washing the hand-plucked wool in the sea, after which they card it (separate the fibres) by making a porridge of wool and plaster and pounding it under foot.

The manufacure of jewellery, traditionally in the hands of the Jews of Houmt Souk and Er Riadh, has declined with the migration of the craftsmen to Israel.

JERBA TODAY: Houmt Souk. Despite the influx of thousands of tourists, Houmt Souk manages to retain its Tunisian character and is a really charming small town which has grown around its core of souks.

If you arrive by bus or louage your first sight of the town will be the Gare Centrale which, despite its name hinting of railways, is the terminal for all buses from the mainland and the starting point for the island's own bus services. Louages have their pick-up point on the road outside and 100m towards the town are the charettes, the touristy horse-drawn carriages. Taxis start from the town centre.

This new gare sets the standard for all others. It has a branch post office, a buffet, café, a self-styled 'drugstore,' a newsagent and tobacconist, and at the far end of the waiting room there are separate toilets for men and women. There is room for improvement here, but the standard is still high compared with other bus station lavatories.

Souks... In the souks of the town centre you can still find merchants selling cloth and craftsmen making leather goods or working in gold or silver. This is where your bargaining skills are needed and you should never pay more than half the asking price of general tourist souvenirs; precious metals are an exception as only the labour element is negotiable.

Nearby is the market for fruit and veg including, in late summer, the ubiquitous pomegranate — but there's no bargaining for these basics of life. Pricing is so strictly controlled that in many fruit markets the stallholders are obliged to display the wholesale as well as the retail price; some work on a remarkably small profit margin for such perishable goods.

...and fondouks. In the days before mass tourism the souks would always have their fondouks or caravanserais nearby, and Houmt Souk is no

The Jerba car ferry terminal at Ajim

exception. Serving as both warehouse and hostelry, many of the fondouks have been restored for tourist appeal and two have adapted to modern needs by becoming hotels; El Arisha, the 'climbing vine,' and the Marhala.

Stay in either of these places for the night and you will be able to appreciate the layout of the fondouk, with a central courtyard opening onto small cells for the storage of goods, and with lodgings on the first floor.

Mosques. The Kharijites of Jerba kept their mosques small but sturdy, refuges for the population in time of trouble. The **Mosque of Sidi Brahim El Jamni** is typical of this type of building, its walls particularly thick because they're made of mud brick. This mosque was more than 30 years in construction and the Bey Mourad Ben Ali eventually finished the work; the mortal remains of Si Brahim are inside in his tomb.

The **Foreigners' Mosque** to the east across the main road has a bizarre roof design with a central dome surrounded by smaller ones. The interior, we are told, is utterly plain, but as it's closed to present-day foreigners there's no way of checking.

Jemaa El Trouk, the **Turks' Mosque,** an 18th-cent structure named from an Arabian religious zealot, has a tapering minaret which some people have mistakenly seen as an oversized rude gesture, forgetting that Islam forbids the sculpting of any part of any living creature. The Turkish connection, by the way, comes from three Ottoman tombs beside the mosque.

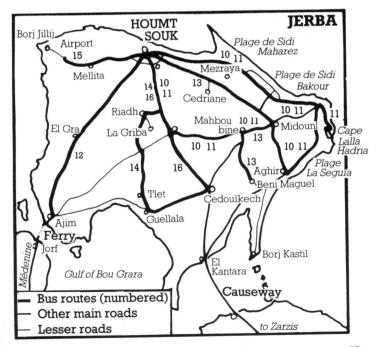

The religious scene is completed with a Catholic church and, in Er Riadh, a synagogue. Both are open to casual visitors except on their respective sabbaths.

Borj El Kebir. The Romans built a fort on the shore to protect their settlement of Girba; in 1289 Roger de Loria, an admiral in the service of Aragon and Sicily, enlarged it and in the mid-15th cent Sultan Abdul Fares El Hafsa used Roger's work as the core for his much larger fortification, Borj El Kebir, the Great Fortress, sometimes known as Borj Ghazi Mustapha.

In the mid-16th cent when Spaniards and Turks were fighting for control over the north African coast, the Turkish pirate Dragut seized Jerba and in 1557 placed his engineer Ghazi Mustapha in charge of strengthening the Great Fortress. The trap was set; all it needed was the victim.

Felipe II of Spain sent his fleet in 1560 and while his army of almost 6,000 men were on Jerba, Dragut's men destroyed their vessels: the victims were ready for the kill. The stranded Spaniards sought refuge in Borj El Kebir but surrendered on 31 July of that year.

Dragut showed no mercy; as they came out he slaughtered them and piled their severed heads on the beach in one of those macabre monuments to mankind's inhumanity. The Borj Er Rouss, the 'Tower of Skulls,' reputed to be 34 feet in diameter, stayed on the beach at Houmt Souk until 1848 when the Bey of Tunis gave the bones burial in a Christian cemetery. A small plaque now stands on the site of the grisly borj.

Museum. The Museum of Arts and Popular Traditions, on the north side of Ave Abdel Hamid El Cadi north-east of town, was opened in 1968 in the former Zaouia of Sidi Zitouni, an attractive building sheltering in a grove of trees.

This museum (which has standard opening hours but which closes from 1200 to 1400 in winter and 1200 to 1500 in summer), houses a wonderful display of costumes and pottery, recalling what were the island's main crafts before tourism and mechanisation upset the established order.

The costumes are arranged according to ethnology — Arab, Berber, Jew — with captions in French, and in the former prayer chamber are Jerban wedding dresses. An extension to this chamber, its floor and ceiling covered in ceramics, leads to a display of jewellery made by the island's Jews, including delicate enamelling and filigree work.

Beyond it a room, part sunk into the ground to increase humidity, holds a reconstruction of a potter's workshop of the type still found at Guellala, and in the courtyard are several examples of the potter's craft including a *duh,* a jar of 300 litres capacity — almost 70 gallons.

A short distance beyond the museum a weaving shed, a *hanout,* of unique Jerban style with triangular end walls and a vaulted roof, is part sunk into the ground, again to control temperature and humidity.

Around Jerba. From Houmt Souk a road runs east along the coast, giving a view over a shallow bay where the low tide exposes around 100 metres of sandy mud — and this in the Mediterranean! Jerba is reputed to have the greatest tidal range in this inland sea but it seldom amounts to more than 18" (45cm).   Along here and depending on the state of the tide you may see men netting fish, egrets and wading birds feeding, or women washing wool.

The first of the tourist hotels marks where the long alluvial spit stretches out to sea, so creating that shallow bay, and where the superb beaches of

Sidi Maharès and **Sidi Bakour** begin, the latter named from a mausoleum that once stood by the shore. A road branches left at the lighthouse, leading to another long spit of land which ends at **Cape Lalla Hadria,** while the main road continues to Aghir.

By the time you arrive work may have started on the biggest hotel complex on the island, the Lalla Hadria station, which has ambitious plans for a 4-star luxury hotel with 1,000 beds, a 4-star without the 'luxe,' of 750 beds, and 3-and 2-star hotels and holiday villages catering for another 5,500 visitors. There will be golf links, a marina, and the usual restaurants and boutiques. It will certainly alter Jerba's character.

Almost all the hotels allow non-guests to use their pools or sports gear, at a price, but outsiders who wander onto the beach behind a hotel soon begin to feel like trespassers. There are, for all that, large stretches of golden sand which the independent traveller can use with a clear conscience, either between the hotels where public paths cross the dunes, or where there are no hotels at all, as for example west of Dar Jerba; by Cape Taguermes east of Sidi Yati where there are some superb sands; north of Tanit Hotel on Cape Lalla Hadria; and by Sidi Slim. For people with their own transport there are some good beaches with scarcely a human footprint on the south of Aghir — but avoid Aghir itself.

The old fort at **Aghir** is now the 162-bed youth hostel which offers basic amenities. There's another fort at **Borj Kastil** at the end of a 7½km track running the length of a sandspit. The Aragonese admiral Roger de Loria built the Borj Kastil — its name translates as 'Castle Castle' — in 1285 and its fair state of preservation is probably due to its isolation.

The sea is shallow all around Jerba and from Borj Kastil you can see a chain of small islands which may, in centuries to come, join to form a natural causeway linking the island to the African mainland.

Meanwhile, there is a perfectly good **causeway** 5km to the west, running from El Kantara on Jerba to El Kantara-Continent on...well, on the continent. The Romans — or maybe the Carthaginians — built the original dyke, broken in several places to allow water wheels to take advantage of the current and drive fulling machines for cleaning fresh-woven cloth.

And then in 1551 the Turkish pirate Dragut found himself and his fleet caught in the Gulf of Bou Grara by the Genoese soldier of fortune, Andrea Doria. Dragut hacked his way to safety through the dyke which then fell into decay although at low tide camel trains could still make their way across. The route, part ford, part causeway, became known as the Trik El Jemel, the Camel's Path, but exactly 400 years after Dragut cut it the Tunisian Government began its restoration.

In 1953 the new highway came into service; 20 years later the causeway was enlarged, and it now supports two carriageways and the island's water supply along a bank 6½km long by 10m wide.

Meninx, the Phoenician settlement at the dyke's northern end, logically became El Kantara with the Arab conquest, as *kantara* is Arabic for causeway.

The highest point on Jerba is the low hill north-east of **Guellala** which provides that village's potters with their raw material. The clay comes from an adit (horizontal shaft) penetrating as much as 50m into the hill, and after being washed in the sea it's used to make hand-thrown pots for a variety of

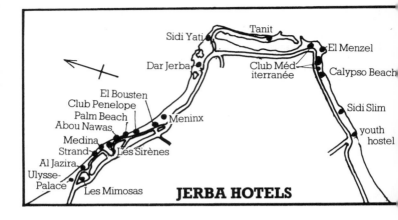

Map labels:
Tanit
Sidi Yati
Dar Jerba
El Menzel
Club Méditerranée
Calypso Beach
El Bousten
Club Penelope
Palm Beach
Abou Nawas
Meninx
Sidi Slim
Medina
Strand
Les Sirènes
youth hostel
Al Jazira
Ulysse-Palace
Les Mimosas

JERBA HOTELS

purposes ranging from the giant *duh* as in the Houmt Souk Museum, to the inevitable tourist souvenir. If you're prepared to wait the necessary few days for drying and firing you can have an 'antique' pot made to order!

When you see the piles of broken pottery overshadowing the houses in the village you can appreciate that the craft has been practised here for centuries. How many centuries more before the clay reserves are exhausted?

A good tarmac road leads to the ferry terminal of **Ajim,** whose fishermen land around 15 tons of sponges a year, either by diving without breathing gear in 15m of water, or by impaling their catch from the boat with a very long trident, but in shallower waters. The sea-god Neptune is famed for his trident, and legend associates the seas hereabouts with the Tritons, Neptune's helpers who also carried the three-pronged forks.

Ajim, known to the Romans as Tipasa, also has Jerba's largest palm grove but the varieties grown — aguioua, lemsi and matata — are not commercial and are eaten by the islanders. Other varieties produce fruit fit only for the camels and some which don't fruit at all are kept only for their lâghmi.

Jerba Airport occupies the north-west corner of the island. From its gate a tarmac road runs 9km east to Houmt Souk, the only wayside feature of interest being the Zaouia of Jamaa El Kebir — literally, the 'Small Mosque of the Great Reunion' — beyond Mellita, surrounded by small cells for the reunion's pilgrims.

And from the airport a dirt track runs 3km west to **Borj Jillij,** started by a Turk, Ali Pasha, in 1745, finished by another Turk, Hammouda Pasha, in 1795, and its ruins now crowned by a lighthouse.

If you look out to sea you'll notice several rows of palm trunks holding mats of woven palm fronds standing in the water in narrow-angled V-shapes open to the prevailing current. These are the *zribas*, fish traps, which propel their catch into darkened death chambers each equipped with one obvious means of escape into the daylight — straight into the keep net which the fishermen empty each daybreak.

In the interior of Jerba, **Er Riadh,** known until recently as Hara Sghira, the 'Small Ghetto,' is one of the two shrinking Jewish communities. The Griba Synagogue — 'The Marvellous' — is 1km south of the village and is still the focus of a Jewish pilgrimage on the 33rd day of the Jewish Pentecost. One of the oldest Jewish holy books in existence is reputed to be kept in this small synagogue, rebuilt in the 1920s.

Midoun is a small village with several mosques — there are around 300 on the island if one includes marabouts and zaouias — but it is much better known for its Friday market when all types of island produce are on sale to the islanders, and to a number of tourists as well. The village was known as Thoar in Roman times.

HOTELS: on the beaches: **4-star:** Abou Nawas, 220r, Mahares; El Menzel, 140r in design of Tunisian *menzel*, or domed house, Seguia; Palm Beach, 200r Mahares; Ulysse Palace, 126r, Mahares; **3-star:** Dar Jerba (see below); El Bousten, 180r, Bakour; Les Sirènes, 120r, Mahares; **2-star:** El Jazira, 340b, Mahares; Hari Club, 424b, new; Medina, 170r, Mahares; Meninx, 160r, Bakour; Penelope, 200r, Bakour; Sidi Slim, 350b in bungalows, Aghir; Sidi Yati, 88b, Taguermes; Tanit, 250r in bungalows, Lalla Hadria; **1-star:** Strand, 120b, Mahares.

Dar Jerba is the largest hotel complex in Tunisia, probably in north Africa. It sits on 65 hectares (160 acres) near Cape Taguermes and offers a total of 2,400 beds divided between 15 4-star apartments, 96 4-star rooms, 509 3-star rooms and 648 2-star rooms. The amenities available make Dar Jerba a small town in its own right: 5 restaurants, 80 shops, hairdresser, bank, tour agency and Hertz car hire offices, night club, cinema, casino, Turkish bath and an 87-bed crèche.

HOTELS: in town: **1-star:** Dar Faïza, 24r; Hajji, 92b; Nozha, 68b; **unclassified:** El Aricha, 35r; Lotos, 17r; Marhalla, 76r; New Hotel (sic), 113b; Nozha, 58b; Sables d'Or, 24b; Sinbad, 23r.

APART HOTEL: Les Mimosas, 24 flats, Mahares, weekly bookings only.

HOLIDAY VILLAGES: Club Méditerranée has two at the eastern tip of the island. Jerba la Douce ('Sweet' Jerba) has 996 beds in rather spartan bungalows; Jerba la Fidèle ('Faithful' Jerba) has 940 bunks and is open from June to September.

CAMPING: ask at the Hotel Sidi Slim, summer only.

HOSTEL: At Houmt Souk, 50b, see map; at Aghir, in the former borj; 162 beds.

RESTAURANTS: The vast majority of tables are in the big hotels. In Houmt Souk there are, in addition, the restaurants Princesse d'Haroun by the port and Blue Moon in Place Hedi Chaker, where you will also find several gargotes, 'working men's cafés.' Other reasonable restaurants are shown on the town plan.

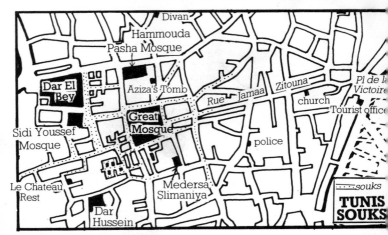

BUSES and LOUAGES: From the bus station south of town there are daily services to Gabès, Médenine, Sfax, Tunis. For details of the island bus routes, see map; for timings, consult the bus station. The most important service for tourists, no 10, runs 7 times daily, stopping at each hotel on request.

YACHT MOORINGS: Houmt Souk and Ajim.

FERRY: Departures from Jerba are at 0100, 0300, 0430, 0530, and then every half-hour until 2030; again at 2130, 2230 and 2330.

CAR HIRE: Africar (at Tourafric office, Ave Bourgiba); Cartha-Rent (at Cartha Tours office, Ave Bourgiba); Avis, Europcar, Hertz, Intercar, InterRent: see map. *Hertz and Avis are also at the airport and Dar Jerba.*

MOTOR-CYCLE HIRE: At Maghreb motor-cycle hire; see map. *Note the speed limit of 70kph on the island roads.*

CYCLE HIRE: At InterRent car hire, also occasionally at Sidi Slim.

AIRPORT: Jerba Airport, which is still spelled Djerba, has a weekly flight to Tozeur, and several daily flights to Tunis and several weekly ones to Monastir, the frequency depending on the season. Economy single fares are surprisingly cheap at 20.900TD to Tunis and 12.400TD to Tozeur, but you must reserve your seat as far ahead as possible: if your plans are fixed in advance you could even do it before you leave home.

MARKETS: Monday and Thursday morning at Houmt Souk, Friday at Midoun.

FESTIVALS: Ulysses Festival, July. Jerba Festival in August with traditional dancing and election of Miss Jerba.

THE OTHER TUNISIA: TUNIS

Tunis, Carthage, and district

TUNIS IS A MAJOR NORTH AFRICAN CITY, becoming a capital in 894 and at one time outshining Cairo. It has seen Phoenicians, Romans, Vandals, Byzantines, Berbers, Arabs, Turks, Spanish, French, Germans and British come as invaders, protectors or liberators.

It is a modern European-styled city built by the French, but its core is still the old Arab medina. Not a tourist centre in its own right it nonetheless has access to Carthage, one of the three great cities of antiquity, and it has a museum of international importance.

TUNIS IN HISTORY

Tines. The Maxitani tribe from Tyre in The Lebanon, settled the town of Thenes or Tines before Carthage was ever dreamed of. Agathocles, the 'Tyrant of Syracuse,' (361-289BC) seized Tunis in 310BC, and soon Rome was looking south for expansion. The general Marcus Regulus tried to capture the now-dominant Carthage in 256, but failed, settling for Tunis and a brutal death at the hands of the Carthaginians.

Rebel soldiers took Tunis, and Rome had no further presence here until the fall of Carthage and its dominions in 146BC. Tunis was quickly rebuilt; Carthage took longer, but both were sacked again in the 7th cent when the Arabs brought Islam to north Africa. Carthage could not recover from this last onslaught, but Tunis survived and soon became the most important city in the region after Kairouan.

Capital. The Aghlabite ruler Ibrahim II made it his chief city in 894 but glory was short-lived because his successor Ziyadet Allah III moved his court back to Kairouan, settling at Reqqada. But Tunis was now unstoppable. It had a port, a fertile hinterland, and reasonable water supplies, which Kairouan could never claim. After the Hilalians came from Egypt on their mission of retribution, Tunis managed to break free and enjoy a period as an independent kingdom.

The Almohad dynasty made Tunis its capital city in 1160, and if there is a date at which the story of Tunisia could be said to start, this is it. Tunis rose to become the most important city in north Africa, greater even than Cairo, and under the Hafcid rulers (1230 to 1574) the people of Tunis restored their trade links with Europe which had been severed by the coming of Islam.

Religion was still a great barrier: followers of the Prophet had conquered Constantinople and reached Vienna, while Christians were driving the Moors southwards out of Spain. In 1270, Louis IX of France led a Crusade to north Africa, seized the ruins of Carthage but died of the plague before he could take Tunis: the Islamic rulers saw the threat and signed a treaty with France agreeing that Christians in Tunis could live on equal terms with Moslems, having their own church and running their businesses. Tunisia was already learning to accommodate other ideas, a gift it would need to develop over the coming centuries.

Spanish Protectorate. Turkish pirates were plundering the Tunisian coast by the early 16th cent, and where trade went the flag would soon follow. The Ottoman Empire seized Tunis by a surprise attack in 1534 — but didn't hold it for long. The next year Carlos V, Holy Roman Emperor and King of Spain, whose flag had already been planted in the New World, sent 400 ships and 30,000 men who seized Tunis and established a Spanish Protectorate.

Tunisia was now the bone between two warring dogs. The Ottoman Pasha Eulj Ali of Alger recaptured the city in 1569 but lost it to Don Juan of Austria. The Turks struck back, with help from their Ottoman liegemen in Alger and Tripoli, and in 1574 Tunisia became part of the Ottoman Empire.

French Protectorate. Little happened on the international front until 1830 when France seized Algeria and, six years later, showed signs of wanting Tunisia as well. The country was by now heavily in debt to countries north of the Mediterranean, especially to France, and knew the bailiffs might come at any day. In 1881, the French claimed that Tunisian tribesmen from the Khroumirie had raided Algeria, which was a good enough reason for France to snatch Le Kef and Tunis. In June 1883 Bey Ali Ibn Husayn had no option but to agree to the Protectorate which was to last 73 years and end with Independence.

TUNIS TODAY: THE MEDINA

Porte de France In 1883 Tunis *was* the Medina plus a few villages outside its walls. From the Middle Ages people had been dumping soil into the Lake of Tunis, which originally came up to Bab El Bahar, the 'Sea Gate' now known as the Porte de France. It was the most important gate in a city which had already lost most of its walls (those each side of the gate disappeared 1950); the British Embassy had been long established immediately outside, and so it is from here we begin our tour of the Medina — on any day except Friday, and on foot.

Victory Square. Inside the gate, one of only two left standing, is Place de la Victoire which commemorates Bourgiba's release from exile on 1st June 1955; in the old days this was where stallholders sold henna and herbs.

Rue Jamaa Ez Zitouna. Two roads lie ahead. Rue Jamaa Ez Zitouna, formerly Rue de l'Eglise, leads to the Great Mosque, *Jamaa Ez Zitouna,* passing at number 12 the deconsecrated **Church of the Holy Cross,** founded in 1662 by a French consul, Père Jean Le Vacher; the Cathedral of the same name, built nearby in 1635, has long gone.

Jamaa Ez Zitouna. The Great Mosque, 'mosque of the olive tree,' is an impressive building almost lost in the press of souks around it. Eleven steps lead to the portico, then eight to the inner court, as far as non-Moslems may go.

The oldest mosque in Tunis, it is supposedly built on the site of an olive tree in whose shade its founder, Obaid Abd Allah Ibn El Habbab, taught the Koran. Founded in 732 as an assembly hall in the widest sense (that's the literal meaning of *jamaa*), the mosque was used for prayers, for teaching the Koran and Koranic law, and ultimately for a university until the modern University was founded after Independence. It also has an extensive library, started in 1451. The Aghlabids enlarged the buildinbg in 864, the Turks added to it in 1638, the minaret was rebuilt in 1894 and there were more restorations in 1962-4.

The **National Library** at number 55, beside the mosque, is in a converted barracks built by the Turks in 1813.

Sidi Ben Arous. Souk des Etoffes leads to the Zaouia of Sidi Ben Arous at number 18 of the street named from him. This zaouia, founded by the Hafcid prince Al Mountasir in 1436, proved too popular with women and was soon closed, to be reopened after protests.

Hammoud Pasha. The lavish and Italianate Mosque of Hammoud Pasha has an octagonal minaret, showing its links with the Ottomans. Built by an Italian who converted to Islam to further his career under the Turks, it was the model for the Bourgiba family mosque in Monastir.

Tomb of Princess Aziza. Rue de la Kasbah leads east to Rue El Jelloud where at number 9 is the privately-owned mausoleum of Princess Aziza Othman who died in 1646. The daughter of Othman Bey, she freed her slaves and gave her fortune to charity, which earned her the name of 'beloved' or 'faithful' — Fatima. The tomb is in the former 13th-cent Medrese (theological school) of Echemmahia, rebuilt in 1647.

Hand of Fatima. The door knockers seen all over the medina model the hand of Fatima; not the Princess Aziza Fatima but the Prophet's daughter.

Dar El Bey. Rue de la Kasbah also leads west to Dar El Bey, an old palace remodelled at the end of the 18th cent and now the Prime Minister's office and the Ministry of Foreign Affairs. The Ottoman **Kasbah**, demolished by the French just before Independence, stood nearby and was for years the seat of government. During extensive town planning shortly after Independence there were suggestions that the Avenue de France should continue from the new city in the east, straight through the medina to the Dar El Bey. Public outrage killed the idea and also gave birth to the *Association de Sauvegarde de la Medina*.

Mosque of the Kasbah. Outside the old city, the Mosque of the Kasbah was built in 1231-5 in the same style as the Dar El Bey; from its heavily-ornamented minaret a flag signals the universal call to prayers of all the city's mosques.

Sidi Youssef. The bey Youssef began the Sidi Youssef Mosque in 1616, and its minaret, the first octagonal one to be built in Tunis, shows the Ottoman influence.

Souks. Each souk was originally restricted to a single trade, as was customary throughout the Arab world. The covered souks which today cluster around the Great Mosque and towards Dar El Bey are much less specialised than they were but retain all their character. **Souk des Femmes,** for example, began catering for women coming on pilgrimage to the tomb of Sidi Mahrez (see below), the patron saint of Tunis and special benefactor to the fair sex , and labyrinthine **Souk des Orfèvres** is still the home of gold- and silversmiths, jewellers, and workers in coral.

Souk de la Laine, beside the Grand Mosque, has little wool these days, but there is a silk-weaving factory in a side-turning where two large looms rumble and vibrate throughout the day. The wool trade has gone to **Souk El Kouafia** a few paces away.

Souk El Attarin no longer deals in perfumes. The English word 'attar' comes from the old Arabic *itr,* meaning the perfume specifically from roses. Three centuries ago this souk stayed open until late at night to serve women coming from their hammam sessions, and before that it dealt in slaves, though the main market for Christian slaves was in **Souk El Berka,** the 'basin souk,' built by Youssef Bey in the early 17th cent.

Souk des Etoffes, also known as Souk El Koumach, was built in the 15th cent in the form of three covered parallel passages with shops opening off them. The **Souk El Leffa** specialised in carpets and blankets, and if you can talk your way to the top floor of the Palais d'Orient carpet shop here, you should have a good view of the medina.

The souk runs into the 18th-cent **Souk Es Sekkajine,,** the saddlers' souk, which has virtually given up trading in leather. **Souk El Trouk** is the souk of Turkish tailors, built in 1630 and now catering to the tourist trade. The M'rabet Restaurant in this souk is one of the best in the city and is built over the tomb of three learned men.

The **Souk Ech Chaouachiya,** built in the time of Mohammed El Hafci — 1675 to 1684 — was a co-operative venture from the start. A *chechia*, as the French call it, is a skull-cap and its manufacture was the monopoly of the Moors driven from Spain early in the 16th cent. Knitted in wool from Ariana, north of the city, it was then soaked in oil and sent to a fuller near Tabarka who converted it into felt. Back in Tunis the material was dyed and pressed to create the skull-cap. Fezzes were made in the same manner but Bourgiba discouraged their use and as they go out of fashion they are taking the chechia with them.

Place Bab Souïka. The northern part of the medina has the liveliest part of Tunis. Bab Souïka, the 'gate of the little souk,' is the place to come after sunset on any day during Ramadan. With the day's abstinence gone and the morrow's yet to come, the people of Tunis come to the cafés here to eat fancy cakes known as *mkharag* and *zalabia*, and to watch belly-dancing. A major rebuilding job has put the traffic in an underpass allowing the square to be pedestrianised.

When Bab Souïka was still a gate it also served as the public gallows. Alexandre Dumas described the execution of a criminal who was brought from the city on a donkey's back, the noose already around his neck. The rope's other end was secured to the gate's arch and the donkey taken away. But, said Dumas, if the animal had put its forelegs on the condemned man's shoulders to speed strangulation, the crowd was ready to pelt the victim with rotten fruit.

Sidi Mahrez. Inside the medina from Bab Souïka on the busy Rue Sidi Mahrez stands the Mosque of Sidi Mahrez, rising like something transplanted from Istanbul. It is the only truly Ottoman mosque in Tunis and glories in its large, Turkish-style domes which dominate the medina skyline.

The Berber Abu Yazid from Tozeur (*q.v.*) who led a revolt against Fatimite Islam, seized Tunis in 944 and treated its peoples cruelly. Abou Mohammed Mahrez Es-Sadiqi urged the citizens to strike back, then to rebuild the city walls and pick up the threads of their lives. Sidi Mahrez wasn't urging the return to the austere existence that the Fatimites demanded, although he chose to live in perpetual penitence. He helped engineer the return to the Malekite way of life and was rewarded in death by being revered as the patron saint of Tunis.

The Turkish ruler Mohammed Bey built this mosque around 1675 after the Spanish had damaged the holy man's tomb, and in 1862-3 the tomb and its zaouia (facing the mosque across Rue Sidi Mahrez) were rebuilt, incorporating a sanctuary where women can buy sifsaris and clothes for their pilgrimage; women consider that the saint has influence over their particular problems.

So why was this large mosque named from a small zaouia and a man who had been dead for seven centuries? Why was it not Mohammed Bey Mosque? Probably because he died before it was finished, his brother was murdered, and his dynasty crumbled. And Sidi Mahrez was so convenient.

Zaouia of Sidi Brahim. The mosque of Sidi Brahim Riahi, alternatively called Sidi Ibrahim, is a smart little place built in 1850 in the reign of Ahmed Bey and extended in 1878. Ibrahim was born in Testour, studied at the Great Mosque and in Morocco, and built this zaouia so he could become a teacher.

Diagonally opposite the zaouia is the first-floor Medersa (Koranic school) of Achouria, with access by a small staircase. The palace Dar Lasram, nearby, is the home of the Association pour la Sauvegarde de la Medina and closed to the public.

Medersa Bachiya. Just to the west, Rue du Pacha is a main street running south past the Medersa Bachiya. *Bachiya* is a corruption of 'pasha' ('pacha'in French) and shows the Turkish connection again. This Koranic school, also known as the School of the Well (Medersa Bir Lahjar), was built in 1756 and was lately used for training the Tunisian national football team.

Rue du Pacha recalls that the pasha once had an official residence in this street, similarly the military chief lived in Rue Agha and the town council met at number 3, Rue Divan (or Diwan). You have now learned the Turkish for 'chief citizen,' 'military chief,' and 'town council.'

Mosque of the Dyers. The southern part of the medina has less sights to offer but has a few interesting hotels — and a smart hammam — on and near the Rue des Teinturiers, the tinters' or dyers' street. The **Souk des Teinturiers,** leading off the street, has a well with a wide opening, its waters used by the dyers. Slightly to the north is the Mosque des Teinturiers or Jamaa El Jedid, the New Mosque, built in 1716 with that octagonal minaret which betrays the Turkish influence. The interior is lavishly decorated with tiles from Iznik, the traditional centre of Turkey's ceramics industry.

Husain Ben Ali, founder of the Husaynid dynasty, built this mosque for his own afterlife and reserved a spot for his tomb between those of two holy men. But his nephew Ali Pasha I dethroned him and buried his own father in the place of honour.

Tourbet El Bey. Ali Pasha II built the Tourbet El Bey to hold the tombs of the Husaynid rulers from 1758, when work began. The uninspiring building is a mixture of architectural styles with Italian predominant.

Ibn Khaldoun. The philosopher and writer Ibn Khaldoun was born at 33 Rue Tourbet Bey in 1332. Khaldoun studied at the Great Mosque, served in the army that defeated Tamburlane ('Timur the Lame'), and died in 1406 in Cairo.

Dar Ben Abdallah. Two converted palaces shine in the southern medina. The 18th-cent Dar Ben Abdallah is now the home of the *Musée du Patrimoine Traditionel de la Ville de Tunis,* the Museum of the Heritage of Tunis (conventional hours, closed Sunday, free entry Friday). Its exhibits give an insight into the private life of the citizen of Tunis from birth to death, including clothes for the newborn, for the boy going to circumcision, a bride's wedding trousseau, and working clothes for men of various occupations: well worth a visit.

Dar Othman. The other palace, Dar Othman, was built by Othman Dey in the early 17th cent. A *dey* was the leader of the Janissaries, the kamikazi warriors of the Ottoman empire who were stolen from Christian homes as infants and, in the modern vernacular, brainwashed. Here, Othman was away from the intrigues of the Kasbah and the Janissaries' barracks, but militarism eventually caught up with the palace which in the 19th cent took on its present role as the **Dar El Aoula,** the 'palace' of Army provisions. Hence the sturdy gate.

Bab Jedid. The dirty trades of dyer and blacksmith were kept well away from the Mosque of the Olive Tree. Rue des Forgerons, 'blacksmith alley,' leads to Bab Jedid, the 'New Gate' of 1276, based on Moroccan Almohade styles. This and the Porte de France, Bab El Bahar, are the only surviving parts of the medina defences.

Mosque El Ksar. Coming north again towards Dar El Bey, we find the simple-styled Mosque El Ksar, built in 1106 by Ahmed Ben Khorassan but heavily restored in 1647 when the minaret was added. Ben Khorassan led Tunis's recovery after the Hilalian invasion of the 11th cent. **Dar Hussein,** a nearby 18th-cent palace, is being converted into the Institute of Archaelogy and as such is closed to the public.

Outside the Medina. Immediately beyond the bounds of the medina to the west is the **Sadiki College,** where Bourgiba was educated. Farhat Hached's tomb is in front of the college while to the south the **Museum of 9 April** tells in Arabic the story of Bourgiba's struggle for independence.

To the north-east, Place Bab Carthajna leads to Rue des Protestants and the Anglican **Church of St George.** The Russian Orthodox Church, by the way, is out to the east on Ave Mohammed V near the Ave du Ghana.

THE NEW CITY

Most of the interest in the new city lies in the Avenue de France from the Porte de France, along the Avenue Habib Bourgiba to the Place d'Afrique, and the streets immediately north and south, particularly the avenues de Paris and Carthage. Let's start again at the Porte de France.

It's not by accident that the short **Avenue de France** with the Porte de France at one end and the French Embassy at the other, feels and looks as if it belongs in central Paris. The arcaded shops, the advertisement hoardings, the pavement voyeurs, all give it that French atmosphere.

Museums. At the Place de l'Independance where the two main avenues meet, the Rue de Rome leads north to the small Museum of Money and eventually to the Thameur Gardens and a **bus station.** The Rue Gamel Abdel Nasser goes south to the main **Post Office** and the **Postal Museum** containing examples of every Tunisian postage stamp issued. Nearby is the **Marché central,** the market for everything edible.

Cathedral. Independence Square's central statue is of Ibn Khaldoun, the city's native philosopher. To the south the French Embassy is housed in the former consulate, but to the north is the ponderous pseudo-Byzantine Cathedral of St Vincent de Paul built in 1882. The two angels blowing trumpets and the gilt figure of Christ over the portico were tasteless in a Moslem land that had not wanted the French protectorate, but the stained glass is good. The original cemetery here, now moved to the equally garish Chapel of St Louis in Carthage, held the body of Ferdinand de Lesseps's father.

The **Avenue Bourgiba,** formerly Ave Jules Ferry, from the Frenchman who intervened in Tunisian domestic affairs in 1881, is the Champs Élysées and the Rue St Honoré of Tunis, a smart dual-carriageway avenue with its trees down the centre and its shops, hotels and prestige offices on each side.

Hotels and restaurants. On the corner of Rue Ali Bach Hamber and the main avenue stands the **Hotel International Tunis,** built in 1977 and originally called *Deux Avenues.* Designed in the grand style, it has its own night-club and the **Sofra Restaurant.** Opposite on the south side are the craft centre and the theatre.

The **Café de Paris** and the **Capitole Hotel** lead on to the **Hotel Meridien Africa** which created such an uproar of protest when it was built in 1970 that Tunisia decided to ban high-rise development. You can't fail to notice the Meridien, its blue walls rising to 21 storeys with a *swimming-pool on the fifth floor,* a night-club on the 20th and the Étoile du Sud Restaurant on the top. Admittedly, it gives a wonderful view of the city.

You can't fail to notice the **Hotel du Lac,** either. It squats by the Place d'Afrique, each of its 10 storeys overlapping the ends of the one beneath. It's a matter of opinion, but I feel it's more an eyesore than the Meridien.

The main branch of the *Office National du Tourisme Tunisien* is on Ave Mohammed V, 100m on the right, but Ave Bourgiba continues, somewhat more drab, to end at the smart new TGM station.

TGM Line. The Tunis — Goulette — Marsa line, from which comes the name TGM (it's not 'Tunis, Gare Maritime') originally came much closer to the medina but was pulled back to allow for the prestigious and impressive Ave Bourgiba: a wise choice. Sir Richard Wood, a British Ambassador in the late 19th cent, suggested to the Bey of Tunis (the king) that a railway be built from near the British Residency at La Marsa, across the shallow Lake of Tunis, to the medina, so he could have a smooth journey from his home to the Embassy. A British firm was awarded the contract but pulled out, leaving an Italian company to do the job in 1880.

Sir Richard had a warning system fitted in the Residency, allowing him to summon a train which would be waiting for him outside his front gate.

"Lake Geneva" at Tunis. The Lake of Tunis is so shallow that a port had to be developed at La Goulette. Sir Richard's proposed rail causeway also carried a road, and the easiest way to find the material for this dyke was to scoop it up from the bed of the lake, so creating the canal which now allows shipping to come into Tunis city and has thus revived the medieval port of Tunis. Work has now begun on creating what the authorities call a 'Lake Geneva' complex, with 5,000 hotel beds, 3,500 holiday bungalows, offices and commercial property, and the expansion of the international fairground.

THE CITY: BELVÉDÈRE

From Ave Bourgiba, Ave de Paris and its aptly-named continuation, Ave de la Liberté, come to the Place Pasteur (the Institut Pasteur is nearby) for the entry to the 250-acre **Parc du Belvédère,** the only true park in the city. The vegetation ranges from palm to pine, olive to eucalyptus, and on its lower slopes is formal and well-watered, turning intentionally to wild scrubland on the drier summit from where, at 82 metres altitude, there is a good view across the city. A belvédère is, of course, a look-out point.

A 17th-cent koubba (tomb) midway up the hill, was brought here in 1901 from its original location in the suburbs. The **zoo,** open daily from sun-up to sundown, features the fauna of Africa, but my sympathy always goes out to creatures caged for the amusement of man. You might find the 17th-cent *midha* (ablutions room), rescued from the Souk El Trouk and relocated here, more interesting.

Near the gate, the **Museum of Modern Art** in the former Casino, specialises in plastic art.

Hilton Hotel. The Hilton International Hotel is on another belvédère to the north-west of the Parc du Belvédère. Opened in 1967 and remodelled in 1971, it has a modest five floors but commands excellent views. And the management offers free transport to the hotel's private beach.

THE CITY: THE BARDO MUSEUM

The Museum of the Bardo has a worldwide reputation for the quality and quantity of its exhibits, many of them from archaeological digs in Tunisia. If you're interested in the Roman and Byzantine sites around the country, you'll be interested in the Bardo and, with time permitting, you could spend a few preliminary hours here then come back for a longer inspection after you've made your tour.

The Bardo as a structure is a complex of palace and outbuildings from the Hafcid dynasty in the 15th cent, plus the excessively lavish palace built by Mohammed Bey and his successor Mohammed Sadok (1854-'59-'82) when the country was going broke. The Museum Alaoui was established in November 1882 but had no home until the coming of the Protectorate forced the Bey out of his palace. While some rooms were retained for state functions, the Museum Alaoui moved into two rooms in March 1885.

With archaeological digs yielding a continuous flow of material, the museum steadily expanded and in 1956 changed its name to the National Museum of the Bardo. It now occupies 35 main rooms and several smaller ones on three floors and continues to expand. Each room is devoted to a specific subject or ancient city site and the most I can hope to do here is whet your appetite with a selection from the major exhibits.

Rooms 2,3,4, Punic Carthage: bas-relief of a priest carrying a child to the sacrifice. **Room 5, Christian:** mosaics and wall tiles. **Room 6, Bulla Regia:** the mosaic of Perseus and Andromeda from the 3rd cent. **Room 7, Cap Bon:** a tiny room with a statue of Tanit as a lion. **Room 8, Thuburbo Majus:** marble statue of Hercules. **Room 9, second floor, Roman Carthage:** large room, formerly the bey's patio, with many mosaics.

Room 10, Sousse: former festival hall, with a major mosaic of the Triumph of Neptune among other excellent exhibits. **Room 11, Dougga:** mosaic of the Four Seasons. **Room 12, El Jem:** mosaics of the Triumph of Bacchus and the Nine Muses. **Room 13, Althiburos:** the palace's concert room holds one mosaic from Althiburos and several from around the country, notably hunting scenes. **Room 14:** the former dining room has cases of jewellery.

Room 15, Virgil: a cross-shaped room with private chambers in the corners. Statues and a mosaic of Virgil with the Two Muses. **Room 16, Prehistory:** one of those tiny private chambers with a few ancient stone implements. **Rooms 17 to 22, Mahdia:** In June 1907 sponge divers found the wreck of a ship which had sunk off Mahdia in 81BC in 40m of water. It was full

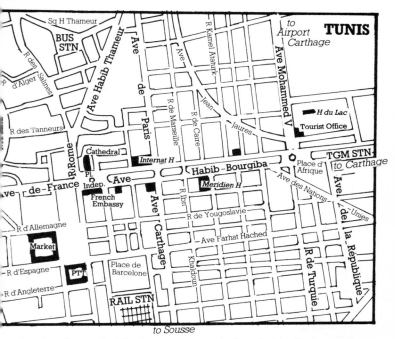

of works of art and while the stone statues had eroded badly the metal objects came up in perfect condition.

Room 23, submarine mosaics: a miscellany. **Room 24, mausoleum:** the Roman mausoleum came from Carthage but the mosaics are of many origins including the Triumph of Venus from Thuburbo Majus. **Rooms 25 to 28, mosaics:** more mosaics! Mosaic of the Seasons from Sbeïtla, of Ulysses from Dougga, of Venus from Kasserine. **Room 29, third floor:** gallery around second-floor room 9 with terra-cotta works. **Rooms 30 to 32, mosaics:** Diana and Bacchus predominate. **Room 33, Acholla:** 2nd cent mosaic of the Triumph of Dionysus and the Labours of Hercules. **Rooms 34 and 35, frescos:** from several sources.

Arab Museum. A museum of Islamic art in the same complex is being rearranged with many exhibits going to Reqqada, Kairouan. Exhibits include prints, weapons, costumes and jewellery, and Jewish artefacts from Jerba and Tunis.

Where, when, how? The Bardo is on the north side of Place de l'Assemblée Constitutionelle, 5km from the Porte de France. It is open daily, except Monday and public holidays, between 0930 and 1630; tickets are cheaper on Friday and Sunday afternoons and card-bearing students may get in free. Take a 42 bus from the Thameur Gardens depot or a 4, 16 or 30 from near the Place de l'Independance.

Houses of Parliament. The *Assemblée Nationale,* the seat of government, is in the building immediately to the south of the Bardo.

HOTELS: 5-star Luxe: Hilton, (Belvédère) 268r; International Tunisia, (Ave Bourgiba), 203r; Meridien Africa, (Bourgiba), 164r; **5-star:** Belvédère (University), 118b; **4-star:** Diplomat, (Ave Hedi Chaker, s of Belvédère), 150r El Mechtel, (Ave Taieb M'hiri, Belvédère), 1010b; **3-star:** Ambassadeurs, (Ave Taieb M'hiri, Belvédère), 182b; du Lac, (Pl Afrique), 202r; Golf Royal, 60r; Ibn Khaldoun, (Rue Koweit, Lafayette), 271b; National, 156b.

2-star: Carlton, (31, Ave Bourgiba), 40r; Dar Slim, (Ave Khereddine, Monplaisir), 14r; Maison Dorée, (6, Rue Hollande, Gare), 54r; Saint-Georges, (16, Rue Cologne, Lafayette), 39r; Tunis Parc, (7, Rue Damas, Lafayette), 36r; **1-star:** Capitole, (60, Ave Bourgiba), 48r; Commodore, (17, Rue Allemagne, s of Medina), 32r; Métropole, (3, Rue Grèce, Gare), 55r; Salambo, (6, Rue Grèce, Gare) 52r; Suisse, (5, Rue Suisse, Gare) 23r; Transatlantique, (106 Rue Yougoslavie, Gare), 42r.

Unclassified: The Tourist Office lists 66 unclassified hotels and will give you names but it cannot make reservations. The majority are small hotels in the medina or around the main railway station south of Ave Bourgiba.

RESTAURANTS: Étoile du Sud, the top-ranking restaurant, is on the top floor of the Meridien Hotel. La Sofra is in the International Tunisia. Le Chateau is a smart establishment at 26 Rue Sidi Bou Krissan in an old Medina palace. Le M'rabet, Souk du Trouk, has waiters in traditional costume. All serve Tunisian cuisine and are pricey.

Chez Slah, 14bis Rue Pierre Coubertin off Ave Bourgiba is the top restaurant for European dishes. The Café de Paris at 62 Ave Bourgiba is popular and has reasonable prices. There are numerous cheaper and smaller restaurants and snack bars south of Ave Bourgiba and in the Medina, but those in the old city close early in the evening.

NIGHTLIFE: Except during Ramadan, Tunis is not noted for its nightlife. The larger hotels have their own night clubs leaving everyone else to the ubiquitous disco, and they're not so ubiquitous in Tunis.

BUSES: The main bus stations are: **Gare Routière du Nord** (for Bizerte to Le Kef), a smart new well-organised building 500m west of Place Bab Sa Adoun on way to Bardo; **Gare Routière du Sud** (for Kasserine and the south), a not-so-new place on Rue Sidi El Bechir south of the main railway station; **Square Habib Thameur** a disorganised departure point for city and short-haul buses 500m north of International Tunisia Hotel along Rue de Rome. A number 50 bus might still run the shuttle between them. All but the most remote destination is served daily from one of these stations.

Some useful bus routes: 1, around Medina; 3, Bardo — Ave Bourgiba; 4, 16, 30, Thameur Gardens — Bardo; 5, 38, Belvédère — Ave Bourgiba; 7, Port de France — Belvédère; 28, Place Afrique — Belvédère; 35, Hotel Meridian — Airport.

LOUAGES: Louages run from several places in the city to destinations as far as Jerba. As the starting points change fairly frequently, consult the tourist office for the latest information.

AIRPORT: 8km from city centre. Check-in for international flights 1 or 2 hrs, depending on airline; domestic flights, 30 mins. Bus 35 from Hotel

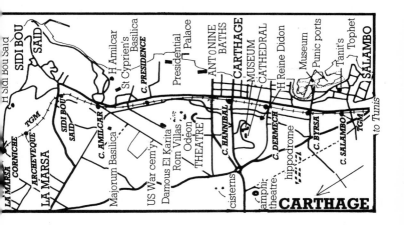

Meridien leaves every 30 mins.

RAIL: The only long-distance passenger rail station is at Place de Barcelone, south of Ave Bourgiba. The TGM station for Carthage is at the east end of Ave Bourgiba. See page 23 for destinations and sample timetables.

FESTIVALS: National Music, February; Theatre, April; Medina, Ramadan.

TOURIST OFFICES:
ONT; Main office, Ave Mohammed V (near Place d'Afrique), tel 255.348, 256.957. Also at Carthage Airport and Place de la Victoire, Porte de France (east entry to Medina).

CARTHAGE and environs

Don't come to Carthage expecting to see vast ruins; there is extremely little remaining of what was at one time the most important city in the world. That city straggled along four miles of coast and climbed the hill inland, but it suffered cruelly at the hands of its conquerors. Over the centuries its stones were hauled away to be incorporated in other buildings, and the weather worked its usual damage. The smart suburbs of Tunis have encroached on the site, making excavation extremely difficult, and the ruins that have been opened are frequently in housing estates.

Come and see Carthage by all means, but be prepared to find more interest in reading about it.

Punic city. Phoenicians from Tyr (Tyre) founded Qart Hadasht, 'New

City,' in 814BC, hoping to escape the menace of the Assyrians, but Virgil claims that the founder was Queen Didon, fleeing from the tyrrany of her brother King Pygmalion. Didon, Virgil said, asked the resident Berbers for as much land as she could cover with an ox-hide, then sliced the skin into one continuous bootlace long enough to encircle a hillside: as the Greek for 'hide' is *bursa,* which became the name of the centre of the city, the legend would appear to have some foundation in truth.

Punic, by the way, is the adjective and noun applied to these new Phoenicians who settled in the western Mediterranean.

Virgil also adds in his *Aenid* that his hero Aeneas, sole survivor of the fall of Troy, was wrecked near Carthage and dallied with Didon, but maybe that was poetic licence.

Empire. The city prospered and in the 3rd cent BC it controlled a maritime empire stretching from Lisbon and Rabat (Morocco) to the Gulf of Sirte (Libya) and including Corsica and Sardinia: it built a satellite city in Spain later to be known as Carthago Nova, the modern Cartagena, and merchants went much further, reaching the Gulf of Guinea for its gold and Cornwall for its tin.

Tanit. At home, paganism was rife and the wealthy families were regularly sacrificing their firstborn children to the goddess Tanit; thousands of tiny skulls have been unearthed near the ancient military port at Salambo.

Roman threat. But Rome, the growing land empire to the north, considered New Tyr a threat. When in 480BC Carthage failed to subjugate Gelon, the first Tyrant of Syracuse, Rome detected weakness. Agathocles, the second and better-known tyrant from Syracuse, inflicted bitter wounds on Carthage which then listened to offers of help from the Greeks.

And then Rome struck. The three Punic Wars (264-241, 218-201 and 149-146) ended with the defeat of Carthage. Cato had warned: "Delenda est Karthago," ("We must destroy Carthage,") and the Romans did so with enthusiasm, glorying in 10 days of pillage and enslaving those citizens who hadn't committed suicide. The centurions ploughed the soil of Carthage then poured salt on it. The city would never rise again.

It did. In 122BC Rome saw the advantages of the site and began rebuilding; in 44AD Caesar made it a colony. The new city became the capital of Roman Africa and a centre for learning, commerce and dalliance. Christianity arrived, but couldn't save St Cyprien from his martyrdom in 258.

Vandals and others. Genseric led his Vandal attack from Andalucia — originally *Vandalucia* — in Spain in 439, destroyed the city then made his capital in its ruins. Belisarius recaptured it for the Byzantines in 534 but in 692 it fell to the Arabs and became a quarry for the builders of Tunis. In 1920 a British encyclopedia commented that "its site is now occupied by a few wretched Arab villages."

ANCIENT CARTHAGE TODAY

If that's an odd title, don't forget that the old city is lost under smart suburbs which have replaced the 'wretched villages.'

Punic ports. Carthage Salambo is the TGM station for the Punic ports, military to the north, mercantile to the south and originally linked. Nearby are the remains of the **Tophet,** the sanctuary of Tanit and Baal, a crater 200m long where were found the remains of an estimated 70,000 sacrificed infants. The modern **Oceangraphic Museum** between the ports (Tues-Sat

1400-1700, Sun 1000-1200, 1400-1700) opened in 1924, is an irrelevant disappointment, and there's little to see of the Hippodrome up the hill inland.

Cathedral of Saint-Louis. Take the train from Byrsa to Hannibal for the main ruins, and walk uphill. Very soon you will see the top of a large cathedral appearing over the roofs of the executive residences. This is the Cathedral of Saint-Louis, built in 1890 and named from Louis IX who died of the plague here in Carthage in 1270 while leading a crusade to capture Tunis. The cathedral is in mock-Byzantine style and looks totally out of place. It was deconsecrated after independence and, in 1964 with Papal agreement, the body of one Cardinal Lavigerie who died in 1892 was exhumed and sent to Rome. It's open to visitors and the terrace has a splendid view.

National Museum. The National Museum of Carthage, in the former convent of the White Fathers, sits on the Byrsa hilltop beside the cathedral. Part-opened in 1972, closed again for major overhaul, it will eventually display the few treasures found in the city, including some of the steles (gravestones) from the sacrificial site of Tanit's temple.

Byrsa ruins. As the Romans levelled this hilltop to build their acropolis, they accidentally preserved a part of the old Punic city. The acropolis has gone, but these fragments of 2nd-cent BC Carthage have, ironically, survived 2,200 years.

Amphitheatre. At the top of the hill and beyond the main road, relics of the great cisterns and the amphitheatre are in open fields and compared with what you can see elsewhere in Tunisia, they are unimpressive. In its glory the amphitheatre was bigger than that at El Jem and could seat 36,000 spectators.

On 7 March, 203, according to precise calculations, saints Perpetua and Felicity were brought into the arena naked to be ritually slaughtered. But the crowd was upset on seeing one had come straight from giving birth and the other was a young girl; they were dressed in loose robes and then summarily killed.

Theatre. Come back down the hill, fork left into the avenue, and follow signs to the 2nd-cent theatre which has been totally rebuilt in the 20th cent and is now the scene of annual pageantry. To the north, the large area of the so-called Archaeological Park of Roman Villas is a 1,700-year-old building site, but in 1960 one house was partly reconstructed to show what may have been. The **odeon** theatre was a victim of Vandalism.

Damous El Karita. Arabic has absorbed the Latin *domus caritas,* the 'house of charity,' to arrive at Damous El Karita. The floor and the bases of some of the columns are all that remain of this Christian church 65m long. If you don't clamber through the fence to the house of charity you'll need to stroll back to the Avenue des Thermes d'Antonin and head downhill.

Antonine Baths. The Antonine Baths, in their own archaeological park (there's a separate entrance fee for each of these parks) are the grandest ruins in Carthage although they're little more than two-dimensional. Using your imagination to its limits you may try reconstructing the schola (school) and the Basilica of Douimes set in a Punic graveyard. A 6th-cent BC tomb survived in this necropolis. The baths, down at beach level, were the largest in Africa.

Basilica of St Cyprien. To the north, 1½km away, is St Cyprien's Church, for which another entrance fee will be asked. Partially restored, this church stands on the tomb of St Cyprien (Cyprian), Bishop of Carthage in 249 who was beheaded in 258 for wanting home rule for the Church.

MODERN CARTHAGE

Modern Carthage and its surrounding villages are the playground of the rich. Habib Bourgiba, who had one of his palaces near the Antonine Baths, opened Tunis Carthage **Airport** on 1 August 1972 and was its first passenger, flying to Monastir Airport to open that as well.

At the south, **La Goulette,** the 'gullet,' is Tunis's port and dormitory town of 25,000 people which has grown around the 16th-cent Kasbah that Carlos V of Spain built in 1535. Miguel de Cervantes, author of *Don Quijote,* was in its garrison in 1574 when (he said) 475,000 Turks and Arabs attacked.

A generation ago, **Sidi Bou Saïd** was the St Tropez of Tunisia, now outpaced by Hammamet but still a town with some charm. At the tip of Jebel Manar, 'lighthouse mountain' but Cape Carthage to Europeans, a lighthouse stands where bonfires formerly marked the way for homecoming Punic vessels. Legend claims that Louis IX, 'Saint Louis' who died here in 1270, met the venerable Sidi Bou, but for once legend is wrong.

Abou Saïd Khalafa Ben Yahia El Temimi El Beji, the original Sidi Bou Saïd, came here in 1207 and died in 1236. He became the village's patron saint but it never took his name until the 19th cent when it was coming into fashion. And if you want to be in fashion today, spend an hour or so drinking mint tea in the Cafdes Nattes, watching the world go by.

Sir Richard Wood, British Ambassador to Tunisia before the Protectorate, quietly told the Bey of Tunis that he didn't have a smart enough residence. The Bey recalled that his treasurer, Ben Ayed, had fled to France to avoid disgrace, abandoning his palace at **La Marsa.** The Bey therefore presented it to the British Government in 1856 and it has been the Official Residence from then on; it was at this address that Sir Richard dreamed up the TGM railway, and it was here in 1943 that General Sir Harold Alexander, later Field Marshal Viscount Alexander of Tunis, had the British HQ after the capital's liberation.

The road ends at **Gammarth,** where in the fifties French expats sunbathed in the nude in what they thought was a secluded bay. Passing fishermen who saw them said that without clothes they looked like monkeys, which is why the spot is called *Baie des Singes,* 'monkeys' bay.' And the smart hotel, now being made smarter, took the same name.

HOTELS: 4-star: Abou Nawas, (Gammarth Beach), 446b; Baie des Singes, (Gammarth beach, been overhauled, should be open); Sidi Bou Saïd, (Ave Sidi Dhrif, Sidi Bou Saïd), 32r; **3-star:** Amilcar, (coast, Carthage Amilcar), 250r; Cap Carthage, (in woods near cape), 324b; Megara, (Gammath beach), 77r; Reine Didon, (near Museum, Carthage Dermech, temp. closed for overhaul)

2-star: Dar Saïd, (Sidi Bou Saïd), 12r (closed winter); Residence Carthage, (16 Rue Hannibal, Carthage Salambo), 23b; Tour Blanche, (Gammarth beach), 170b; **Unclass:** Abou Ghazi, (167 Ave Bourgiba, Le Kram) 80b; Beau Rivage, (28, Rue Ibn Battuta, Kherredine), 18b; Corniche

Plaza, (La Marsa beach), 28b; Palm Beach (7, Rue S S Youssef, Le Kram) 14b; Predl, (La Marsa), 10b; Residence Africa, (Sidi Bou Saïd), 100b; Sidi Bou Fares, (Sidi Bou Saïd), 8r.

HOLIDAY VILLAGE: Dar Naouar, Gammarth, 1,064b.

YOUTH HOSTEL: at Carthage Demerch, 110b.

RESTAURANTS: Fish is the speciality along this coast. Le Pêcheur at Gammarth goes in for all the trimmings; DarZarrouk is in an old palace at Sidi Bou Saïd and is pricey; there are plenty of smaller and cheaper places.

TRANSPORT: Up to La Marsa the TGM is unbeatable for price and reliability and is easy to locate. At Gammarth, catch a number 40 bus for La Marsa (and the TGM) or a 20G for Tunis.

FERRY: La Goulette — Rades, every 15 mins from 0530 to 2030, free.

SOUTH OF TUNIS
The beach begins at Rades and runs unbroken to Soliman Plage on Cap Bon, dirty at first but becoming progressively cleaner.

Hammam Lif. Hammam Lif tries to be a resort: after all, Bey Ali Pasha built himself a pavilion here and it has thermal baths, the 'hammam,' which cure nasal complaints: *Lif* is a corruption of 'El Enf,' 'the nose.' But it also ships phosphates and has several factories. And the casino is closed.

PLO. Borj Cedria, slightly inland up the hill, was still too close to the sea for comfort. The Israelis sent in an assault boat in 1988 and assassinated one of the PLO leaders in his HQ here.

HOTELS: Bon Repos, 12r, Casino, 14r, both unclassified.

YOUTH HOSTEL: at Rades; 56b.

Vegetable market in Tunis

THE CORAL COAST

Bizerte, Tabarka, Béja, Bulla Regia.

NORTHERN TUNISIA IS A TOTAL SURPRISE. The springtime green fields look as if they belong on the lower slopes of some Swiss mountain, though the summer sun scorces much of it brown; the houses have pitched roofs to shed the rain; and here is the country's only sizeable permanent river, the Mejerda which rises in Algeria as the Mellègue — but it's only 15m wide when it reaches the sea.

The Mountains of Mejerda, west of Bulla Regia, have an annual average rainfall of 65", around 1,600mm, three times the level for London. Almost all of it falls between early October and March, typical of a Mediterranean climate, but it sustains the oak forests of the Khroumrie, a thriving farming industry, and extensive wildlife — though this is coming under increasing pressure as hunting is promoted with the growth of tourism. The Tunisian Government must learn the lessons of conservation, preferably before it is too late.

Even more surprising is that these mountains have snow in the winter, yet down at sea level the water is sufficiently warm to allow coral to grow.

Over the centuries this region has been called many names: the granary of Ancient Rome, the Barbary Coast, and now with expanding tourism in mind, it has become the Coral Coast.

BIZERTE

The French influence is still very strong In Bizerte — Bizerta, if you want the English spelling— where the new town laid out on a grid system is in distinct contrast to the nearby medina with its narrow and meandering streets.

Skirmish with French. This town was the last outpost of French colonialism in north Africa. France agreed in 1955 to Tunisian independence and granted it on 20 March 1956, yet it refused to pull its troops out of Bizerte which was, according to Paris, an essential outpost for NATO. Relations between the former colonial power and the former protectorate, uneasy for several years, worsened as France remained adamant. There was a confrontation in 1961 followed by the Tunisian Army's baptism of fire as its troops attacked the French.

A thousand African soldiers died in the skirmishes but eventually France agreed to withdraw and named the day as 15 October 1963. It was a national holiday until Bourgiba's departure in November 1987. And the irony of it is that France is no longer a member of NATO!

The French began fortifying Benzert, as the Arabs called it, in 1882, only months after establishing the Protectorate of Tunisia. Britain had taken legal title to Malta in 1814 after the débacle with Napoleon, and following the opening of the Suez Canal in 1869, Malta became an important naval base. France saw the danger and converted Bizerte and its lake into a Gallic navy yard on the south side of the Mediterranean.

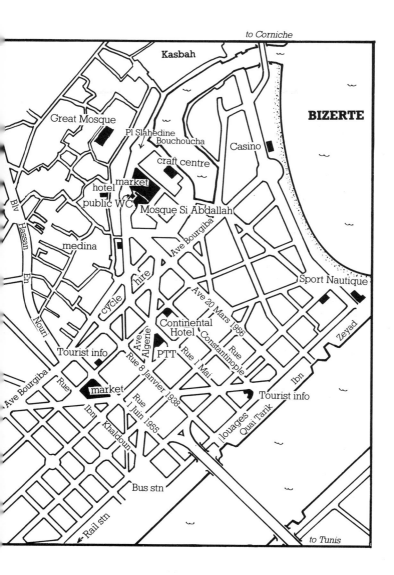

The base was important, but not crucial, in the First World War; in the Second War Rommel's Afrika Korps seized the town in November 1942 and held onto it until the US Army liberated it in May 1943.

Bizerte in history. Bizerte was founded by the Phoenicians, who probably dug the first simple canal from the Old Port to clear access to Lake Bizerte which is really a saltwater lagoon.

Agathocles, the Tyrant of Syracuse, seized it in 307BC (310BC according to some authorities), gave it the strange name of Hippo Diarrhytus, then lost it to the Roman Empire. Rome left little mark here, the Vandals left none, and the Arabs made little impression until the 13th cent when the Hafsid Caliphate of El Mostancir built a palace and gardens.

The year 1492 is memorable in Spain not only for Columbus's landing in North America but for the conquest of Granada and the expulsion of Islam from Iberia In the years that followed, many expelled Moslems settled in north Africa, including those who built the Andaluz quarter of the medina, north of where the Kasbah would be built.

Spaniard versus Turk. Spain came back on the scene in the 16th cent as the Ottoman Empire spread itself west from its small beginnings in Turkey. Kheir Ed Din Barbarossa had seized Tunis and Bizerte in 1534 on the orders of the Sultan of Constantinople, driving the Hafsid caliph Moulay Hassan into exile in Sicily.

The Pope and the Italian princes saw the threat and begged the Holy Roman Emperor, Carlos V of Spain, to intercede. He did; he sent a punitive raid to Bizerte which was now set to join other ports on the Berber coast as a haven for pirates, and his large force of 30,000 men in 400 ships recaptured Tunis, where Carlos reinstated the caliph with the order: "Go get the Turks!"

The Pasha of Algiers took the region in 1569 and four years later the battle swung the other way when John of Austria seized it, holding it for only one year. When the Turks came back in 1574 they were there to stay, starting work on the Bizerte Kasbah and establishing the Husaynid dynasty which lasted until independence in 1956.

Bizerte today. The enormous Kasbah that stands at the northern entrance to the Old Port is a 17th-cent fortress incorporating the so-called Spanish Fort which the Turk Euji Ali built between 1570 and 1573; since 1968 it has been used as an open-air theatre. On the south side of the approach to the picturesque port, nowadays lined with equally picturesque fishing boats, is the recently-restored Borj Sidi El Hani, built at the same time as the Kasbah and now holding the small Oceanographic Museum.

Bridges. A lift bridge across the entrance to the port allows larger fishing vessels and the occasional small cruise liner to pass, but the town's main bridge, built in 1976 over the canal, stands high enough to give mast clearance. Before '76, traffic crossed on ferries or drove around the lake via Menzel Bourgiba.

Old canal. Rue Slahedine Bouchoucha, which runs from the Old Port past the market — and a tolerable public toilet — is on the course of an ancient canal, probably the one the Phoenicians dug, which ran through where the new town now stands. It was filled in during the late 19th cent.

West of Rue Slahedine Bouchoucha is the medina, its streets named from the crafts which were practised there, and on the medina's eastern edge stands the 17th-cent Great Mosque with its octagonal minaret.

Bizerte began to nibble at the tourist market in 1963 with the opening of the Hotel Corniche, the first of the conglomerates to go up on the sea-front road which leads to Cap Blanc. The Nador and Sidi Salem came in 1967, and the Jalta in 1970, but the town has failed to attract crowds on the scale that Sousse manages: maybe that will change if the planned 'Tunisian Disney World' comes to Ghar El Melh.

HOTELS: 3-star: Corniche, 174b; **2-star:** Jalta, 204b; Nador, 200b; P'tite Mousse, 24b, all on Corniche; **unclass:** Auberge de Remel, 16r, at Remel Plage; Continental, Rue Constantinople, 52b; El Khayem, 24b; Sidi Salem, both on Corniche, 60b; Zitouna, Rue de la Régence.

APART HOTEL: Aïn Meriem, on Corniche, 126b in flats.

HOLIDAY VILLAGE: El Kebir, on Corniche, 740b.

HOSTELS: Youth hostel, north of town on Blv Hassan En Nourri, 120b; and a privately-run and dirty hostel at Remel Plage, 50b.

RESTAURANTS: Most popular but 6km out of town is La P'tite Mousse, on Corniche, with Zoubaïda nearby under its pagoda roof. Bar-Restaurant Sport Nautique, where the canal meets the sea, is basic — and there's no sport either. Restaurant de la Liberté, Rue de Constantinople, is the best in the town.

CASINO: it's on the seafront, but it's closed.

The Vieux Port at Bizerte

CYCLE HIRE: available from 2 shops in town.

PTT: Ave d'Algérie; phones at rear on Rue 1 du Mai.

BUSES and LOUAGES: Twelve buses daily to Tunis; five to Mateur; three to Jendouba, Le Kef; one to Ghar El Melh, Jebel Plage. Bus station near new canal bridge; see map. Louages leave from Quai Tarik Ibn Zeyad almost under bridge.

RAIL: Rail station is 500m west of bus station near canal bank. Three trains daily to Tunis.

FERRIES to France: they don't run any more.

TOURIST OFFICE: SI; Ave Bourgiba. ONT; Quai Tarik Ibn Zeyad-Rue Constantinople.

AROUND BIZERTE

If you hire a cycle in town, **Cap Blanc** is within easy reach. The headland truly is a white cape, but it is not the most northerly point in Africa as so many people claim; that title goes to Rass Ben Sekka (Rass Engelah), 5km to the west which beats Blanc by some 100m. Catch a bus to the village of Béchateur — a tiny place where a Roman water catchment is still in use — follow a rough track for 25km, and you'll reach the beach of Sidi Abd El Ouabed and you won't be surprised to find it deserted. You'll also see Rass Ben Sekka on the way.

On the other side of Lake Bizerte, **Menzel Bourgiba,** the former French naval base of Ferryville — named from Jules Ferry and not from a ferry boat — is an industrial town producing chemicals, steel and cement, and running a shipyard.

Yet 2km away is **Lake Ichkeul,** the most important wildlife sanctuary in north Africa (see 'wildlife' on page 42) and a refuge for many thousands of migratory birds. The surrounding hills are home to wild boar, hyenas, foxes and jackals, and there were buffalo until the trigger-happy US Army used them for target practise after defeating Rommel. The last wild lion and leopard suffered the same fate here earlier this century and if hunting is allowed to continue unchecked the wild boar will soon be extinct. Meanwhile, there are plans to expand hunting way to the west...

The lonely but beautiful **Remel** beach is a few km off the main road back to Tunis; if you're relying on public transport get off the bus at Menzel Jemil and walk.

The small village of **Ghar El Melh,** 'Salt Hole,' but Rusucmona to the Phoenicians, is another of Tunisia's surprises. Around 4,000 people live off the land in one of the most beautiful settings in the country. A 30 sq km lake, as big as Lake Tunis and formerly fed by the River Mejerda, lies between the town and the sea.

It was here that the Holy Roman Emperor Carlos V anchored his fleet before attacking Tunis in 1541; it was also here that the pirate Ousta Mourad built his private harbour with its own fort; and it was this port, with the fleet of Hammouda Bey at anchor in it, that Admiral Blake destroyed in 1654.

And when the French came they had ideas of making this harbour a second Toulon, until they opted for Bizerte instead.

Now? The village slumbers into its old age, tranquil and beautiful. But perhaps not for much longer, for this is the spot where the Tunisian version of Disney World will arise, according to the plans of Saudi businessman Sheikh Salak Kamel who proposed in 1981 spending 160,000,000 dinars to create the fantasia on a vast site, and provide 30,000 hotel beds for the expected visitors.

Across the ridge lies **Raf Raf,** another pretty village and where you will see women dressed in traditional costume if you chance to arrive when there's an important local event. Embroidering wool and growing large muscat grapes are the local industries, both tempting to the visitor, but the biggest attraction is undoubtedly the splendid beach, sweeping in a white semicircle on the pivot of the rocky Ile Pilau in the middle of the bay.

To the south and 2km from the main Tunis road lies **Utica,** the first Phoenician city in Africa. The Elder Pliny claimed that Utica was founded by the people of Tyre (the one in The Lebanon) in 1101BC, 287 years before Carthage, but 3,000 years after the event we are still no nearer confirming Pliny's statement.

Agathocles took Utica in 308BC while Greece and Rome squabbled, then in the War of the Mercenaries (240-237BC) it supported Carthage, the losing side; in defeat, Utica surrendered unconditionally and became part of the Roman Empire.

When the Second Punic War broke out (218-210BC) Utica was again siding with Carthage and was again attacked by the Romans; so at the start of the Third Punic War it was comfortably in the Roman camp: as a reward it was granted the status of a free city and became the capital of Ifriqya.

The most gruesomely memorable period of Utica's history came during the power struggle between Caesar and Pompey in 49-45BC. Cato the Younger was commander of Utica when he heard of Pompey's supporters' defeat at Thapsus in 46BC; he vowed he would never serve under Caesar and chose to fall on his sword in the honourable fashion. Doctors tried to save him, but he thrust them aside and pulled out his own bowels with his bare hands.

The Emperor Augustus reinstated Carthage as the chief city and Utica gradually went into decline though it had a spell of prosperity in the 2nd and 3rd cents as a trading station. Today there is not a great deal to see except foundations covering a site 1½km across; excavations began in the 19th cent and the finds are in the Louvre, Paris, or the archaeological museum on the Utica site.

The main attraction at Utica is the **House of the Cascade,** named from the fountain which played in the central courtyard of the house, which was presumably the home of a wealthy Punic merchant. You can study the ground-floor plan of this 75m by 40m mansion, but the walls are rudimentary. The main room, the 'grand triclinum,' has multicoloured marble relics, some of Tunisian origin but the green stone has been identified as coming from the Greek island of Euboea.

In the north-west corner the treasury is so-called because of the coins found there; opposite was the hunting house, named from the design on its mosaics. The eight-roomed living quarters filled another corner and were almost separate from the remainder of this stately home.

Across the street lies the other main attraction of Utica, the **Punic cemetery,** which was buried under the later Roman town. And a short but unknown distance to the north was the shore, so the wealthy merchant who lived in the House of the Cascade could presumably watch his ships come and go.

HOTELS: Menzel Bourgiba: 1-star Younes, 16r in bungalows; unclass Moderne, 20r; **Menzel Jemil:** unclass Rimel, 60b; **Raf Raf:** 1-star Dalia, 22b.

MARKETS: Wednesday, Menzel Bourgiba; Friday, Rass Jebel.

TABARKA

The coral reefs off Tabarka are closer to Europe than any others and have even made their mark in English literature. Shakespeare wrote in *The Tempest* in 1611 of a wedding party sailing back from Tunis being wrecked on these reefs. He uses a little poetic licence when he gives the sprite Ariel these lines in act i, scene ii:

> *Full fadom (fathom) five thy father lies;*
> *Of his bones are coral made;*
> *Those are pearls that were his eyes;*
> *Nothing of him that doth fade*
> *But doth suffer a sea-change*
> *Into something rich and strange.*

Thabraca. The Phoenicians established the small port-city of Thabraca on this beautiful bay, and under Roman dominion it became one of the wealthiest communities on this coast. In the 3rd and 4th cents ships sailed from here carrying cereals and olive oil from the 'breadbasket of Africa' to Rome, but there was also trade in timber from the mountains, wild animals for ritual slaughter in the amphitheatres, lead ore and fine marble — and a small amount of coral.

Thabraca became the centre of Christianity in Ifriqya with its own bishop and a scattering of monasteries; a church between Borj Messaoud and Borj El Jerid a little way up the hill behind the town, had some splendid funerary mosaics which now adorn the entrance hall of the Bardo Museum in Tunis.

Île de Tabarka. The old town slumbered through the Arab conquest and beyond, coming to life again with the struggles between Spaniard and Turk in the 16th cent. In 1541, shortly after Carlos V of Spain seized Tabarca town, Barbarossa gave him the little rugged island in the bay in return for the freedom of Dragut who was then languishing in jail in Corsica having been taken by the Genoese.

Carlos sold the island to the Genoese family of Lomelli who built a castle on it and stayed firmly in place for the next 200 years, although the Turks ruled the mainland.

The Lomelli family and their successors became agents in the sordid business of negotiating the ransomed release of Christian slaves held in Moslem jails by the Barbary pirates, and they managed to do some fishing and coral gathering as a sideline. In the 17th cent their success as intermediaries aroused jealousy among the French who were establishing forts to the west at El Kala in what is now Algeria, and to the east at Cap Negro, and who desperately wanted to seize the Île de Tabarka as well.

Resorting to intrigue, in 1741 the French persuaded Ali Bey that he could drive the Genoese out; they even allowed themselves to be ousted from Cap Negro. Then in 1781 they came back in force, seized the town of Tabarka and its rocky isle, and by 1804 had established themselves so well they could open a consulate.

With the coming of the Protectorate in 1881, the French aimed their cannons at the island castle of Tabarka and made certain it would never again dominate the mainland nearby. Castles were outdated long before the Second World War but the fortress would have helped the French in 1942-43 when they held Tabarka in a gallant stand against the German Afrika Korps. After the war they built a causeway linking the island and the remainder of Africa, and the former Genoese stronghold is now part of the tourist circuit.

Tabarka today. Tabarka is in Tunisia's north-west corner, far enough from the public eye to be considered a safe place of exile for the troublesome Habib Bourgiba in pre-independence days. He stayed for a while at the Hotel Mimosas but after a disagreement with the management moved to the Hotel de France which now bears a plaque commemorating its guest who rose to become president.

"Ne pas bronzer." At the moment there is little else in the town to excite the visitor, but it is nonetheless a pleasant spot for a short break — though in July and August the Coral Festival becomes an excuse for a six-week-long street party with the bizarre slogan *"Je ne veux pas bronzer, idiot!"* ("I'm not going to get sunburnt, numbskull!") The so-called 'University of Summer' draws thousands of young people from Tunisia and France, and a few other lands, for a range of activities from music festivals to serious conferences.

Basilica. Many of the festival's events are held in the grounds of the Basilica at the west end of town, which is really a 3rd or 4th cent Roman cistern capable of holding 2,700 cubic metres of water; the White Fathers converted it into a church and it's now open every day with no entry fee.

Coral fishing. Around 500 people are still engaged in the coral industry, relying on the efforts of one or two divers who scour the shallower reefs between September and April, and the grabline contractors who drop large hooks onto coral as deep as 150 metres; this last operation is haphazard, with chunks of the living rock plunging to inaccessible depths.

Diving. It's possible to hire diving equipment and have air bottles refilled in the port, but *it is forbidden to gather coral without a licence,* obtainable from the Regional Fishing Office.

The town's other industry is raising poultry, with plans to expand annual production to 120,000,000 eggs and 2,000,000 table birds a year; in contrast the manufacture of cork products from the oak wood of the uplands is very small.

Montaza Tabarka. But all this is changing. Already work has begun on the Montaza Tabarka project which plans to build hotel accommodation for 10,000 visitors who will come in either through the new Tabarka International Airport or by train to the enlarged rail terminus. These visitors will be offered a marina, 27-hole golf course, a sea-water spa, sport and culture, as well as the beach, with the first of the hotels due to open in November 1988.

HOTELS: 3-star: Mimosas, 154b; Morjane, 320b; **1-star:** de France, 38b; Mamia, 36b.

HOLIDAY VILLAGES: Festival de Tabarka, 1,200b in huts, open 15 June to 15 Sep; Village des Pins, bungalows or **camping.**

YOUTH HOSTEL: 20 beds.

RESTAURANTS: Le Corail, non-alcoholic; Les Agriculteurs, low-priced fish specialities; Café Andalous; Navetty. Restaurant Khroumir is on the beach and specialises in giant prawns.

Local specialities are prawns and lobsters in summer and wild boar in winter, although this latter is forbidden food for the devout Moslem.

BUSES: Poor services; one daily to Tunis and Jendouba, three weekly to Le Kef. Bus station on Rue du Peuple, west end of town.

LOUAGES: Poor service, operating from Place du 18 Janvier 1952 on sea front.

RAIL: One daily train to Tunis from the station on the sea front.

MARKET: Friday.

TOURIST OFFICE: SI; in the Municipalité at west end of Ave Bourgiba.

BEYOND TABARKA

The cluster of six volcanic rocks known as the **Galite Islands** 65km north-by-east of Tabarka is Tunisia's northernmost territory. The only one inhabited is La Galite, 5.3km long by 2 km wide, supporting a scattering of lobster fishermen and grape growers.

The others are Galiton de l'Est and de l'Ouest (East and West Galiton), Pollastro, Gallo, Gallina and Chiens. The archipelago briefly belonged to the infant Louis of Spain, grandson of France's Louis IX, and this Spanish connection might explain why several of the islands' names are in Spanish — *gallo* and *gallina* are cock and hen and *pollastro* is pullet. But *chiens* is definitely French for dogs.

The only way to reach the islands is to negotiate your passage with a fisherman from Tabarka, preferably one who may well be planning to drop his nets in the shoals of fish around the rocks. There are European fur seals here too, rightfully protected by law.

Within sight of Tabarka, *Les Aiguilles, 'The Needles,' is a group of jagged rocks rising to only 25m. Much of the mainland coast is equally rugged, testimony to Shakespeare's choice of location for his shipwreck in The Tempest.*

There is no other town or village on Tunisia's northern coast, but *Sejenane,* a few kilometres inland, is a useful base if you are independently mobile and want to explore the remote and deserted beaches at Cap Serrat and Sidi Mechrig, or visit the ruins of Cap Negro where the French had a coralling station until Ali Bey captured it, with Tabarka, in 1741. Sejenane lives by its lead and zinc mines, by growing tobacco and processing cork, and by catering for wild boar hunters in winter. It has a small Thursday market.

The road south leads high into the mountains, and into the **Khroumirie,** countryside which is utterly unlike anything you would expect in a dry land such as Tunisia. Moss-covered cork oaks cling to fern-clad mountain slopes much as you would find in the French Pyrenees, while the white-walled houses have russet roofs reminiscent of an Alpine landscape. And if you come here in winter you're liable to be snowbound.

Aïn Draham, 'Silver Spring,' the tiny village at the centre of this wooded wonderland is so unlike anything else you will find in the Arab world that it is being developed as a major international tourist centre — for wealthy Arabs from the Middle East rather than for Europeans.

The focal point of this expansion is the **Col des Ruines,** a small plateau in the cork woods near the summit of Jebel Fersig at around 800m. The first part of the project, due for completion in 1988, has 1,400 beds in hotels, chalets and bungalows, with an open-air swimming pool, sports ground and an amphitheatre; the second stage, planned to be ready by 1992, should add another 2,400 beds, including some in a small holiday village.

Aïn Draham was, and hopefully will remain, a small and very picturesque village living off the products of the forest. Before the Col des Ruines project it had nothing artificial to offer visitors whose sole enertainment was the pure delight of walking in the woods. While the Jebel Fersig trail will presumably lose its appeal, I trust other trails will remain open, notably the 13km hike to Jebel Bir for vast panoramic views across the Medjerda Mountains.

A trail that's less exhausting goes down into the Lil valley to the dam of **Beni M'Tir,** 483m long by 78m high and built in 1955 to hold back a 700-acre reservoir. It provides the city of Tunis with 80,000 cubic metres of water each day and drives a power station downstream which generates 17,000,000kw-hours per year; to the south is the smaller Bou Heurtma reservoir which adds 3,000,000kw-h-yr to the system.

With your own transport or a taxi you can travel the 12km to **Hammam Bourgiba,** a small spa village where the ex-president used to take the waters. The place is tucked into a small valley lined with cork-oaks and the access road almost touches the border with Algeria.

The Khroumirie is a delightful but small region with the highest rainfall and the lowest winter temperatures in the country. It's also rugged and was for ages the hideout of a band of Khroumiri tribesmen whose 19th-cent raids into French-held Algeria prompted the European movement into Tunisia to 'protect' the country...from itself?

HOTELS (exclusive of the Col des Ruines development): **3-star:** Hammam Bourgiba, in village of same name, 80b; **2-star:** Les Chênes, 6km south, a smart and overpriced hotel used for training hotel staff, 68b; **unclass:** Beau Séjour, used by hunting parties so try for room in annexe, 31r.

YOUTH HOSTEL: 7km south, in the forest, 120b.

BUSES: Daily to Tabarka and Tunis; 3 weekly to Le Kef.

TOURIST OFFICE: SI; in village centre.

BULLA REGIA

Bulla Regia, 35km south of Aïn Draham, is unique among Roman cities in that its inhabitants had their living and sleeping quarters underground, almost certainly to escape the extremes of temperature at the surface. Windblown sand and soil had helped bury the city even more effectively after its destruction, probably by an earthquake at some era as yet unknown.

The site was certainly abandoned for centuries, which has helped preserve the treasure of superb mosaics, most of which are now on display in the Bardo Museum in Tunis.

There is, not surprisingly, little to see above ground, though excavations have exposed the foundations — and the subterranean chambers — of this surprising city.

As you enter the site (open every·day, sunrise to sunset) the most noticeable ruins are the 3rd cent baths of Julia Memmia with their cisterns beside them. Beyond them a Roman street runs east to west, which may deflect you from the underground dwellings to the north.

Nobody knows who owned or lived in any of the mansions, which are optionally called palaces, but they have been named from the most characteristic find in each one. The Treasure House, therefore, the first you will come to as you strike across the site, had some Byzantine coins among the tons of soil that were removed from its basement. You can now stand at ground level and examine the exposed subterranean dining room of some wealthy Roman, the floor mosaics probably showing where he placed his furniture. Beside it are two other rooms, at least one of which was a bedroom.

Ahead again, passing the more visible remains of two 6th-cent churches, you suddenly reach the crossroads in the town centre and see before you the exposed basement living and sleeping quarters of some of the wealthiest citizens of Bulla Regia. Palaca, mansion or house, call it what you will, but each is named from a dominant mosaic found during excavation.

Palace of the Hunt. The Peacock Palace on the left had a large inlay of that particular bird, but the Palace of the Hunt to the right, the most lavishly decorated residence in the city, had the ultimate luxury, an underground courtyard flanked by columns and leading to a dining room and to bedchambers, each with a raised platform to carry the bed. Scenes of the hunt decorate all the rooms.

The ground-floor plan almost duplicated this basement lifestyle, with two colonnaded courtyards to allow sunlight to filter to that lower court. Here, too, were the baths and lavatories of this once-splendid palace.

The Palace of the New Hunt, sometimes called the Grand Hunt, was discovered in 1973 immediately to the north and containing a mosaic showing horsemen looking down at lions and a disembowelled boar. A mosaic near this palace proclaimed HECDOMUSDEI, 'this is the house of God,' but the Romans studiously avoided God's sixth commandment about not killing, whether it applied to animal or fellow man.

Palace of Amphitrite. Beyond the Fisherman's Palace, with its basement strengthened with four sturdy columns, the road leads north to the Palace of Amphitrite whose ground floor had a splendid mosaic showing the Deliverance of Andromeda, now in the Bardo Museum.

A backstreet in Le Kef

Andromeda, the beautiful daughter of Cassiopeia, was troubled by a monster which Poseidon had sent to ravage her lands. An oracle warned that the only way the monster could be defeated was by sacrificing Andromeda, which made the remedy worse than the affliction. Andromeda was already chained to a rock, awaiting her doom, when Perseus came to the rescue, turning the monster into stone and so delivering the beautiful maiden.

Amphitrite was the wife of the sea-god Poseidon, which is probably why the Palace was named from her, but it's a mistake. The mosaic on the dining room floor — and still there today — is not of Amphitrite but of Venus, carried in triumph by two sailors.

Bulla Regia's other relics include a natural spring which still provides water, temples to Isis and Apollo, with marble statues from the latter now gracing the Bardo, and, on the other side of the approach road, some baths 60m by 55m and not yet excavated.

Beside them stand the ruins of another wrongly-named building, Alexander's Church. The mistake arose from an inscription from the Psalms on a lintel which is no longer in place, but a closer inspection of the building shows long troughs of stone and a metal hitching ring inset into a column. This 'church' was probably a sampling house for grain merchants, an early corn exchange.

JENDOUBA

There is no hotel at Bulla Regia. The closest is in Jendouba which, despite having 16,000 inhabitants, is unappealing except, possibly, for its Wednesday market during the grain harvest. The town is a French legacy, established to trade in the cereals grown on the surrounding plain, the former home of the Jendouba tribe.

DETAILS: 2-star Atlas Hotel, 16r, beside the **railway station** which is near the **bus station**.

119

BEYOND JENDOUBA

West of Jendouba the main road runs past Oued Meliz to **Ghardimao,** a tiny frontier town which grows tobacco. The town itself has no more attraction than does Jendouba, but it's set on the edge of some beautiful mountain country.

Unless you're going into Algeria you will normally come to Ghardimao only as a jumping-off point for the ruins of Thuburnica, but if you have transport or are prepared to hitch a lift you could explore the **Forest of Feija** to the north. As this is so close to the border, you'll need to clear customs and immigration before venturing into Tunisia's second largest forest. There are several paths for hikers or for people who just fancy a leisurely stroll.

The track up here is poor, little more than a service road for the foresters, and some way into the woods it passes close to **Kef Nekcha,** an enormous freestanding boulder probably 200 feet (60m) tall, with steps cut into it. The view from the top, I'm told, is worth the climb. And at journey's end, near the village of Aïn Soltane, is a large hostel where lovers of solitude can congregate overnight.

Otherwise, Ghardimao's only **HOTEL** is the Thibournik of 26 beds. The town has **buses and louages** to Jendouba and is on the main **railway** between Tunis and Algeria.

Without your own transport you will need to take a louage to the ruins of **Thuburnica,** scattered in an olive grove several kilometers along another poor road. This Roman settlement has much less to offer than has Bulla Regia, mainly two triumphal arches, one of them with a triple-span, the remains of a two-storey mausoleum, temples to Juno and to Mercury, and a Byzantine fortress occupying the highest point. Modern buildings nearby belong to an agricultural co-operative.

With your own transport you can now take a short cut back to Jendouba on equally poor roads, passing the more impressive quarries of **Chemtou,** otherwise you will need to walk about 4km from Oued Meliz. But be careful — floods cut a vital ford in 1986; check that the road is open again.

These quarries began yielding their distinctive pink, yellow and green marble in the 2nd cent BC, and in 27AD the Romans built a small town on the site, Colonia Julia Augusta Numidica Simmithus, which not surprisingly soon had its name shortened to Simmithu, and hence Chemtou.

The stone is particularly attractive and a little softer than most marbles, qualities which made it highly prized among affluent Romans and Byzantines. The tremendous effort involved in getting the stone across the Mediterranean, either by dragging the blocks across country to Thabraca (Tabarka) or floating them down the Oued Melah on rafts, added to the cost and made the marble the status symbol of its day which in turn boosted its price.

The little community of Simmithu had its own theatre and amphitheatre, its basilica and its nymphaeum, traces of which still perch on the southern rim of the quarry, but the most impressive Roman relic is the aqueduct which strides across the Oued Melah on the northern edge of the site.

Quarrying began again in the 19th cent but ceased for ever in the 1980s and the area is now of archaeological interest. The little on-site workshop holds some splendid miniature examples of statuary carved from this so-called Numidian marble.

If you judge artefacts by their intrinsic merit rather than by their size, you will be interested in a stone with three deep channels carved across it, claimed to be part of the only water-powered turbine the Romans built in Africa.

BÉJA

Béja, now sitting on the main road and railway west from Tunis, was Vaga to the Romans and was at the centre of the granary of Africa. As far back as the 1st cent BC Sallust, the governor of Numidia, recalled the people of Vaga worshipping Demeter, the Greek goddess of agriculture whom the Romans called Ceres, and having a three-day feast and orgy at harvest time. Béja still enjoys the role of being the prairie town of Tunisia, except that the rolling hills all around are nothing like the grain lands of the United States.

The town was built on a hill inside a sturdy wall, but despite those precautions it was still vulnerable. In 109BC the Numidians under their king Jugurtha sacked the city in the general uprising against Rome. The Vandals — dare one say it? — vandalised the community in 448AD when their leader Genseric took brief control of this part of Ifriqya.

Abou Abdulla, the Fatimite caliph, wrought vengeance on the people in the 10th cent when they were reluctant to concede the Mahdi's interpretation of Islam (see Mahdia), and when the Hilalians raided the province the following century in retribution, Béja suffered again.

The town today. Modern Béja is built in a grid system, showing the colonial influence, but in the old quarter of Mzara there are still a few cave dwellings in use. The town's streets are steep, several being a series of steps cut into the bedrock.

A strange building dominates the town square; it began life as a church and had a dome added when it became a mosque. Now unconsecrated, it is the *Maison du People* — the English translation of 'People's House' doesn't do justice to its role as a community hall.

Kasbah. The Byzantine fortress of Justinian once had 20 towers and three doors. It became the Kasbah after the Islamic conquest but was restored and repaired many times during the centuries. Very little of that original now remains, but as it's in use as an army barracks it's impossible to inspect the dungeon, which is among the oldest parts surviving.

HOTELS: 3-star: Vega, 36b; unclass: Phenix, 30b.

HOSTEL: 60b.

TRANSPORT: There are good **bus** connections; two daily to Tunis, one daily to Tabarka, Jendouba, Aïn Draham, Bizerte, and three a week to Le Kef. Three **trains** a day run to Tunis. The bus station, railway station, louage stand and the youth hostel are all close by at the foot of the hill.

Beyond Béja. With your own transport you could drive carefully for 13km down the badly-rutted road south of town to see **Trajan's Bridge,** built around 29AD and probably the work of Tiberius, but later restored, probably by Trajan. What is certain is that the bridge was on the main Roman road from Carthage to Bône in Algeria and is now close to the waters of the vast Sidi Salem reservoir, but safely above the flood level.

TÉBESSA HEARTLAND

Thuburbo Majus and Dougga, Le Kef, Kasserine.

THE TÉBESSA MOUNTAINS which roll in from Algeria lack the grandeur and the timber cover of the mountains to the north. They mark the beginning of what we would expect inland Tunisia to look like — treeless, somewhat featureless, and above all open to the searing skies of summer.

In the north they are still well-watered in winter, which is the farming season; after harvest, in April and May, the land is too dry to be worked until the winter rains come again. As you travel further south, the mountains give way to hills which become no more than a gentle plain sloping down to the salt pans of the Chott el Jerid. The rainfall, too, diminishes until you pass from the zone of dry-land farming into the desert where only the oases yield any produce.

The southern fringe of this heartland of Tunisia was the limit of Roman influence and few Europeans ventured beyond until relatively modern times. Two thousand years ago when the rains were more plentiful the Romans had a scattering of city-forts across the countryside, but today it is an empty zone with few towns though with a grandeur and appeal of its own.

THUBURBO MAJUS

The Berbers had a higgledy-piggledy town which they called Thuburbo. The Romans chose it as the site for a colony of their veterans and, as Augustus was emperor, they called it Colonia Julia Thuburbo Majus: there was a Thuburbo Minus near Carthage.

Emperor Hadrian made it a municipium in 128AD and in 188 under Emperor Lucius Aelius Aurelius Commodus it took the unwieldy name of Colonia Julia Aurelia Commoda Thuburbo Majus and was again a colony.

The 'Happy Republic.' The city-colony began prospering under Hadrian (117-138) and reached its peak in the closing years of the 2nd cent and the first half of the 3rd, the time when most of the monuments and the smart mansions were built. It went into decline in the latter part of the 3rd cent for reasons not yet fully understood, though this was when Christianity arrived. By the 4th cent Thuburbo Majus, now called Respublica Felix Thuburbo Majus, was prospering again and there was considerable restoration work done; many of the mosaics of this period are dated according to the Christian calendar, which makes archaeology so much easier.

Ruined city. The Vandals destroyed much of the city in their reign between 439 and 534, and the community never recovered its past glories when the Byzantines returned. The Arabs renamed the declining city Henchir El Kasbate but never occupied it. Shortly afterwards it was abandoned to the winds, and was rediscovered by the Frenchman Tissot in 1857.

Excavation began in 1912, using First World War prisoners as navvies, then in 1937 Poinssot began restoring several of the more prominent monuments. The Second War put a stop to all archaeology which never began again until 1957 and then in a haphazard manner. By the mid-1970s Mrs Alexander of the University of Iowa and Mrs Ben Abed of the Bardo Museum had begun their study of the mosaics, and the story of this important city became public knowledge.

Thuburbo Majus today. Entering the site from the north — it's open from sun-up to sundown — you first notice the restored Capitol, otherwise known as the **Temple of Jupiter.** Jupiter, 'jove pater' or father of light, was the god of the heavens and controlled thunder and lightning. His temple was built in 168AD and is the most impressive capitol building in Africa although most of its former glory has gone for ever. Among the rubble the prisoners of war moved were the remains of a 7m-tall statue of Jupiter, parts of which are now in the Bardo.

With the coming of Christianity and the fall from favour of the ancient gods, the crypt — visible today — probably took on some purely practical use such as storage, and in the area immediately behind the capitol several olive oil presses went into production.

Steps lead down from the capitol to the great **forum,** 49m square, which had columns lining three sides. Traces of those piers now rise no more than 5m and some of the marble flagstones have suffered the ravages of time. The builders were surprisingly considerate towards future historians as an inscription over a doorway has enabled us to date the building of this forum to some time between 161 and 192AD, and it was restored in 376 precisely.

South of the forum is the oddly-shaped **Temple of Mercury,** the Roman god of trade and patron of merchants. Only the floor plan is visible but this clearly shows a circular 'nave,' unlike anything else the Romans built; again, we can date it accurately to 211AD.

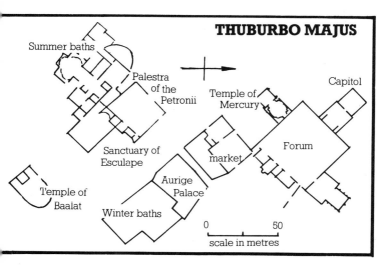

THUBURBO MAJUS

Summer baths

Palestra of the Petronii

Temple of Mercury

Capitol

Sanctuary of Esculape

market

Forum

Aurige Palace

Temple of Baalat

Winter baths

0   50
scale in metres

South-east, along one of the main streets of the city, lies the market, lined on three sides by tiny cubicle-like shops, and at the far end of the street are the **winter baths,** probably built at the same time as the capitol but restored — according to the mosaic artist — between 395 and 408. Twenty bath-chambers allowed a kind of intimacy in the cooler weather while at the **summer baths** to the west, a complex covering 2,800 square metres, there were just three large baths, restored in 361AD.

The baths, and the most luxurious houses in Thuburbo Majus, had hypocausts incorporated in the construction. This is one of the earliest-known forms of central heating in which hot air was passed under the marble floors and up through cavities in the wall and shows, with piped water and public sewers, the standard of living which civilized man was not to regain for another 1,500 years. While much of the city's treasure is in the Bardo, there are sufficient mosaics still on site to give a good indication of the quality of life in the 4th cent, and on some you will find the ancient insignia of the swastika which by a twist of fate was the symbol of the last foreign power to conquer Tunisia.

North of the summer baths is the **Palaestra (gymnasium) of Petronii,** built in 225 and named from the 'mosaic of the fat boxers,' which is now in the Bardo. Youths exercised here, either boxing or running, before going to the baths.

The furthest ruin worthy of interest — the amphitheatre beyond is in a bad state — is the **Temple of Baalat,** the female version of Baal, who was not so much a goddess as the personification of all the goddesses in one. Built around the 2nd cent the tiny temple was at the top of a flight of nine steps leading from a small court.

EL FAHS

The town of El Fahs has nothing to offer the tourist. They don't come to the Saturday market although it is so close to Tunis, and only a few visit the June Festival of Cérès when there is dancing in the streets and fun and games on horseback.

The market, the bus and rail stations, and the louage stand, are all conveniently close. There's no hotel.

ZAGHOUAN

Around 28km east of Thuburbo Majus is the picturesque little town of Zaghouan, dominated by the rugged peak of Jebel Zaghouan, a 1,295m tall grey granite outcrop that looks as if it belongs in the Dolomites or the centre of France. The mountain is probably the most picturesque in the country, particularly when seen as backdrop to the **Temple of the Waters,** Zaghouan's other attraction.

The temple is really an elaborate fountainhead with a raised semicircular platform 30m in diameter on which the statue of some god once stood. He has long gone, as have the 12 nymphs who each occupied an alcove in the platform's rim. Most of the alcoves remain, as well as the fountain itself.

Two kilometers below the temple is the town, known to its Phoenician founders as Ziqua. The Romans enlarged Zaghouan, but the only trace of their passing is in a triumphal arch and, of course, the temple, both built under Hadrian's rule. The Great Mosque is of little interest but the **Marabout**

of Sidi Ali Azouz is remarkable for the green varnished tiles on its roof. But this is one of those towns which is attractive in its own right, with tiled fountains at most street corners.

Surrender. Zaghouan has a place in modern history too, for the German general Von Arnim, retreating from Montgomery's attack, made his last stand in the lowlands between the town and Hammamet. On 11 May, 1943, the remains of the German and Italian armies here were encircled, and the next day Indian troops with the British Eighth Army captured Von Arnim. On the 13th his successor surrendered the Axis forces and so brought to an end the African theatre of the Second World War. The town's next illustrious resident was Habib Bourgiba who built himself a villa here.

HOTELS and TRANSPORT: The only hotel is the small Nymphes. There is a basic bus and louage service with connections to Tunis and El Fahs.

DOUGGA

Dougga has the most impressive ruins after the coliseum of El Jem, and its Capitol features on a number of posters advertising Tunisia. Access is the only problem as the ruins are 6km from Théboursouk and there's no public transport.

Thugga. The 4th-cent BC Phoenician city of Thugga was known to be large, but the first recorded details are from the time of Rome's defeat of Carthage in 146BC. The Numidian king Massinissa (160-155BC) had pledged his support to the empire and in return had been allowed to retain his independence when Rome seized the Carthaginian spoils. Thugga opted to join the Numidians and so preserved its lifestyle for two further centuries.

By 205AD Rome was in control everywhere, and under Septimus Severus Thugga became a municipium; the arch at the eastern end of the city was built to mark the event. In 261 Thugga received colonial status but went into a gradual decline in the closing years of the Roman Empire. The Byzantine reconquest brought some improvement of prospects but the Arab invasion signalled the end of the golden age for Thugga as for many Christian cities. A few people stayed on amid the ruins and, strangely, there were always one or two families living in Dougga until modern times.

British Museum. Dougga's impressive ruins made it a tourist attraction even in the 19th century, and in 1842 the British Consul in Tunis, Sir Thomas Reade, cut a valuable bilingual inscription from the Lybico-Punic Mausoleum and sent it to the British Museum where it remains. The French carved a replica in 1910. Exploration began in earnest in 1882 with the first digs in 1899; almost a century later excavation is still in progress with the last of the citizens of old Thugga now rehoused in the purpose-built village of Nouvelle Dougga.

Dougga today. The city occupies a gently sloping hill ranging from 500 to 570m altitude, not the kind of location the Romans would have chosen though it offers a commanding view across the countryside.

Capitol. The most impressive building by far is that much-illustrated Capitol, a temple dedicated to the trinity of Jupiter, Juno and Minerva who were jointly the protectors of the Roman state.

Jupiter, whom the Greeks called Zeus, was the god of the heavens and therefore in control of the weather and the daylight; by association he became the patron of justice and later he was Deus Fideus, the god of oaths and fidelity. His wife Juno was naturally the queen of Heaven and also the patroness of women and the goddess in charge of childbirth. Minerva was the goddess of wisdom, of the arts and crafts, and later joined Mars in supervising wars; the Romans had their Feast of Minerva in March, the month which was named from Mars. This trio, therefore, controlled virtually all the basics of life in a polytheistic Rome.

The Capitol, built in 166-7AD, has been restored to an excellent state of repair and exists in all its three dimensions, unlike the two-dimensional ground plans that are so often all there is to see on many ancient sites. The building dominates not only the city but the valley, and gave pride of place to its three deities. Fragments of the 6m statue of Jupiter are now in the Bardo but there is nothing left of Juno and Minerva.

Forum. As you stand on the Capitol steps looking out, the Forum is on your right. It is small as Roman forums go, a mere 38m by 24m due to the constrictions of the site, but its multicoloured marble flagstones enhance its dimensions. The reconquering Byzantines, fearful of a Vandal return but not realising that a greater menace would soon come from the east, cannibalised several of the surrounding buildings to create a fortress which engulfed the capitol and the forum.

DOUGGA

Compass of the Winds. To the left of the Capitol steps is the Compass of the Winds, a public square with one side extended into a hemisphere, an unusual design for the Romans who loved their straight lines. Built between 180 and 192 it takes its name from a 3rd-cent compass rose carved in the stone and showing the twelve winds.

Temples. Several temples face this odd-shaped square. The Temple of Mercury on the north had three rooms, possibly for the Roman trinity. Beside it are the tiny 2nd-cent Temple of August Piety, and the Temple of Fortune which became a mosque for the few followers of Islam who stayed on.

Brothel. Beyond this town centre complex other buildings, mostly two-dimensional, extend for a kilometer across the site. The Trefoil House, the Maison du Trifolium, was the brothel of Roman times with a flight of 21 steps leading up to the business quarters. The name comes from the shape of the basement floor.

Cyclops' baths. Is there subtle humour in having a set of public toilets near the baths of the Cyclops? These one-eyed gods were responsible for delivering thunderbolts, an apt description for any Roman who used one of the 12-seat communal latrines placed above a sewage outfall — and particularly as the toilets were located just outside the baths and convenient for the brothel. The mosaics of the cyclops are, of course, in the Bardo.

Summer baths. There were several other bath houses as one would expect in a Roman city, the 2nd-cent summer baths to the south being the largest structure in Dougga.

More temples. West of the town centre stands the Temple of Calaestis (*caelum* is the Latin for 'heaven') dedicated to Juno Calaestis, the Queen of Heaven. Built by Alexander Severus, emperor from 222 to 235, it is in a semicircular plot, another instance of the Romans of Dougga diverting from their established style. The restored sanctuary in the centre, once again surrounded by columns, graduated from temple to church with the coming of Christianity. Alexander Severus, by the way, also built a triumphal arch 100m to the north-east.

There is little to see of the Temple of Minerva to the north, not much more at the Temple of Saturn, begun in 195BC, nor of the temples of Concorde, of Frugifer and of Baal (Liber Pater) in the town centre.

Theatre. Thugga had a small theatre, built in 168 and 169 with a capacity of 3,500 though the city had a population estimated to be 5,000 at its greatest. The theatre, 63m in diameter, is being restored.

TÉBOURSOUK

When you make your way back to modern Téboursouk you may be surprised to learn that this, too, was once a Roman town — Thubursicum. The Byzantine emperor Justinian II built the city walls, but there is little to see today. The town's main attribute, particularly for visitors who've walked to and from Dougga, is that it has the only **hotel** in the vicinity, the 2-star 33-room Thugga, in an olive grove on the road to Tunis.

There are **buses** to Tunis and Le Kef, a **market** on Thursday, and the Syndicat d'Initiative has a kiosk in the town centre.

OTHER RUINED CITIES

This corner of Tunisia abounds with ruins of Phoenician and Roman cities, most of them reduced to little more than a few stones or the hint of foundations in the dry earth.

Not far from Dougga, **Agiba** has a Byzantine citael with the remains of two of its towers. To the north, Aïn Tounga is the Roman **Thignica** at the base of the Jebel Laouej. Its 6th-cent Byzantine fortress is among the best preserved in the country, showing tangible evidence of five of its square towers and two doorways. Archaeologists have yet to investigate the fortress, or even clear the accretion of wind-blown soil from the base of its walls, but in 1961 they found the outlines of houses beyond the triumphal arch at the rear of the fortress. There are also vestiges of a temple, a theatre, and a small amphitheatre.

Ksar Lemsa stands on the site of **Limisa,** which prospered in the 2nd and 3rd cents. The small village is still dominated by its 6th-cent Byzantine fort, restored in 1961 except for its north wall which has vanished, and subject to further digs in 1968. The fort, 29m by 31m, was built of material cannibalised from the pre-Vandal city and had a tower at each corner. There are traces of a Roman theatre a few hundred yards away.

Bou Arada is on the site of the old **Aradi,** with nothing to show for it beyond a triumphal arch built by Commodus. Nearby are **Suo** and **Sucubi,** the latter with a temple to Pluto, **Bisica** which has the remains of a temple, and at the modern village of Fétisse there are the vestiges of **Avitta Bibba:** two arches, two temples and three mausolea. **Tepelte** has two temples but there is virtually nothing to see of **Thimisua** at the modern village of Gaâfour.

Sbiba is the old **Sufes,** where the Christian basilica has been restored as far as available materials will allow: the church was at one stage the mosque of Sidi Oqba.

The Numidian capital of **Zama Regia** and its nearby satellite city of **Zama Minor,** near the present-day village of Jemna, have been identified as the site of the Battle of Zama of October 202AD, when Scipio defeated Hannibal and so ended the second Punic War; he also earned the accolade of Scipio Africanus.

South-west lies the mausoleum of **Ksour Toual** and the nearby Numidian stonework of **Kbour Klib** measuring 45m by 15m by 6m high. El Ksour, **Uzappa,** has traces of a Temple of Baal but is better known as the place where Safia water is bottled.

Musti, sometimes called Mustis, stands close to the main road in view of passing traffic yet has not suffered badly at the hands of latter-day vandals. This small city was probably founded in the 2nd century by one Marius, for his veteran soldiers. It became a municipium, though nobody knows whether Julius Caesar or Marcus Aurelius, two centuries apart, made the decree; it never reached colonial status.

Archaeologists moved in in 1959 but the only indication of the name found on site is the adjective MVSTITA; as Ptolemy called the place Mubsi some modern confusion is permissible.

There was a triumphal arch at each approach to the town, with one of them now back in place. A large Roman house, olive oil presses, and a Temple of Pluto indicate affluence under the Romans but the Byzantines plundered much of the masonry — which the Vandals had probably dislodged — to build their citadel.

Approaching Makthar, we come to the modern Zannfour on the old colony of **Assuras**. The site is large, with remains of three arches, one traced to 213AD, two mausolea, a temple, a theatre, and a Byzantine fort which, once again, helps to explain the near destruction of the earlier buildings.

Ellès lies to the east, noted for its 2nd-cent BC Numidian barrow-like tomb built with large stones. A low passage leads deep into the tomb and reveals several small grave chambers. A 4th-cent mosaic of Venus from Ellès is now in the Bardo.

MAKTHAR

And then there is Makthar. A 2nd-cent BC Numidian chief chose this hill site for a castle to deter the nomadic raiders who would come out of the desert; tombs found here have yielded early Libyan as well as Touareg script. The town of **Mactaris** dates from the 1st cent BC though its name is probably of later origin.

Phoenicians. Following the fall of Punic Carthage, displaced Phoenicians moved south beyond the immediate reach of Rome and settled in Makthar with Numidian blessing. In the long term the Romans were unstoppable; they inevitably came and conquered, and in 46BC Makthar was granted the status of a free city within the Roman Empire.

Prosperity. It became a colony in 180AD when Marcus Aurelius settled Roman citizens here, and for more than a century Makthar prospered. The Vandal invasion ruined its economy which the Byzantine reconquest could not restore, and the 11th-cent Hilalian invasion brought ruin.

French town. A French officer saw the site's potential in 1887 and decided to build a town here, not knowing anything of ancient history. New Makthar was built a little distance away and in 1890 the pioneering science of archaeology began investigating the old city, returning in 1910-2 and again after the Second World War.

Old Makthar today. A museum by the gate has a small geological collection, some coins from the site, and a 6th-cent mosaic that never found its way to the Bardo. The site itself is a mere 600m north to south, with a flagged Roman road snaking up a gentle slope from the rear of the museum. On the right, an amphitheatre no more than 40m long sets the scale, and even has an undersized aperture inferring that small animals were urged through to their deaths.

To the left is the Temple of Hoter Miskar, a Carthaginian god. Rebuilt in the 3rd cent and incorporating the House of Venus, it has a crypt for the storage of so-called holy objects.

Triumphal Arch. Ahead, at the top of the rise, is the forum with its paving stones near perfect. At the far end stood Trajan's Triumphal Arch which carried the inscription, loosely translated: *To the Emperor Caesar Nerva Trajan Augustus, great among princes, conqueror of Germans, Armenians and Parthians, in his 21st year as Tribune.* The date was therefore 116AD. The Byzantines later used part of this arch for a small fortress-tower.

South of the forum stands the triple-naved Basilica of Hildeguns, several times altered and with a resulting confusion in its ground plan.

Bath-fortress. Beyond it are the Great Southern Baths — the Northern Baths are much smaller — built around 200AD and measuring 85m by 45m.

The returning Byzantines converted these baths into a fortress, indicating just how insecure they felt on reoccupying the old Roman Empire after the departure of the Vandals.

From the Trajan Arch a Roman road leads west, past the Temple of Baal, to the old forum of Numidian times. Beyond, in a small cluster of buildings, are the remains of the Scola of Youth where the Juventus, an association of young men of Makthar met, according to an inscription of 88AD. The building later served as a grand house and in the 3rd or 4th cent became a Christian church.

Cemetery. The cemetery beyond it was in near-continuous use from early Numidian to Byzantine times, except for the Vandal incursion, and investigations in a 1st-cent BC Numidian tomb show that each catacomb was used for several interments.

Modern Makthar. The modern town that Frenchman built is small and insignificant, but a few years ago it surprised its summer visitors by having a snowplough parked near the main road. No wonder; the altitude is 900m which makes it one of the highest towns in the country.

HOTELS and TRANSPORT: Marhaba, 12r; Mactaris, 24b; both unclassified. They are near the bus station at the bottom of town; SNT runs two buses daily to Tunis and local companies serve Le Kef and Kairouan. Louages leave from further up the hill.

LE KEF

Le Kef, still sometimes called El Kef, takes its name from the great rock — *kef* in Arabic — on which the town stands. *Le* is, of course, French for 'the' — *el* in Arabic, and can cause problems for visitors who don't speak French. *Le Kef* literally means 'the rock,' but 'to the rock, to El Kef,' which you will see on bus timetables, is *au Kef*, and 'from El Kef' is *du Kef*.

The Arabic name is Chakbanaria, a corruption of Sicca Veneria, which was what The Rock was called in Roman times, but to everybody it is now simply Le Kef.

Mme Bourgiba was born here so it's no surprise to learn that during his presidency Habib Bourgiba had a palace built in the town; it's on the hillside just below the giant Kasbah, and enjoys a splendid view across the countryside to the south.

Venus. Veneria was a corruption of 'Venus,' the goddess of love or, as some forthright historians choose to put it, of sanctified prostitution. After the first Punic War which ended in 241BC, this Venusian outpost received a contingent of Sicilian soldiers who then found themselves fighting in the War of the Mercenaries (240-237BC), a local civil uprising.

Sitta Veneria became a colony under Augustus and grew rich in the 2nd and 3rd cents AD, taking the title of city in 256 and then becoming the seat of a bishopric and, by the 5th cent, an important centre for monastics who revered Saint Augustine, a complete reversal of its earlier role as devotee of Venus.

Islamic adventures. The Arab invasion which brought Islam to Ifriqya also brought ruin to Sitta Veneria. It remained in the backwoods until the Ottoman caliphs of Algier and Tunis began arguing over territory and, as a result, the Bey of Tunis built a sturdy kasbah here at Veneria. Now properly

Le Kef from the Kasbah ramparts

known as Chakbanaria, the town thus found itself in the emerging nation of Tunisia and since it was a so close to the border it soon became an important administrative centre, which it still is.

Free French. After the fall of France early in the Second World War, Le Kef became the seat of government of a Tunisia opposed to Vichy and the collaborators; later, it was the headquarters of the Free French.

And yet, when France granted Tunisia's demand for independence in 1956, it held on to two outposts: Bizerte and Le Kef. Bizerte stayed in French hands for almost eight years but Le Kef fell quickly when its menfolk climbed the hill to the north of town and fired on the foreign soldiers holed up in the crumbling Kasbah.

Le Kef today. The Kasbah is still there, a vast fortress built in 1612, probably on the foundations of a Byzantine castle (the site is too good to ignore) and extended in 1679 by the Ottoman Mohammed Bey, using stone from earlier constructions.

Kasbah plans. The kasbah has been closed to the public virtually since independence but I found somebody willing to show me around and explain the impressive plans that the National Institute for Archaeology and the Arts has for this vast complex. By 1990, I'm told, it will be converted into a smart hotel, a restaurant, a night club and perhaps a casino.

Distinctive room. For the moment, though, Le Kef has just two hotels of which the Hotel de la Source is probably unique in the land. Its manager, Fethi Galia, is proud to show off the ground-floor four-bed room. T-shaped, with the door opening into the crown of the 'T,' its main section is vaulted and very ornately tiled, giving the impression that the building once knew far better days.

131

The hotel is on the universal plan of small buildings with a courtyard open to the sky so that from every floor it's possible to step from your bedroom onto a cool balcony. De la Source is unusual in that the court has been glazed in and fitted with a fountain, a 'source,' which regrettably seldom works.

Holy spring. The source, the spring of Ras El Aïn, rises in the walled-in enclosure just below the hotel and has supplied the town since the beginning. Traces of the Roman conduit remain, but you're more likely to notice the small shrine set into the wall, remembering an Islamic holy man whose followers occasionaly leave offerings.

Mine of information. A privately-run organisation, the Association pour la Sauvegarde de la Médina, runs the town's only tourist office from a quaintly-furnished room leading off the Place de l'Independance; look for a blue door and if it's ajar, the office is open. Its principal is Mohammed Tlili who has made a detailed study of Le Kef's history and will sell you photocopies of his town map and French-language information sheets.

Monument à Auge. M. Tlili is particularly interested in the Sidi Bou Makhluf quarter, which contains the kasbah, the Bou Makhluf mausoleum, and the basilica, formerly the Great Mosque but now the *Monument à Auge*, the Trough Monument.

This former basilica is a gaunt-looking building, 35m by 25m, in the shadow of the kasbah, with a wrought-iron gate leading to a small courtyard. From here a door opens into an X-shaped chamber totally without windows, light from the door allowing you to pick out the details of the vaulted ceiling. In each of the four corners is a tiny, pitch-black cell and there's a fifth cell outside with a built-in latrine. Byzantine carvings in the court confirm the antiquity but don't explain the building's role in the community — was it a counting-house for grain merchants (a Roman granary was not far away) or a secret store for the town's treasures?

The Byzantine basilica became one of the first mosques in the country that was not purpose-built and later became the Great Mosque, and this despite its cruciform plan — Islam is so wary of anything reminding it of the cross of Christianity that even the Red Cross has to operate under the symbol of the Red Crescent.

Now deconsecrated, the Trough Monument is to become a museum of local antiquities but at the time of writing has only a few statues in the court.

Sidi Bou Makhluf. The open space outside the basilica is the Place Sidi Bou Makhluf, the centre of Le Kef until the French improved the roads and built their grid-plan new town further down the slope. A short distance uphill is the Mosque of Sidi Bou Makhluf, whose octagonal minaret is much more impressive than its white dome. The mosque was the powerhouse of the Aïssaoua Confederate, founded in Meknès, Morocco, in the 16th cent and who developed the bizarre habit of eating scorpions, lizards, cacti complete with their spines, and poisonous plants.

Jewish quarter. Coming down from the Place Sidi Bou Makhluf via the narrow and stepped Rue Bahri Babouch, you find yourself in the former Jewish quarter with its now-decaying synagogue which might become a museum some day.

Dar El Kous. Near the bottom of the street is the restored Dar El Kous, a 4th-cent Christian church dedicated to St Peter. The three naves have lost their roof so the building is now an open-air theatre for occasional performances.

LE KEF

Museum. Near the presidential palace is the Museum of Arts and Popular Traditions (standard museum hours, cloed Mon) in the former Zaouia of Sidi Ali Ben Aïssa. The museum has a splendid display showing the nomadic way of life, and local costumes and trinkets. Facing the palace is the Zaouia of Sidi Mizouni, built in 1834.

HOTELS: unclass: De la Source, 18b; Auberge, 17r (not recommended); **2-star being built:** Sicca Veneria.

BUSES: Good bus connections; 4 daily to Tunis, 3 to Tabarka, one to Bizerte, Sakiet (frontier), and to other local destinations. Bus station is downhill in new town (see map).

LOUAGES: The louage stand is on the main dual-carriageway which serves the bus station.

MARKET: Wednesday and Thursday.

FESTIVAL: Bou Makhluf in July.

TOURIST OFFICE: Association for Safeguarding the Medina, near Place de l'Independance.

AROUND LE KEF
The Algerian frontier is within easy reach by louage or the daily bus to **Sakiet Sidi Youssef,** the former Numidian city of Naraggara and, according to some historians, the site of the decisive battle between Scipio and Hannibal although the concensus is that this happened at Zama. The town also saw some bloody fighting in 1958 during the Algerian war of independence and several of the gutted houses still stand empty as witness to the slaughter of the innocents.

Jebel Dyr. Jebel Dyr, the 'mount of the monastery,' rises to 1,084m to the north-east of town, the monastery clinging to its flanks. It's well preserved but off limits as it's now a farmhouse.

Further north is the village of Nebeur, from where a scenic road plunges into the valley of the Oued Mellègue, a tributary of Tunisia's only permanent river. A dam 470m long by 65m high holds a power station producing 16,000,000 kw-hours of electricity a year — but for how long? The water surges through like soup, inferring that there's heavy silting of the reservoir.

SOUTH TO KASSERINE
Medeina. South of Le Kef the rather jumbled ruins of Medeina, known to the Romans as Altiburos, lie south of Dahmani (Ebba Ksour) and are notoriously difficult to reach without your own transport: you may have to walk 10km each way.

Altiburos crowns a gentle hill lying between two oueds, the first sight of it being a 3rd-cent triumphal arch far to the left. As you approach you see the well-restored capitol standing to the right of the forum, a dedication to Commodus dating the work to 190AD. A street running between the capitol and the forum passes beneath the now-ruined Hadrian's Gate, built to honour the city's founder.

House of Sixteen Bases. A ruined temple is on the far side of the forum, with the foundations of the House of Sixteen Bases beside it. The peculiar name comes from the carved reliefs on each of 16 bases which formerly supported columns.

East of the forum the excavations reveal a town-planner's nightmare which archaeologists have tentatively called an industrial zone. Beyond, to the south, are a theatre and several mausolea, with two possible megalithic sepulchres.

Away to the north-east is the House of the Muses, excavated early this century, its mosaics now transferred to the Bardo Museum in Tunis. The Building of Asclepia, beyond, dating from the 3rd and 4th cents, has more baths and washing basins than one would expect for a normal house, and a mosaic with the word *Asclepeia* written on a crown seems to infer a connection with Asclepios, the Greek god of medicine.

Jugurtha's Table. Tajerouine is the only town you will see on the road south from Le Kef; the countryside is empty and the road is scarcely wide enough to allow two cars to pass, all other traffic being forced onto the dusty verges. At Henchir El Baida crossroads the route leading east towards Jerissa takes you into a stark industrial region of iron-ore mines: at 55% metal the ore is particularly rich but is nearly worked out.

The road to the west, towards the frontier, also leads through mining country but with the ultimate scenic interest of Jugurtha's Table. Passing Sidi Amor Ben Salem, which had a mine yielding lead and silver, you reach Kalaat Es Senam and the approach to a table mountain composed of 20,000,000 cubic metres of solid rock sitting on a dome of softer soil. The megalith is around 40m thick and its gently-sloping summit is accessible only up a flight of steps which the Byzantines carved.

According to legend the Numidian chief Jugurtha had a last retreat up here in the 2nd cent BC, and the more recent bandit Senam, who gave his name to the village beneath, is said to have followed Jugurtha's example. A marabout to one Sidi Abd El Jouad shows that somebody appreciated the summit for more etheric reasons.

The view is magnificent, but as the countryside is now a series of gently rolling, treeless upland, it's unphotogenic.

Haïdra. The road passes through Kalaat Khasba where you may notice a station on the railway to Tunis; the line earns more from carrying ores than from passengers. A side-road to the frontier post takes you through the centre of the modern village of Haïdra which is on the site of the ancient the Roman city of Ammaedara.

Ammaedara. Ammaedara is in the metaphoric backwoods today, but it was at the parting of two major Roman roads, from Teveste (Tébessa, in Algeria) to Carthage and Teveste to Hadrumetum (Sousse). The first dig began in 1883 and, with later excavations, it has revealed a surprising wealth of history.

Third Legion. Emperor Augustus installed the Third Legion here to prevent the nomadic desert dwellers invading the more fertile lands of Ifriqya, but Vespasian moved the troops west to Tébessa and brought in veterans in their place.

Citadel. Ammaedara became the seat of a bishop, according to records of 256, and with the return of Christianity under the Byzantines it was once more an important military outpost of empire, with Justinian building the large citadel between 527 and 565. This fortress, 200m by 110m, with its curtain wall originally up to 10m high, had six square towers and must have been a formidable sight rising from the north bank of the Oued Haïdra. Most of its walls are now in ruins, with modern floods further damaging the south-west tower. The part-visible south-east tower had a gate which led to a bridge over the oued, and the slightly better-preserved north wall was rebuilt in Ottoman times.

Basilica of Mellus. A triple-naved church snuggled against the citadel's inside wall with another outside, but the most important and best-preserved church, the Basilica of Mellus in the city centre, has two altars which are said to contain relics of the local good man, Saint Cyprien, whom Bishop Mellus deposed in the 6th cent.

Of the capitol, next to Mellus's Church, only the base and one re-erected column remain, and we can but speculate that the area beyond was the market place.

Maison à Auge. There is a building with trough-like carvings in the tops of stone tables, similar to the one in Le Kef, but here the troughs are still in situ fuelling speculation that this was where farmers brought samples of their grain, either for sale or as a tax tribute.

Triumphal arch. The most impressive work on the site is the triumphal arch of Septimus Severus, built in 195AD across the old Roman road (a little to the south of the present road) and in very good state of preservation. The Byzantines surrounded it by a fort which probably helped it survive 15 millennia.

Access. There is no public transport from Kalaat Khasba as the tiny modern village of Haïdra is on the frontier, but hitch-hiking is possible.

THALA

Thala, at 1,017m, has the distinction of being the highest town in Tunisia, and early mornings here are often quite chilly, even in summer. Thala has its own small collection of antiquities, mainly a well-preserved Christian basilica and a mausoleum, but the town is better know for its marble and kaolin quarries, kaolin being the raw material for porcelain.

South of Thala are 48km of rolling, lonely, empty, semi-arid countryside. And then there is Kasserine.

KASSERINE

The Romans called it Cillium and built two towers. The Arabs came and renamed the city 'two towers' — in Arabic, Kasserine...or so runs the legend.

Flavian Mausolea. The towers are the Flavian Mausolea, between the modern town of Kasserine and the main road Y-junction to the west. The larger one, built in 110AD and dedicated to Flavius Secundus, is three storeys tall and in very good condition. It's possible to read parts of the 110-stanza Latin verse praising Flavius which is inscribed on the lower part of the building, while the upper part has the further information that other members of the Flavian family are also interred here.

Arc de Triomphe. West of that Y-junction, along the road to Gafsa, a 3rd-cent triumphal arch some way from the road, completes the attractions of Cillium — and of Kasserine, too. The arch, standing dramatically on the lip of a ravine, was rebuilt in the 4th cent and has survived the passing 1,600 years in good condition.

There *are* other ruins. There are the last traces of a theatre to the south of the arch, and by the Y-junction is the main cluster of Cillium's relics, though scarcely worth seeing.

Cillium was founded as a municipium by Vespasian or Titus, some time between 69 and 81AD; it rose to colonial status under Septimus Severus who died in 211, and in the 5th cent St Augustine's followers built a monastery here.

Esparto grass. The modern town of Kasserine is primarily involved in the growing of esparto grass which is fed into the local American-financed factory for the manufacture of cellulose and a low-grade paper; the Americans were here in February 1943 under unhappier circumstances, their troops suffering heavy losses in the col between Jebel Douleb and Jebel Chambi. Oil was found in the Jebel Douleb to the north but the precious fluid is piped direct to the terminal at Sakhira on the Gulf of Gabès without benefiting Kasserine.

Jebel Chambi. And Jebel Chambi, of course, is Tunisia's highest peak at 1,544m, 5,098ft. It's an utterly unspectacular mountain with no rugged screes and no precipitous crags: it's rather like a hill that grew to a mountain's stature without realising it. You can drive to its upper flanks but even that isn't particularly rewarding as the countryside also lacks drama.

Kasserine is the kind of place that you go through, rather than go to. But if you find yourself benighted here you have a choice of accommodation.

HOTELS: 3-star: Cillium, at base of hill by the Roman town of Cillium, 72b; and in the town centre, **1-star:** Pinus, 14r; **unclass:** Hotel de la Paix, 15r; Ben Abdallah, 24b.

BUSES: To Tunis, Kairouan, Sfax, Sousse, Le Kef, Gafsa. Buses leave from the town centre.

MARKET: Tuesday.

FESTIVAL: Music and folklore, May-June.

SBEÏTLA

On your journey south through the heartland of Tunisia, Sbeïtla is the last modern town to have an important ancient Roman city as its spiritual twin, but it has a temple complex worthy of the best.   The history of Sbeïtla, the Sufetula of Emperor Flavius in the 1st cent AD, is almost a closed book. The oldest inscription found on the site was from the time of Vespasian, 67 to 71AD; we know the place achieved colonial status and was mentioned in Antoninus's *Itinerary* and in episcopal lists in 256.

Virtually the next we know was that in 646 the Byzantine bishop-prefect Gregory, seeing the wave of Islam sweeping across Ifriqya, declared the city to be independent of Rome. It did him no good: Abdallah Ibn Saad sacked Sufetula in 647 and Gregory was among the victims. This was the first Arab incursion into Christian Africa and Abdallah took back to Egypt a great load of booty and the news that the Byzantine empire would be easy

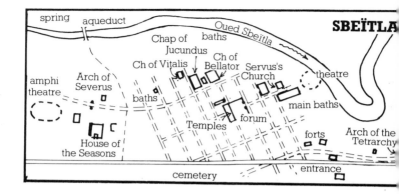

prey for further attacks.

Sufetula. Entry to the site, from dawn to dusk, is direct from the main road and between two Byzantine forts. The three churches are away on your left, standing shoulder to shoulder.

Vitalis's Church. On the left is the Church of Vitalis, a great structure with five naves and which probably served as the city's second cathedral. It was built on and overflowing the site of a 4th-century house, and samples of the house's floor mosaics are visible almost alongside those of the church.

On the right is the three-naved Church of Bellator, built on the site of what may have been a temple; it was Sufetula's first cathedral but presumably lacked the desired grandeur. Between them is the 5th-cent Chapel of Jucundus.

Temples. South of the holy Christian trinity stands the well-preserved forum and the magnificent ruins of temples dedicated to the holy Roman trinity of Juno, Jupiter and Minerva. An intriguing building technique is evident on closer inspection, for the columns at the front of these temples were purely ornamental and never carried any great weight.

The temple on the left has been sufficiently restored to allow you to appreciate its original immensity, and you can venture into the crypt.

House of the Seasons. To the north the most impressive ruins are of the House of the Seasons, named from its mosaic which is now in the Bardo with its 5th-cent altar. A large central courtyard suggests that the place may have been the private home of somebody of importance. The amphitheatre beyond is now merely a low rise in the ground.

Triumphal arches. The ruined triumphal arch of Severus Septimus at this north end contrasts with the Arch of the Tetrarchy at the southern end of the city. There is also an impressive arch dedicated to Anthony the Pious on the eastern side of the forum and opposite the temples.

The theatre, down by the Oued Sbeïtla, is in ruins but the nearby baths are still well enough preserved for the original hypocaust (under-floor) heating system to be visible.

138

Church of Servus. Across the street stand the ruins of a church. In Roman times the original building was a temple to one of the many pre-Christian gods; in Vandal times it served other gods, which is not quite the image we have of this wandering tribe of raiders; and in Byzantine times it was the Church of Servus and probably acted as the city's third cathedral, used by Donatists who followed the breakaway Christian cult founded by Bishop Donat of Carthage and which turned from the pomp of the established church.

Sbeïtla. The modern town has nothing to delay the tourist.

HOTELS: 2-star: Bakini, 40r; Sufetula, 50r, near the amphitheatre of the Roman city.

BUSES: The town is on SNT's Tunis-Kairouan-Gafsa-Tozeur route and there are also local buses. All leave from the bus station south of town.

MARKET: Wednesday.

SOUTH TO THÉLEPTE

The road south from Kasserine enters the semi-desert fringing the Sahara, and it shows. The soil gradually becomes sand, often eroded by flash floods into deep gulleys. Nomads graze their sheep and goats on whatever vegetation they can find, and the most noticeable plant is the prickly pear cactus, the *figuier de Barbarie*.

Thélepte. The last Roman town but one lies here at Thélepte, although it is merely a random assortment of stones scattered widely across the countryside. The Arabs call this site Medina El Kedima, 'the old town,' an apt description. There are traces of a few churches and a Byzantine citadel, a theatre and baths, but you would need the skills of an archaeologist to interpret them.

Saint Fulgence of Ruspe, who died in 532 at the age of 65, spent much of his time here during the Vandal occupation and his diaries are our best indication of this Dark Age of Mediterranean history.

Horse carriages wait to take the tourists into Gafsa oasis

THE OASES

Gafsa, Gabes, Tozeur, Nefta, Kebili and Douz.

WHEN YOU REACH TUNISIA'S OASES you know you are in a foreign land for there is nothing like them anywhere in Europe. The countryside is dry, dry, dry, and in high summer scorchingly hot, but you are not yet in the land of the vast rolling sand dunes, the great ergs. This *is* the desert, and you *are* in the Sahara, but you will still find hard ground underfoot and a scattering of greenery across the landscape, for it does rain here... sometimes.

Human life, however, centres on the few places where ground water surges to the surface and vegetation can luxuriate. And how it thrives! The oases exist at three levels, rather like the rain forests of equatorial regions. At the top the date palms fruit 15 to 25m above the sandy soil; much closer to the ground the pomegranate and the banana produce their crop; and at the bottom, cabbages and other vegetables exist in the patches of sunlight which filter through the double canopy. Nowhere is any patch of irrigated soil wasted, and when you have walked to the far boundary of an oasis another five paces take you into the desert.

The land here is low and flat, much of it only a few feet above sea level. The winter rains on the mountains to the north dissolve salts and other minerals as they slowly filter south through the rocks, so that much of the desert between the oases is flooded. But not with lifegiving water; this water is saline, bitter, and deadly to almost all forms of life. This is the region of the chotts and in particular the Chott El Jerid, a salt lake that was impenetrable to man and animal until the Tunisian army built a roadway across it.

This, indeed, is the north Africa of *Beau Geste,* of *Ice Cold in Alex,* and of those dreams in *A Thousand and One Nights,* though none of those stories was set here in Tunisia. This is a fascinating, wonderful, cruel, unique, landscape. Don't miss it.

GAFSA

The children of Gafsa will assume you've come to their town for the sole purpose of seeing the Roman baths and, given the opportunity, they'll lead you there. On your own, you would find the baths more by luck than judgement, but if signs were put up they would deprive the youngsters of their means of livelihood, for life is economically hard in the oases and becomes harder the further south you travel.

Roman baths. The baths are certainly worth seeing. The only remaining evidence that the Romans were ever in this town (unless you count the occasional carved lintel), they are two stone-lined square pits around 10m square, with steps leading down the 5m to water level. An arched tunnel links the baths below the surface and boys delight in swimming through it and diving two or three metres through the crystal-clear waters at 31 ° for coins.

The bath on the west, known as Aïn Es Sakkan, is overlooked by the sturdy but otherwise unimpressive House of the Bey, built by an earlier ruler and recently restored.

Capsa. Prehistoric man left fragmentary evidence of his passage through this region, and he became known in the text-books as Capsian Man, from Capsa, the name the Romans were to bestow on this Numidian settlement when their governor Marius seized it from Jugurtha's men in 106BC, making it their most southerly outpost of Ifriqya.

A chronicler of Jugurtha's War wrote "the conquest of this place (Capsa) is the highest point of Marius's ambition," and described the capture of the town by stealth and surprise after a war that had been dragging on for six years. But there was no mercy to be shown: the Romans imprisoned all those whom they didn't put to death by the sword.

Capsa thrived under Rome, becoming a municipium during Trajan's emperorship and later a colony, but we don't know exactly when the baths were built. The local Byzantine prefect Solomon built a wall around the city — nothing remains of it — and named it Justiniana from his emperor, which gives us the approximate date of 540.

Arab arrival. In 668 the Arabs arrived. Oqba Ibn Nafi showed no more mercy than the Romans had done, seizing 80,000 prisoners in the southern part of Ifriqya and sending many into slavery. The Berber townspeople who had ceased their nomadic way of life were devout Christians speaking in dog Latin, and they took unkindly to the notion of having to convert to Islam without the option.

Kasbah. The Hafsid caliph Abu Abdallad Mohammed started work on Gafsa's Kasbah in 1434, partly on the site of the Byzantine city walls and using some of their masonry. Little more than a century was to pass before north Africa became the battleground between Spaniard and Turk, and in

The Roman pool at Gafsa   Sfax: the Archaeology Museum

1551 Dragut laid siege to the Kasbah. He failed to take it. The Ottoman pirate Turgut Reis, Dragut to Europeans, was not the kind of man to accept failure lightly and in 1556 he tried again, and succeeded. *(Dragut makes an appearance in two other books in this series, 'Discover Turkey,' which recalls the place of his birth, and 'Discover Malta,' which tells of his death in the siege of that island, his only irrevocable failure.)*

Ammunition dump. The Kasbah had a major restoration in the 19th cent but suffered its greatest disaster in 1943 when an Allied ammunition dump inside its eastern wall exploded, and suddenly there was no eastern wall any more. That was a bad year in other ways, for the retreating Germans counter-attacked and the town of Gafsa changed hands three times.

Law Courts. Twenty years after the big bang the dreadfully uninspiring Law Courts filled the gap in the Kasbah walls. The building is so much like modern European architecture at its worst that we can turn with relief to the picturesque old town across the Ave Bourgiba.

Theatre and baths. West of the Kasbah, on the opposite side to the Law Courts, the modern Theatre of the South is a cinema offering French-language films. Posters outside have bosoms carefully painted over in black, as you will see in other parts of the country, yet postcards on sale elsewhere in town specialise in cleavage rather than landscape. Beside the cinema is a thermal bath where the water gushes forth at a constant 25°C.

Great Mosque. South of the Kasbah and overlooking the oasis, the Great Mosque, restored in 1969, has the same ground plan as the Great Mosque of Kairouan, but as Nazranis (Christians) are allowed no further than the courtyard there's no point in describing the blue geometric-pattern tiles which I hear decorate part of the interior. Every child in Gafsa seems to know that it's *défendu* for us to enter.

Artisanat. The Office Nationale de l'Artisanat Tunisien, the ONAT, which runs the craft centre on the town's western fringe encourages visitors and shows some of its young craftsmen and women making *ferrachia,* the traditional Bedouin blanket with strong colours and geometric designs. The ONAT, with an eye for business, also encourages its protegés to weave much smaller and cheaper items purely for the tourist trade. Yes, life in the oases can be hard.

Rebellion. It was particularly hard on the night of 27-28 January, 1980, when 300 armed men stormed the town. The Army, which now has barracks here, took three days to recapture Gafsa, leaving 21 townspeople and 13 rebels dead as well as 24 of its own men. Sixty rebels stood trial in March 1980 and on 17 April, 13 of them were executed despite pleas for clemency from abroad.

The motive for the uprising was never explained and is still a mystery. It's assumed the men were Libyans, but they chose a town notoriously difficult to defend with modern weapons, as the Eighth Army already knew. There had been a major strike in Ksar Hellal in October 1977, a riot in Tunis in January 1978, and there were to be bread riots in Kasserine in January 1984. But why Gafsa in 1980? Perhaps because there is an underlying feeling here that other parts of the country are prospering while Gafsa languishes. Spend an hour or two in the town centre and you find yourself fending off the self-appointed tourist guide or the man who wants to tell you outright about his financial problems.

The Oasis. Gafsa exists solely because of its oasis, yet the 100,000 palm trees don't dominate the town. Not until you go down Rue Ali Belhaouane looking for the Roman baths, or walk past the Great Mosque, do you realise the palms are there. They produce low quality fruit, which doesn't help the borderline economy of the town, although apricots, oranges, lemons, figs and a few pistachio nuts spread the harvest season a little longer. The water here is sweet — drink some and you'll agree — and comes from natural springs and artesian bores.

Around Gafsa. There are two smaller oases nearby. The **Oasis of Sidi Ahmed Zarroug,** 4km to the north-west, has a thermal spring which issues sulphurous and slightly brackish water, Since 1964 some of this water has been diverted to supply the thermal baths in the luxury Jugurtha Hotel which nestles in the oasis. The Jebel Ben Younès on the fringe of the irrigated area offers a gentle climb for a view of the surrounding country — rugged and barren, but not sandy. Take a taxi from town but if walking, follow signs to the hotel.

The small **Oasis of Lalla,** 7km south-east, is what you would expect an oasis to be like, with a gentle stream trickling over the sands. Go by bus from town or, in your own transport, take the Gabès road and turn left immediately after the level crossing.

Twenty kilometers south of Gafsa are the **phosphate quarries** of Mdhila which began yielding in 1920 and now produce 1,500,000 tons a year from a seam 3½m thick; 2,000,000 tons a year is the yield from the mines of Jebel Sehib a little to the south. Production began in 1970 and the reserves are likely to be exhausted early in the 1990s.

And if you leave Gafsa on the P3 road to Kairouan, watch for the impressive ravine of Bir El Hafey, at 70km.

By the market at Tozeur

HOTELS: 3-star: Jugurtha, in oasis 4km west of town, 152b; **2-star:** Gafsa, 102b; **unclass:** Ennour, 36b; Khalfallah, 24b; Maamoun, had 42r, extended and due open 1988; Oasis, 48b; République, 34b; Tunis, 43b.

RESTAURANT: Semiramis, at the Gafsa Hotel.

BUSES: Three daily buses to Tunis; frequent minibus services to Tozeur, Nefta and Gabès. Bus station in town centre; see map.

RAIL: Up to two trains daily in each direction, to Metlaoui and Tozeur and to Sfax and Tunis. Railway station 3km south-west of town at Gafsa-Gare village.

MARKET: Tuesday.

TOURIST OFFICE: ONT; town centre, 100m from bus station.

Lost oases. The wayside community of Metlaoui is of no real interest — the mine workings, the railway and the overhead ore conveyors dominate the town — yet it is the gateway to one of the most fascinating regions of Tunisia far from the normal tourist circuit, taking you to the lonely mountain oases of Tamerza, Midès and Chbika and showing the spectacular Selja Gorge.

If you are on route to or from Tozeur with your own transport and with two days to spare in your itinerary, then you'll never regret making this détour. Travellers relying on public transport will find the going gets tough and they may need to allow three days to cover the circuit. And package tourists who tire of endless days on the beaches can buy an excursion into this fantasy land.

Metlaoui. The road begins at Metlaoui, a town which is totally devoted to the production of calcium phosphate, used as a fertilizer. A French army vet with a keen interest in geology came to this remote area of Tunisia in 1885 to study the diseases of goats. Instead he began exploring a narrow cleft in the hills outside the town and realised the rocks were rich in phosphates, derived mainly from fossilised animal dung though to a lesser extent being the fossilised remains of the creatures themselves; there is a small museum in town displaying dinosaurs' jaws and suchlike relics.

The vet also made a collection of the flora and fauna of his era and took home 200 species either as stuffed birds, reptiles in preserving jars, birds' eggs, or butterflies pinned to boards. He knew there was little prospect of his phosphate discovery being exploited due to the lack of suitable transport, but in 1896 the railway from Sfax reached Metlaoui, and a sattelite village bearing the vet's name, Philippe Thomas, grew up on what is now the main road from Gafsa to Tozeur.

Thomas received an award of 6,000 francs and a pension of 2,000 francs per annum, but he died on the year payments began.

Superphosphate. The railway was extended in 1904 and '05 on metre-gauge tracks from Metlaoui, through the Selja Gorge, to two further phosphate deposits at Redeyef and Moularès, but the First World War reduced the quantities mined. When peace returned, Morocco announced the discovery of a higher-grade phosphate, so Tunisia's response had to be to enhance the value of its deposits by converting them, at source, to superphosphate. This means crushing, adding water, then taking it away again, making the finished product much easier for plants to absorb than the basic slag. And that was not going to be easy on the edge of the world's greatest desert.

Sabre Cut. Let us leave the chemical industry for a while and follow in Thomas's footsteps. The narrow cleft which intrigued him was known as the Sabre Cut and was the work of Al Mansour, a warrior of long ago who ran away with his master's bride, the beautiful Princee Leila. Al Mansour hacked into the hill with his sabre and thus carved his marriage bed. Unbelievable? Then so is the Selja Gorge which lies hidden behind this cleft.

Selja Gorge. The entry to the gorge is only a few metres wide but it gradually expands to reach 40m, its red-brown cliffs of waterworn sandstone rising almost precipitously to 100m and making this incredible chasm something of a lost world. The noontide shade on the canyon floor is a welcome relief from the searing sun, and the Oued Selja, which flows throughout the year, cascades over the boulders in its bed.

Ahead, the gorge opens into a cirque, a natural amphitheatre carved from the stone, before narrowing again with its cliffsides rising to 200m overhead. But the river bed is also rising steeply and a few kilometers further on you emerge from this wonderland onto a searing plateau.

The Romans built a series of dams across the Oued Selja to aid irrigation of the soils around Metlaoui (which wasn't there then), so the people planning to convert phosphate into superphosphate had the answer to their water problem.

By rail. Today, diesel-powered trains follow the sinuous track through the Selja Gorge, bringing phosphates and superphosphates down from the deposits of Moularès and Redeyef. At the ridiculous hour of 0520 and again at 1620, a passenger coach is tagged onto the end of the train allowing you to go all the way through the gorge to the railhead at Redeyef, or to drop off at the Selja signalbox and walk back — being careful of other trains on the line. If you choose to drop off, you have the option of waiting around 80 minutes for the passenger-carrying train to return.

And, in the tourist season, there are the special excursions aboard the *Lézard Rouge*, the train that once served the Bey of Tunis.

On foot. If you have the constitution for walking you can take the track above the gorge (it's suitable for cars) and at 5km clamber down to the bottom of the canyon. And from there you can make your way back to Metlaoui on foot. But be careful: this can be a gruelling walk in the heat of the day. Wear a hat, have light clothing, and take as much water as you can carry.

By road. There is no motor road through the Selja Gorge but an adequate road meanders across country from Metlaoui to Moularès and Redeyef. The first few kilometers are sinuous and you'll meet big lorries bringing phosphate down from the open-cast mine of Kef Schfaier to the north of town.

Vital statistics. You want statistics? Kef Schfaier has 90,000,000 tons of phosphate reserves in eight beds with a total thickness of 12m; the mine went into production in 1975 and yields 2,500,000 tons a year. Metlaoui's two phosphate beds are two and three metres thick.

Moularès has a seam 4m thick from which 800,000 tons are dug each year, and it also entrains 1,000,000 tons a year from the mines of Jebel Mrata to the north. No wonder a cloud of phosphate dust hangs permanently over the little town.

Redeyef has a two-metre seam yielding 1,500,000 tons a year which is converted on site into superphosphate. This is the last of the industrial towns which give a nightmarish, other-planet atmosphere to the landscape; from here we're in the rugged, rock-desert with its fascinating, almost fairy-tale oases.

Tamerza. An infrequent minibus service is the only public transport over the unmade road to Tamerza; there are plans to lay a tarmac surface at some unspecified date but in the meantime tongues of fine sand occasionally drift over the hard-packed earth and add to the problems of motoring.

The town is on the site of the Roman and Byzantine outpost of Ad Turres and is totally different from its mining neighbour. The old part of town, with its houses built of the local yellow sandstone and yellowish mudbricks, has been abandoned following a disastrous flash flood of 1969, but the tombstones of its holy people are still tended.

Cascades Hotel. From the centre of town a track leads down to the Cascades Hotel which can sleep 120 guests in the rustic splendour of bamboo-and-grass bungalows clustered around a refreshing pool. The Cascades is a popular stopover on the itinerary of travel firms organising Land Rover safaris around these remote mountain oases, and almost all the visitors are bussed in on these mini-packages.

Other cascades. Take a walk from the Cascades Hotel to the mini-gorge of the Oued El Khangat and see two natural cascades, one hot and one cold, tumbling into the ravine.

Midès. If you find it difficult to accept the stark, rugged beauty of this mountain oasis, then hire a donkey or camel from the Cascades Hotel and go 5km west to Midès, an incredible village whose houses stand on the rim of a gorge which cleaves its way around three sides of the tiny community, leaving a vertical rock face as the fourth side.

This is geology gone mad, but it gives fantastic rock formations whose russet colours contrast with the green of the tiny oasis where oranges and pomegranates grow under the palms. The Romans were here, calling their frontier post Mades, and with Algeria just a stone's throw away, Midès is still a frontier post. In fact, if you're travelling alone you're likely to have to show your papers to the police.

El Khanga. From Tamerza there's a choice of road: the good one direct to Chbika or the poor but scenic one which detours through the mini-oasis of El Khanga at the head of a gorge 150m deep. Neither road has any form of public transport, nor is there any from Chbika to Tozeur, and traffic is so light that hitch-hiking is unpredictably slow.

Chbika. Chbika is only around 150m above sea level at the base of a range of hills. The Romans had a lookout post at the top of the jebel and used mirrors of polished metal to flash the news of any camel trains coming across the desert to the south; their name *Ad Speculum* means 'to the mirror' and prompted the early Arab name of Kasr El Sham, Castle of the Sun.

The picturesque mud-brick houses of the old village of Chbika, which is also called Chebika, are crumbling into decay as the people move into newer and more convenient homes that look far less attractive, but that's often the way of progress. The equally-picturesque oasis is 500m away at the entrance to a gorge whose walls are of rust-red rocks.

Chott El Gharsa. From Chbika to Tozeur the road varies from good to so-so, with occasional stretches partly covered by drifting sand. The track crosses the corner of the Chott El Gharsa saltpan which is 20m below sea level at its greatest depression.

HOTELS: Metlaoui: Ennacim, on road to Tozeur, 36b;   **Tamerza:** Les Cascades (see text), 120b. Both are unclassified.

TRANSPORT: Metlaoui is on the bus and rail routes Gafsa-Tozeur, and louages leave from the town square in both directions. Buses and trains (see text) also go to Redeyef, the buses via Moularès. *Tamerza* can be reached from Redeyef by infrequent minibuses, and the best you can expect from Tamerza to Midès is donkey or camel. There is no transport from Tamerza to Tozeur.

FESTIVAL: of Mines, Metlaoui, in July.

TOZEUR

Tozeur is a remarkable town by any definition. Living in an oasis is little different from living on an island and choice of occupation becomes strictly limited. For centuries Tozeur has been involved with growing dates and receiving camel caravans — and then came tourism with its totally different values and demands.

Mixed character. The modern Tozeur is therefore a town of many characters, all trying to mix. It is still a desert outpost and oasis where a bale of animal fodder, grown under the palm trees, is a valuable commodity. But it's now a tourist town where independent travellers prepare for their venture into the desert and where organised Land Rover safaris are continually passing through.

Tozeur has cheap and basic hotels for its own people, such as the Essaada, for example, at 4TD a room; and now it has smart tourist hotels like the Oasis, which charges 16TD per person in mid-season and is out of reach of the average Tunisian.

You will find shops selling harness for donkeys and camels; there are others with television sets for the few affluent locals; and there are the craft shops selling locally-made souvenirs to the visitors. Tozeur the tourist town has several banks and there is now an international airport, yet Tozeur the oasis town has still to come to terms with its age-old unemployment problem.

Architecture. Even the architecture reflects these twin cultures trying to coexist in harmony. The older houses, particularly in the 14th-cent Ouled El Hadef quarter, are built with small yellow bricks baked from the local sand and mud and laid according to traditional Berber designs — you can see the same designs woven into their blankets in the craft centre and on the streets — but many of the modern buildings are those square blocks that could be anywhere in the world.

In fairness, some of the old houses are simple mud-brick affairs and some

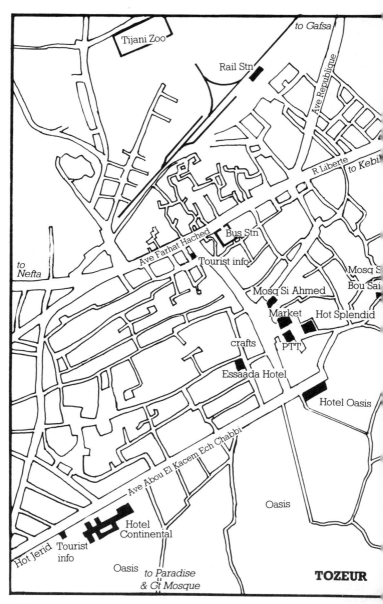

Tijani Zoo

to Gafsa

Rail Stn

Ave Republique

R Liberte   to Kebil

Bus Stn

Ave Farhat Hached

to Nefta

Tourist info

Mosq S

Bou Sai

Mosq Si Ahmed

Market   Hot Splendid

crafts

PTT

Essaada Hotel

Hotel Oasis

Ave Abou El Kacem Ech Chabbi

Oasis

Hot Jerid

Tourist info

Hotel Continental

Oasis   to Paradise & Gt Mosque

TOZEUR

of the new buildings, such as the better hotels, are preserving Berber building design: it is, after all, part of the charm of the Jerid and what the visitors come to see.

Building materials govern architecture at all levels, and you will notice that in this part of Tunisia the mosques are also made of these same thin bricks and the plastered domes of the north have given way to the square minarets of the south.

Thursuros. The Romans controlled the Bled El Jerid area, the 'land of palms,' in the 2nd cent but never colonised the old Berber settlements. This oasis took the Latin name of Thursuros and although the later Byzantines brought in Christianity, they never left a legacy in stone, or even brick.

The conservative Berbers accepted the teachings of Christ and history recalls the names of several bishops of Thursuros, then in the 7th cent the proselytising Arabs introduced the doctine of Islam and gave the Berber population the choice of death or religious conversion. But who are we to criticise: Christianity's record is no cleaner.

Kharijites. Once the Berbers had come to terms with the new faith they were loath to change. In 944, for example, the local man Abu Yazid saw no reason for abandoning the Kharijite cult in favour of the Fatimite doctrine that the Mahdi was proclaiming from Mahdia. Abu Yazid mounted his donkey and led a rebel band across the country to besiege the gates of Mahdia for three years. But the legendary 'man on a donkey,' as well-known to Tunisians as Robin Hood is to the British, was killed in 947.

Tozeur, known as Kastiliya in the Middle Ages, also resisted the Almohades and the Hafsids, but had to concede to the overpowering force of the latter.

Slave trade. Cholera killed half the townspeople in the 16th cent but Tozeur survived economically because of its vital place in the chain of oases which dictated the caravan routes across the Sahara. Two centuries later it was much more a city of the desert to the south than a town of Tunisia to the north; it received caravans of up to 2,000 camels and traded in anything that was merchantable, building up a profitable line in slaves from black Africa. And on one occasion the Bey of Tunis had to send an expeditionary force to collect his taxes.

Khammes. Some of those slaves stayed on to work in the oases, and their mixed-blood descendants are in town today, by force of circumstance still employed in the oases. A plantation worker with an almost full-time job is known as a *khammes*, from the Arabic *khamsa*, meaning 'five.' A khammes receives one fifth of the value of the harvest he helps to produce from his year-round labours of fertilising the blossoms, irrigating, tending and then harvesting the fruit.

The date harvest. In the main harvest season of November and December there is work for almost all the able men of the town who come in as day labourers for 120TD a month. And when the last date is gathered these unfortunates begin an enforced period of unemployment which will last until the next harvest.

A man in his twenties explained it to me forcefully. "There is no unemployment pay in Tunisia. There are pensions for the old, but we who have no work have no income. There are 30,000 people in the town and 10,000 of them are unemployed for 10 months of every year." He might have added that there are 15,000 people in Nefta and their employment prospects are the same, with the phosphate mines of Metlaoui offering the only other work in the area — but not for an extra 15,000 adult males.

A date with economics. Throughout the Jerid the income from dates scarcely keeps the region solvent, and the lesser crops grown in the shadow of the palms are not enough to meet local demand. In the Bled El Jerid region, the oases to the north of the Chott El Jerid, 1,600,000 palms yield up to 30,000 tons of fruit a year, of which 1,000 are of the high-value exportable *deglet en nour*, 'finger of light' variety.

And if you like statistics, the oasis of Tozeur has 200,000 palms on 1,000 hectares (2,400 acres) fed by 200 springs giving 2,500,000 litres (480,000 gallons) of water an hour.

Phoenix dactylifera. The date palm, phoenix dactylifera, reaches up to 25m tall with leaves from 2½ to 5m long and lasting for several years. The female tree begins fruiting after five years and trees of either sex can survive up to 200 years although 150 is a more normal old age.

The palms are planted at around 720 to the acre (around 1,100 in the Corbeille of Nefta where water is more plentiful and there is less undercropping) and are tended manually: small plantations grown for mechanical harvesting are at only 350 trees to the acre which doesn't justify wasting the precious land and certainly does nothing for the unemployment problem.

Pollination. The single-sex trees need human help from April to June to achieve pollination, then from September the workers begin wrapping plastic bags around the choicest fruit, and harvest it with machetes from October onwards: the job involves a tremendous amount of tree-climbing with no ladders at all.

The oasis of Tozeur

Oasis impressions. The casual visitor sees none of this. His impression is usually one of total serenity and an almost cathedral quiet, broken only by the twittering of wagtails and other small birds and the occasional grumbling camel. Small fish live in the streams, the *seguïas,* whose flow is controlled by concrete sluices. The air is hot, but out of the direct sun it feels refreshingly cool, and flies don't make themselves a nuisance.

Seeing the oasis. At 3TD for 45mins you can hire a camel at the oasis entrance beside the Hotel Continental, but as the camel guide travels at walking pace you may as well do the same and save your money. Donkey carts are available, carrying three or four people a time and are the more practicable way of appreciating the size of the oasis and going on to Paradise, but I would still recommend walking a few hundred yards if only to sample the sights and sounds of an oasis.

No driving. Don't try taking a motor vehicle into the oases of Tozeur and Nefta: it's not advisable.

Bled El Hader. The adequately-signposted oasis trail to Paradise winds for three km from the Hotel Continental to the small village of Bled El Hader, on the probable site of the Roman Thursuros. The village square has a much-restored brick minaret built on a stone base, suspected as being the only visible evidence of Rome's presence. The mosque nearby was built between 1027 and 1030 by Ali Ibn Ghaniya who came to Tozeur to preach revolution but preached religion instead.

This little village also holds the tomb of Ibn Chabbat who died in 1282; he was instrumental in organising the irrigation of the oasis, and a timetable which he compiled is among the exhibits in the Museum of Arts and Popular Traditions in town.

Jujube tree. The trail snakes on to the tiny village of Abbes overshadowed, quite literally, by a jujube tree so important that it is marked on the Michelin map of Tunisia: look for *jujubier.* The jujube, *zizyphus* to botanists, is a native of Afria and subtropical Asia and bears fleshy fruits up to an inch (3cm) long; some authorities claim it was *zizyphus lotus* which fed the lotus-eaters of Homer's Odyssey and perhaps of Tunisia's Jerba as well. Certainly the fruit was used in flavouring confectionery and gave its name to the jujube sweet which older readers may remember.

This jujube is supposed to be 700 years old, and legend claims it was planted by Sidi Ali Bou Lifa whose remains lie in his marabout in the shade of the jujube tree.

Paradise. On the other side of Abbes lies Paradise, a small private garden created by the late and locally lamented Amor Rehouma, who could recite from memory the names of all the flowering plants in his garden. He picked strawberries in February, plums in June and grapes in July.

Its present owner has inherited the collection and still offers for sale liqueurs made from their blossoms — but you can buy identical drinks far cheaper elsewhere in the village! Next door is the smaller of the town's zoos, whose animals excite more sympathy than interest.

Belvedere. Starting at the Hotel Continental (in your donkey cart?) head west down the Avenue Abou El Kacem, pass the Hotel Jerid, and in 2½km you will eventually reach the Oued El Machraâ, the main irrigation channel of the oasis. The now-dusty little track continues to the desert's abrupt edge by some large sandstone rocks, the Belvedere, from the top of which you have a good view across the Oasis of Tozeur and the Chott El Jerid.

Tozeur town. The Ouled El Hadef quarter, behind the bus station and the market, has several religious buildings of which the Koubba (Marabout) of Sidi Bou Saïd is distinctive. The koubba is in two triangular sections, one each side of the street, linked overhead by Bou Saïd's tomb which forms a bizarre archway.

Museum. The Museum of Arts and Popular Traditions (closed Monday) in the marabout of Sidi Bou Aïssa holds the original manuscript of Ibn Cabbal's timetable for irrigating the oasis but its most impressive display is the room reconstructed as a bridal chamber and displaying the gown which the Berber bride of olden times would wear on the seventh day of her marriage; the feast usually lasted a full week. There are also the clothes a lad would wear on his journey to be circumcised, an exhibition of Berber kitchen utensils, and of carpets and kilims woven in the town. (*A kilim is a special kind of carpet described in detail in 'Discover Turkey.'*)

Modern costume. Avenue Bourgiba and its produce market are the best places in town to see the modern Berber female dress which is essentially a thin black cloak thrown over the head and coming down almost to the ground but worn so that a white stripe appears as a belt. Some women have their cheeks exposed, some have one eye peering through a slit, and some are completely covered, looking through the mesh. They are all camera-shy.

Across the Ave Bourgiba lies the Zebda quarter, whose inhabitants were totally hostile to the people of the Ouled El Hadef until the mid-19th cent. This quarter holds several craft shops, the low-priced Hotel Essaada, and beside it, a Turkish bath.

Zoo. Tozeur's larger and better-presented zoo is to the north of town, signposted beside the Rapid Voyages tour operator on Ave Farhat Hached. The founder was Sidi Tijani, an acknowledged expert in Jerid and Saharan wildlife who kept a small snake farm — including the deadly poisonous horned viper — and milked them of their venom in an attempt to isolate a vaccine. His son now runs the zoo which has hyena, jackal, desert fox, fennec and gazelle among its inmates, plus Hercules, a lion who made it big in the French film *One hour 45 minutes BC.*

AROUND TOZEUR

El Hamma du Jerid has an oasis of 110,000 palms fed by six springs pouring out slightly sulphurous waters at 38°C. **Degache** is a sprawling village of ochre houses and a date packing works in the Oasis of El Oudiane which grows 220,000 palms and a wealth of other fruits. And west of Tozeur the new oasis of **Ibn Chabbat** has 75,000 deglet-en-nour palms in an experimental resettlement scheme.

HOTELS: 3-star: Continental, 300b; Grand H de l'Oasis, 92b; **1-star:** El Jerid, 110b; Splendid, 52b; **unclass:** Aïcha, 78b; Essaada, 35b.

YOUTH HOSTEL: on edge of town, a long walk, 26r.

CAMPING: Les Sources, at the Belvedere; Camping Oasis at Degache, 5km east.

RESTAURANTS: Paradis, in town centre by Hotel Essaada; République, on Ave Bourgiba; Splendid, opposite hotel of that name, popular with organised tours and overpriced; El Hamma, 9km on Gafsa road, specialising in Tunisian dishes and with grand views.

TRANSPORT: Buses: daily service to Tunis via Kairouan; local buses and minibuses to Gafsa and Nefta. Minibuses to Kebili via the Chott El Jerid at 0930 and 1415. Bus station on Ave F Hached east of junction with Ave Bourgiba. **Rail:** daily service to Tunis in peak season. **Air:** Airport 6km along Nefta road; take a taxi from Ave Bourgiba.

SPORT: Hotel Jerid occasionally hires small sand-yachts for use on the edge of the Chott El Jerid.

FESTIVALS: Festival of the Oasis, 3 days of carnival and camel wrestling and racing in November.

TOURIST OFFICES: SI; Place Ibn Chabbat; main square at top of Ave Bourgiba, 0800-1200, 1500-1800. ONTT; Ave Abou El Kacem Chabbi, beside Hotel Jerid, standard hours.

NEFTA

Nefta will surprise you. Formerly the Roman way-station of Nepta it is now the second holiest town in Tunisia and has one of the smartest hotels in the country, yet it shares with Tozeur the crippling problem of finding permanent jobs for its menfolk: the women are not so unfortunate as many of them weave blankets and rugs for commercial markets as well as for the tourist trade.

Corbeille. The Corbeille is the town's main attraction for visitors. It is an irregular-shaped depression up to 30m deep around which the town has grown; several springs on the northern side irrigate its date palms which are among the tallest you will see, as they are planted closer than normal and protected from the winds.

The stream escapes at the south end of the Corbeille, under the main road and into a oued, at one of several places where paths give access to the plantation; other paths come down the rugged clay cliffs near the Great Mosque.

Oasis. The main oasis on the south side of the town's bypass grows 400,000 palms, of which 70,000 are of the valued deglet en nour variety, on 1,100 hectares (2,600 acres). According to somebody who must have done the counting, there are 152 springs, some hot, some cold, yielding 700 litres a second, or around 560,000 gallons an hour. In the 1960s several wells were drilled, the deepest going t0 657m (2,055 feet).

Pilgrimage. If you were to come to the oasis on a Moslem holy day, particularly on the third day after Aïd El Kebir, you would find yourself in a pilgrimage with everybody heading for the Marabout of Sidi Bou Ali deep in the palm groves. The marabout, permanently closed to non-Moslems, marks the spot where Bou Ali died in the 13th century after journeying from Morocco to preach against Islamic cults not following the mainstream ideology. They say he also brought the date palm to the oasis, but that is

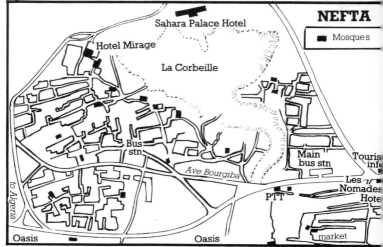

NEFTA

■ Mosques

Sahara Palace Hotel

Hotel Mirage

La Corbeille

Bus stn

Ave Bourgiba

Main bus stn

Touris[t] info

Les Nomades Hote[l]

PTT

market

to Algeria

Oasis

Oasis

nonsense: with no palms there would have been no people.

Sufism. The Berbers of the Jerid have for centuries held on to the religion currently in vogue, and Bou Ali's message therefore met local approval. His message is still preached today and has become a sect in its own right, Sufism, although its followers stress that they are in no way deviating from the holy word of the Koran; instead they are trying to get nearer to the fountainhead of truth. Sufism, therefore, leans towards mysticism and meditation and its holy men are the *fakirs* who, in an unholy world, are remembered more for their ability to lay on a bed of nails.

Holy city. Sufism has made Nefta the holiest city in Tunisia after Kairouan and, in addition to the Mosque of Sidi M'Khareg deep in the oasis beside the marabout, it has 24 mosques and more than 100 marabouts.

Zaouia of Sidi Brahim. The 15th-cent Zaouia of Qadriya, also known as the Zaouia of Sidi Brahim, is at the centre of Sufism and several of its most devout adherents choose to be buried in its tombs. The building is by the western lip of the Corbeille and — with the nearby Café de la Corbeille — has a wonderful view over the palm grove.

Town centre, Matmata

Intricate architecture at Nefta

Great Mosque. Several small mosques are in the maze of backstreets to the south but none holds any interest for the tourist — and that is also true of the rather insignificant Great Mosque, the 15th and 16th cent Mosque of Sidi Salem. But it *does* command another viewpoint over the Corbeille, and nearby is another track down into the grove.

Sahara Palace. Probably the best view over the palms is from the five-star Sahara Palace Hotel on the northern rim. Built in 1968 in Tozeur ochre-brick this splendidly-designed 'palace in the desert' offers everything the well-heeled tourist could want: a pool, tennis courts, riding stables, bars, boutiques, a night club, bank, car hire agency, and its own Land-Rovers for that executive-styled expedition into the real Sahara. The hotel originally had 50 rooms and six suites but with the coming of Tozeur International Airport the Palace was extended in the late 1970s and now has 114 rooms and nine suites.

Brigitte Bardot declared it her favourite hotel, and the cast of *The Little Prince* stayed here while filming in 1973.

Mirage. As the Sahara desert extends south into the Sahel it is increasing the hazards that migrating birds must endure on their two annual migrations. It's comforting to note that a growing number of swallows no longer face that ordeal: they overwinter in the oases of Nefta and Tozeur.

And if you want to begin to appreciate the rigours of a desert crossing for yourself and you have a car, drive west out of town for 10km along the road towards the frontier post of Hazoua until you reach the edge of the Chott El Jerid. In front of you lies a vast, empty, dead landscape, one of the most inhospitable places on earth. If you time your visit to near noon in high summer, when the glistening salt is dust dry and at its hottest, you will almost certainly see one of those wonders of the natural world, a mirage.

And that's where we're going next — across the Chott El Jerid.

HOTELS: 5-star: Sahara Palace (see text), 114 rooms; **1-star:** Mirage, overlooking Corbeille, 54r; **unclass:** Marhala Touring Club, 76b; Les Nomades, 88b.

RESTAURANTS: Les Sources, Les Amis and Le Paradis, all good without being expensive. Café de la Corbeille has tables with a view.

BUSES: Buses for long-distance journeys leave from the main bus station on the western edge of town (see map); minibuses for shorter runs (Kebili bus goes at 0830) leave from Place de l'Independance.

MARKET: Wednesday.

POST and TELEPHONE: On Ave Bourgiba (see map); no international calls possible at weekends.

FESTIVALS: Carnival and camel wrestling, April; Festival of Sidi Bou Ali and Festival of the Oasis, both in November.

TOURIST OFFICE: SI; at eastern end of town (see map).

THE CHOTT EL JERID

The 50km journey over the Chott El Jerid between Kriz and Bechri is the longest crossing of a wet saltpan anywhere in the world and has been possible in the safety of a motor vehicle only since 1985 when the Tunisian army completed the asphalted highway.

The road passes through conventional dune desert for a kilometre or two before venturing out on a causeway across dry, crusted salt. Soon it is evident that there is moisture beneath that crust: a thick black mud giving way to small patches of open water, particularly near the road where earthmovers have scooped up the lake bed to built the dyke.

The salinity is at its maximum in late summer, with every drop of water lost to evaporation causing more salt to crystallise out. Rafts of floating salt from a metre to 50m across, gently nudge each other like ice floes, building up ridges around themselves until they look like the leaves of giant water-lilies.

There is no noticeable wildlife here. The water is too bitter to support fish, so there are no birds. Yet there is human activity out on the pans where small trucks venturing far from shore manage to load salt. There are also three ramshackle roadside restaurants built of palm-leaves and offering the added attraction of a 'WC,' the effluent going straight into the lake.

Mirages. In the middle of the journey there is nothing to the south-west of you for 100km, and that's only the invisible border with Algeria. Beyond that there is a further 250km of total emptiness, part of the vast dune-desert of the Grand Erg Oriental, before you meet the first human settlement. And yet you think you can see houses, towns, oases, and buses speeding along a highway. This is the fantasy world of the mirage which brings home the truth that you cannot always believe your eyes.

Crazy plans. Camel caravans have crossed the Chott for centuries, following trails staked out with palm-trunks and with a raised overnight resting place somewhere near the middle of the trail — but not the middle of the chott which is pure brine under its crust. In 1876 an army officer on the staff of the French war ministry saw this chott, around 190km long by a maximum of some 75km wide (it's impossible to give firm dimensions since it's impossible to define the boundaries with precision), as a possible inland sea and suggested digging a canal from the Gulf of Gabès. The idea was preposterous as the Chott El Jerid is above sea level — Chott El Gharsa is below — and the only result would have been a slightly drier salt lake. In more recent times the United States' Atomic Energy Commission has made the even more preposterous suggestion of testing nuclear weapons on the chott.

KEBILI and DOUZ: the Nefzaoua

As the region north of the Chott El Jerid is the Bled El Jerid, so the region to the south is the Nefzaoua, the northernmost outpost of the true nomad and centred on the ragged hills of the Jebel Tebaga, rising to 469m.

Leopardskin landscape. This region of small oases living under the constant threat of annihilation by the Grand Erg Oriental, has also been called the leopardskin landscape from the colour of the ever-present sand. Inhabited since neolithic times, its peoples have been forced to follow an annual migratory circle, so there are no ancient ruins.

Roman era. That's not to say the Nefzaoua hasn't seen outsiders. The Phoenicians probably knew the area and, according to legend, they introduced the date palm (*phoenix* dactylifera has obvious connections with *Phoenicia*). The Romans certainly came to the Nefzaoua and Trajan

A roadside restaurant on the Chott El Jerid

founded Civitas Nybgenorium in the territory of the nomadic Nybgene tribe; Hadrian renamed it the municipality of Turris Tamalleni and today it's known as Telmine, west of Kebili.

The only relics which might have been in Turris Tamalleni are a few stones re-used in modern buildings and a well-head which was heavily restored in 1780.

Nomads. The Vandals and the Byzantines never touched these desert regions; there was neither commercial nor military profit and the warrior tribes had too many allies in the desert, particularly the Touareg.

These southern peoples were ultra-conservative. They had resisted Rome and deterred Byzantium; they went unwillingly under the Arab yoke of Oqba Ibn Nafi in the 7th cent; they later formed the main body of troops that Abu Yazid took on his donkey-ride to Mahdia; they backed the incumbent Almoravids against the Almohade invaders from Morocco; and the Ottoman invaders wisely left them alone.

From the 13th to the 18th cent the nomads of the Nefzaoua lived their own life, cultivating the palm in season, raiding neighbouring tribes, trading in slaves from black Africa, following their sheep from oasis to oasis, and making woollen goods for barter or trade. And then with colonialism their role began to fade. There was no need of them as protectors of the oases; the once-great caravans began declining, and there was the incentive to settle down and enjoy the benefits of education, health care, and gradually improving water supplies.

Tribes. In the early 1980s there were around 15,000 nomads remaining, with numbers diminishing year by year. The **Adhara** have settled around Zaafrane, the **Ghrib** are at Nefta and El Faouar (the end of the tarmac road beyond Douz), the **M'Razig** are at Douz, the **Ouled Yacoub** now live in Gafsa and a scattering of communities in the Nefzaoua, the **Rebaya** have taken roots in remote Remada and in Algeria, and the **Sabria** are in Es Sabria.

Climate. Strangely, the climate of the Nefzaoua is not as extreme as that of the Jerid. The maximum recorded temperature south of the chott is 38°C (102°F) while in the Jerid 49°C (120°F) has been recorded — and a minimum of -4°C (28°F). The *gebli* and the *chehili* (sometimes called the chilli) are hot winds off the desert which nonetheless have a cooling influence. They also make the rainfall totally unpredictable. The Jerid averages 120mm a year, with wide fluctuations, but the Nefzaoua averages 90mm, with a range from zero to 450mm.

KEBILI

Kebili is a modern town of kerbed streets built to a planner's design and surrounding the old business quarter of the Souk El Biaz. Sand is everywhere, as you would expect, which helps to create the illusion that this is a permanent building-site.

The bus station is supposed to be on the road to Douz, but buses and minibuses stop in several streets. The few road signs still use Latin script but most other signs, including the destination cards in the buses, are in Arabic.

It is difficult to find anybody with a good command of French, and English is totally unknown, but language doesn't seem to matter as the town has that wait-and-see mentality so typical of Africa south of the Sahara. Not surprisingly, the French considered it a suitable place to send Habib

Bourgiba in 1934 on one of his internal exiles.

Fort Ostrich. Kebili is, however, interesting as a crossroads of cultures. Its Tuesday market, little troubled by tourists, is busy with local produce, and its only hotel has an unusual history: converted from a barracks but retaining its crenellated watchtower, it became in the early days of this century the centre of an abortive attempt to rear ostriches, which explains its unusual name of Borj des Autruches. Ostriches were common here until the mid-18th cent when somebody decided their fat had medicinal properties; after that their value increased and their numbers decreased, each factor governing the other until the bird became extinct.

HOTEL: Borj des Autruches, unclass, in Souk El Biaz, 100b.

RESTAURANT: Chez Saad, on main road.

BUSES: Buses and minibuses for Gabes, Tozeur and Nefta, Douz and beyond. No recognised bus station: see text.

FESTIVALS: Music and popular arts, in May; date harvest, in November.

DOUZ

Douz is a total contrast to Kebili. It is a picture-postcard town that is popular with operators of organised tours, and its Thursday market brings packaged tourists anxious to see camels being traded. The craft centre has benefited from this minor invasion and Douz now has the reputation of producing the best traditional-style clothes in southern Tunisia, particularly camelskin shoes in the style of the North American moccasins, and fine woollen burnouses (cloaks with hoods).

Packaged Douz. The package tourist began arriving in Douz in 1975 with the opening of the Saharien bungalow village which has failed to gather a single star rating despite being smart, clean and comfortable. The Roses de Sable hotel is named from that peculiar geological formation, the sand rose, which you will see on offer in all the craft centres from Tunis to Tozeur to Tataouine. The sand rose is a brown quartz crystal formed in a water-worn hollow underground and, I must admit, it makes an attractive souvenir.

Camel rides and safaris. You've come here independently and want to join the fun? Ask at the Syndicat d'Initiative for details of hiring a camel by the hour or the day, or ask Douz Voyage on Place de l'Independance about an organised excursion into the desert or around the oases.

HOTELS: Marhala Touring-Club, 115b; Roses de Sable, 180b; Saharien, 235b in bungalows. All are in the oasis, all unclassified, and all get close to the soil without charging the earth.

CAMPING: Grad, 48b; Nouaiel, 80b; Paradis, 100b; all in the oasis. *Camping Zaafrane (40b) is in Zaafrane Oasis.*

RESTAURANTS: Le Calme and Les Palmiers are restaurants; Ali Baba and Oasis are snack bars.

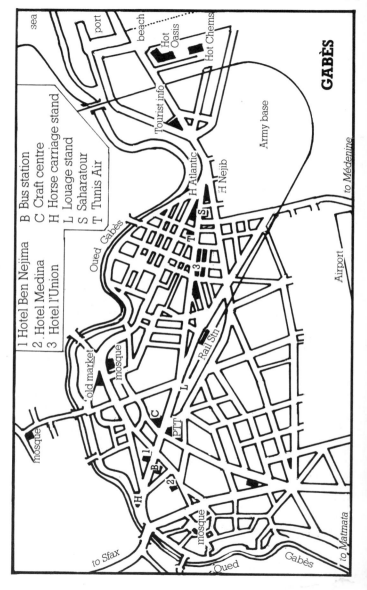

GABÈS

1 Hotel Ben Nejima	B Bus station
2. Hotel Medina	C Craft centre
3 Hotel l'Union	H Horse carriage stand
	L Louage stand
	S Saharatour
	T Tunis Air

sea
port
beach
Hot Oasis
Hot Chems

Tourist info
H Atlantic
H Nejib
Army base
to Médenine

Oued Gabès
old market
mosque
mosque
PTT
C
H
B
Rail Stn
L
T
S
3
Airport
mosque
Oued Gabès
to Sfax
to Matmata

TRANSPORT: Buses to Kebili, Gabès and Zaafrane. Louages to smaller oases. Buses and louages leave from roundabout near Avenue des Martyrs.

FESTIVAL: Sahara Festival with parades, camel wrestling, hare hunting, theatre and dance, Bedouin art and photogaphy, mock departure of nomads for fresh grazing grounds (the real departures are in spring and autumn); January.

TOURIST OFFICE: SI; Avenue des Martyrs.

BEYOND DOUZ

The road from Douz to El Faouar deteriorates with each passing mile and the last stage is better tackled with a four-wheel-drive vehicle or, at best, a truck with good sand tyres. Buses leave at 0700 and 1500, or sometimes before the scheduled time, but go no further than Zaafrane: after that the traveller without wheels must hitch a lift.

The dunes begin pressing in on the road at **Offra**, 3km along the track, from where several camel expeditions set out into the desert. **Glissia**, at 6km, has been covered by the encroaching sand.

At **Zaafrane**, (14km) there is a small oasis and the so-called Guelta of Mimoun. *Guelta* means 'sea,' but the small lake or large pond of Mimoun is certainly well stocked with fish and is an unexpected find on the edge of the Grand Erg. Zaafrane, the home base of the Adhara tribe who still make the annual trek to Ksar Ghilane, also has a few brick kilns.

A diversion 8km to the north-west over a poor track brings you to the village of Nouaïl and its 1,800 or so people who live from its oasis. Earlier inhabitants distilled a wood-creosote which had the reputation of curing mange in camels, but the only camels you see in Nouaïl today are fit beasts, ready to take tourists on treks into the desert.

At 29km you reach **Sabria**, where 1,000 people of the Sabria tribe have almost lost their nomadic way of life. Their oasis is fed by two springs but is under permanent threat from the dunes. Or you can bypass Sabria and go direct to **El Faouar**, (35km), a village of Bedouin tents and brick houses where the dunes appear to be awaiting the order to invade.

El Faouar is reputed to be the only place in the country where the newly-wed girls preserve their traditional wedding dances for their own sake and not for tourist appeal. The most impressive is the *danse de la chevelure* in which the girls swirl their heads incessantly, swinging their long black hair around to the rhythm of the tambourine.

GABÈS

Gabès is a quiet town with an oasis of 300,000 palms coming down the delta of the Oued Gabès to the seashore. The oued meanders around the north of the town and spills its waters over a small dam the Romans built.

Massinissa. The Phoenicians probably landed here in 'Little Syrtes,' a smaller version of the Gulf of Syrtes (Sidra) in Libya: if they didn't, from which other port of entry could they have carried the date palm to the Jerid? The Carthaginians certainly had a small outpost here, for history records that it was seized in 161BC by Massinissa, the Numidian chief. The Romans eventually took control of the community and made it their colony of Tacapa.

Pliny the Younger (61-113AD) wrote in his ponderous *Natural History* that "in the middle of the sands of Ifriqya, when one goes to Syrtes and to Leptis Magna, one comes upon a city named Tacapa where, under a very tall palm grows an olive, under which a fig, under which a pomegranate, and under that a vine, beneath which one sows wheat followed by vegetables — and all that in the same year and under the shade of the same tree."

Prophet's barber. There was little of Tacapa standing when the Arabs arrived in the 7th cent. Sidi Bou El Baba, often called Boulbaba, who had been barber to the Prophet, had reached Ifriqya with the first wave of invaders and deposited his greatest treasure, three hairs from Mahomet's beard, in safe keeping in the new city of Kairouan. (They must surely be the same hairs featured at the Mosque of the Barber?) He had then come down to Gabès to die in a more benign climate.

Mosque of Sidi Bou El Baba. His tomb was built on the site of old Tacapa, and the Mosque of Sidi Bou El Baba which was built around it, is the oldest surviving structure in Gabès although it has been restored so heavily that little of the original remains. The mosque, distinguished by the 10 arcades on decorated columns which surround its entrance, has a smartly tiled courtyard open to all visitors, and the non-Moslems among them may sneak a peep into the prayer-hall which is covered in quality carpets given by El Baba's followers.

(The mosque is out of town on the road to Matmata, 20 mins walk from the PTT or a few minutes on a town bus; get off at the river bridge.)

Pilgrims who came to see El Baba's tomb, and later to pray in his mosque, helped the town grow, and Sidi Bou El Baba is the patron saint of Gabès in recognition. El Idriss, a 12th-cent chronicler, recorded that Gabès was "a great city surrounded by walls and a moat" but when the French came the place was in decay.

Military strategy. The French soon realised the military significance of the location of Gabès, if not of the city itself. It commanded the very narrow gap between the chotts and the sea, along which any land-based invading force had to come. They made Gabès a garrison town, which it still is, and once again its people prospered.

Gabès suffered severely in the Second World War until Montgomery's Eighth Army, with the help of the Free French under General Leclerc, liberated it in March 1943. There's a statue of Leclerc at Ksar Ghilane on the edge of the desert 100km to the south; if you want a monument to Montgomery it could be the rebuilt city of Gabès.

Gabès today. There is little to see in Gabès, but the craft centre (artisanat), has women weaving the traditional local-style carpets and making palm-frond baskets. The Great Mosque on Ave Bourgiba was built in 1952 — and flooded, like the rest of the town, in 1962 — but the Grande Jara, the Old Market, opposite the mosque, is worth more than a passing glance.

Jara. Try the covered souk in the Grande Jara. One section is given over to the whitesmiths, making ornaments and jewellery in silver and gold, with another section for the blacksmiths, forging iron and sharpening steel. Across the Oued Gabès at the convenient bridge, the small village of Petite Jara lies in the oasis and holds the 11th-cent Mosque of Sidi Driss (Idriss), a descendant of the Hilalians who brought havoc to the country at that time.

Oasis tours. To see the oasis in comfort, take a ride in a horse-carriage from the stand at the entrance to town, the western end of Ave Farhat Hached, or take your own car. This is the largest oasis in Tunisia, reaching 6km from the so-called cascade by the Roman dam, to the railway and the beach, and 2km at its widest. It has 300,000 palms, none of them producing fruit of exportable quality, and it also has, as Pliny noted, a variety of other fruiting trees: bananas, lemons, oranges, pomegranates, peaches, apricots and even olives. The ground-cover vegetation would have confused Pliny for it includes tobacco.

Chenini. Chenini is the main village in the oasis and lies near its western end. Its Marabout of Sidi Ali El Bahloul will not detain you long.

Museum. Gabès's remaining attraction, apart from its prime beach, is the Museum of Arts and Popular Traditions in the former medrese (school of Islamic teaching) beside the mosque of the patron, Sidi Bou El Baba. The design of the medrese is a major attraction, with a yellowstone door leading to a courtyard lined on three sides by small cells. The exhibits specialise in Berber customs, featuring handicrafts that the women practised, offering a reconstruction of a nomadic Berber kitchen, and ceremonial clothes for the elaborate wedding rituals.

Industry. You would never guess that Gabès is an industrial city, as the planners have wisely sited the ugly side of life well away from the oasis, in the anticipation that tourism will expand. There are factories producing cement, bricks, a range of chemicals including potassium, sulphuric acid and superphosphates; then there is a petrochemical and plastics industry, canneries for tunny and for jam, an aluminium works, and offshore natural gas wells.

Sponge-catchers' boats at Ajim

HOTELS: 3-star: Oasis (on beach), 144r; **2-star:** Chems (beach), 556b; Nejib (town), 128b; Tacapes (town), 56r; **1-star:** Atlantic (town) 120b; **unclass:** Chela-Club (oasis), 140 beds in bungalows; Ben Nejima (town) 25b; de la Poste (town) 20b; Medina (town) 40b; Marhab (M'Rabet) (town) 60b; Kilani (town) 40b; Regina (town) 30b; Union (town, basic).

YOUTH HOSTEL: now closed and derelict.

CAMPING: Sanit El Bey, at Petite Jara.

RESTAURANT: El Mazar, Ave F Hached; good menu.

BUSES: Good connections around the country; buses start from gare routière at west end of Ave Hached (see map). Six daily to Sfax, five to Matmata, four to Jerba, three to Tunis, two to Sousse. **Buses to Chenini in oasis** leave every hour from Rue Hal Jilani Lahib.

LOUAGES: There is a good louage service, with vehicles leaving from near the railway station on Ave Hached.

RAIL: Gabès is at the end of the line with two departures a day northbound.

AIRPORT: The airport is on the southern edge of town. Services to Tunis only; enquire at Tunis Air office at east end of Ave Hached.

LOCAL TOUR OPERATOR: Saharatours, for Land-Rover expeditions into the desert (see page 28); Ave Farhat Hached 5.

MARKET: daily, except Monday.

FESTIVALS: Fête de Tacapa, traditional dances, etc, July; Festival of Sidi Bou El Baba, almost a pilgrimage, last three days of Ramadan; Gabès Trade Fair, March-April.

TOURIST OFFICE: At far end of Ave Hached; neither ONTT nor SI and often closed. Information sheets in window.

AROUND GABÈS

The 14th-cent oasis of **Teboulbou** comes down to the beach, as at Gabès. It's off the tourist track, but the beach is wide and welcoming. **Kettana** is reputed to grow the best pomegranates in Tunisia in its small oasis. North of Gabès **Aouinette** has 'little springs' as its name infers; the Romans called it Ad Palmam. And **Ghannouche** oasis is fed by artesian bores.

Thermal springs at 47°C give **El Hamma de l'Arad** its modern name, though to the Romans it was Aquae Tacapitanae. The town and its satellite villages of Sombat and El Ksar hold the Festival of Hammam (with a final 'm') in March.

Until the 10th cent El Hamma was the home of a Berber tribe that was driven into the hills. We now turn our attention to the tribe's new home in the troglodyte town named from its people — Matmata.

THE DESERT

Matmata, Médenine, Tataouine and the South

MATMATA IS ONE OF THOSE TOWNS YOU MUST SEE. It's set in a shallow valley of sulphur-yellow tufa, which is somewhere between hardpacked earth and crumbly sandstone. The town has 5,000 people but there is only a scattering of modern brick huts on this arid landscape, for the people live underground in 700 crater-homes hacked from the tufa.

When the Matmata tribe was driven from El Hamma it settled in the Jebel Dahar, this barren range of hills, at first digging itself semi-communal cave homes guarded by small forts, but with the end of inter-tribal conflict in the early 19th cent the people moved into the valley and began carving these newer homes which certainly could never have been defended.

Why underground? Tufa makes poor bricks but excellent caves, and a hole in the earth has a more equable temperature throughout the year.

Cave community. The average cave home begins with a *haouch,* a hole around 7m to 10m deep by 10m to 15m across, with access along a sloping tunnel beginning maybe 20m away. Caves dug into the base of the haouch wall are for family use; eating, sleeping, stabling the animals: caves nearer the top are for storing grain, olives and fodder, and usually have a small delivery chute accessible from the level ground above. The people reach these upper floors either by steps cut into the wall or by clambering up or down a knotted rope.

Underground hotels. The community is so different from a conventional town that it is an obvious tourist attraction, like Guadix in Spain and Göreme in Turkey. Three hotels that have sprung up — or should we say gone to earth? — to cater for the influx have several interconnected haouches with individual caves dug into their walls, equipped with steps instead of the knotted rope.

Tourists arrive by the coachload from mid-morning, but few of them have much chance to see the town as they spend their precious few hours in this unusual community buying postcards and dining in the hotels' underground restaurants. And by mid-afternoon they have headed back to their other hotels at the seaside.

True, there is not much more to *see* in Matmata (pronounce it with equal stress on each syllable), but it is well worth spending a night in a cave hotel if only for the experience. And when the crowds have gone some of the cave dwellers will invite you into their homes for a dinar!

Star Wars. A few of the people of Matmata quite naturally resent this mass intrusion by another culture and have erected barbed wire fences around their haouch. Public awareness of Matmata rose with the shooting of part of *Star Wars* in the Marhala Hotel, and I heard talk of the creation of a fourth hotel involving the compulsory purchase of several cave homes at 160TD each.

HOTELS: Marhala Touring Club, 100b; Les Berbères, 80b; Sidi Driss, 140b; all are unclassified.

RESTAURANTS: At each hotel, but non-guests may find difficulty in being served at midday when there are full coach bookings. All three serve wines with meals. There is, of course, above-ground the Café Auled Azaiz in the town centre: you can't miss it.

POST OFFICE: Conventional building opposite the café: look for the Tunisian flag above the Garde Nationale beside it. No international telephone.

BUSES: The Bus station is 200m from town centre along the Médenine road. There are five buses to and from Gabès daily in peak season dropping to three in low season. *There is no other public transport from Matmata in any direction.*

AROUND MATMATA

The lack of public transport to the surrounding villages and the poor state of the roads, mean that the other cave communities in the neighbourhood have yet to be touched by tourism: if you manage to see some of them you cannot fail to notice the difference in their demeanour.

The are a few cave dwellings at **Beni Zelten,** but **Haddèj,** fairly near the bus route, has quite a number, mostly well hidden beyond few conventional houses in the village. This was the home territory of the khalifa, the traditional Matmata tribal leader, until the relatively settled life of modern times.

Téchnine is at the end of a bad road, its mosque, shop and marabout being the only visible buildings. The villagers have the reputation of making their own built-in cave furniture from palm-wood, its porous grain filled with clay or plaster. **Tijma,** 4km north of Matmata and convenient to the road, has no more than three or four conventional houses amid its scattering of caves, but just to the north is the **Maison de Fatma,** a cave that has been sold to the tour operators. Many coaches pull up here to allow the tourists to see a 'genuine' cave dwelling and to admire Fatma (or was it her mother or her daughter — they all call themselves Fatma) in her traditional clothes and Berber jewellery. It *is* geniune, but when you see the souvenir cave beside it you realise it's not quite the real thing.

Remote outposts. Two other villages in this range of hills are worth seeing, if you have the time and the transport. The road to **Tamezret** is well-surfaced but narrow and twisty, passing several isolated caves and pockets of cultivated land with a scattering of olive trees. The village itself sits proudly atop a pointed hill crowned by a white, battlemented mosque. Backstreets are narrow and steep and have eroded down to the bedrock which is too hard to allow the digging of caves. At the top, a simple bar gives a wonderful view of the shimmering landscape.

By contrast, the road to **Toujane** is bad, whether you come from east or west. The village sits on top of an even more impressive hill, straddling a gorge that makes you catch your breath — if you have any left. Time your visit to the relatively cooler winter season and you may see the village camel ambling round a large flat circular stone, pulling a smaller vertical stone wheel which crushes olives: the simple olive press of antiquity.

The only French spoken in these remote villages is frequently difficult to understand, and Berber is more common than Arabic.

MARETH

In 1938 the French anticipated an Italian attack from Libya and so built a defensive line from the Gulf of Gabès to the Jebel Dahar; the Mareth Line. In 1941 the Italians brought their German friends, and Feldmarschall Rommel's Afrika Korps breached the Mareth Line from the east to hold it against the advancing Eighth Army led by General Montgomery.

Monty's troops, with the Free French under General Leclerc, regrouped in Médenine before attacking the line. The battle lasted 40 days and when the Allies drove Rommel back towards Tunis there was nothing left of the Mareth Line. Nor of Mareth either. Today the little village is rebuilt and goes about its business tending its oasis. Two kilometres south-east, a conical monument is a memorial to the Free Frenchmen who died in the action.

Nearby is **Arram**, a 15th-cent village founded by Berbers who had migrated across half the Sahara from Rio de Oro, later known as Spanish Sahara, then Western Sahara, and now claimed by Morocco.

MÉDENINE

Médenine is a prosperous-looking small town with no apparent means of support. At the western end of the Ave Bourgiba are the Banque Nationale de Tunisie, the Banque du Sud and the Banque de France, all offering to exchange currency. There are four petrol stations, two PTT buildings — the postal side of the business is in a prestigious office in a well-tended park that actually has lawns with real grass — and finally the ODS edifice which probably explains this affluence. The Office du Développement Social is the skyscraper of southern Tunisia and its lights burn on into the night.

The town grew around the Ksar El Touazine, which became its name, then in the early 19th cent a holy man living at Ghomrassen near Tataouine suggested his people should move up to here. They built their *ghorfas*, and by 1960 there were around 6,000 of these grain-stores around town. By the late 1980s only one remains, converted into a souuvenir shop along the Rue des Palmiers. The ksar has gone, too.

Frogs. Médenine's modern name is a corruption of 'two towns,' divided by the small canal-straight oued which not only has water all year but also has a resident population of frogs.

شرل The town's Sahara Hotel beside the PTT's telephone office is impressively large and reasonably smart but is the only hotel I saw in the country that did not have its name up in Latin script. If the situation is no better by the time you need to stay the night in the town, look for the Arabic شرل — or stay at the Essaada, which is the smartest hotel I saw to bear that name.

Road checks. I was unable to find out why the roads around Médenine are subject to the most stringent police checks in the country, with private cars and buses equally coming under strict scrutiny. "Orders," or "It's our job," were the only answers I had. Could it be the proximity to the Libyan border? After all, old soldiers of the Eighth Army may recall seeing a sign in town, pointing east and proclaiming *Cairo, 2,606km*.

HOTELS: 2-star: Agil (not on map), 26b; **unclass:** Sahara, 82b; Essaada, 16b; Hotel du Sud; Palmiers (on road to Jorf).

YOUTH HOSTEL: on Rue des Palmiers.

RESTAURANTS: Several in town; try on Ave Bourgiba opposite the Mobil station.

BUSES: Bus station in Rue 18 Janvier. SNTRI and SRTGM each pretend the other does not exist. SRTGM has 0730 and 1600 buses to Tataouine and 0300 (!) and 0830 to Zarzis. SNTRI has one bus each day to Gabès, Tunis, Jerba, Zarzis and Tataouine.

LOUAGES: Much better for shorter journeys. Louages leave from yard off Rue Aflatoun (see map).

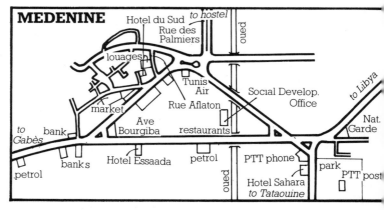

AROUND MÉDENINE: GIGHTIS

There is little to see at this ancient city and port, but as it's conveniently close to the road and to Jerba, it's popular with excursions from the island. Independent travellers visiting by public transport, almost certainly louages, will have no trouble in getting here but getting away could be difficult: unless a louage stops to drop off another visitor you'll have to rely on being squeezed into an already full vehicle. The lesson is clear: come early in the day and alone — or hire a car. But Gightis isn't worth too much effort.

Probably founded by the Phoenicians, developed by the Carthaginians, Gightis was attacked by Rome in the first two Punic wars but fell to the Berber Massinissa in 202BC. Rome took the city-port in 46BC and Caesar incorporated it into New Africa.

It prospered because of the sheltered Gulf of Bou Grara, trading in oil and wine, pottery and cloth, spices and dried fish, as well as slaves and exotica from south of the Sahara. It was on the overland route from Carthage to Leptis Magna (100km east of Tripoli), and trade improved further after Tiberius built the causeway to Jerba.

Punic spoken here. Inscriptions from the 2nd cent AD, now in the Bardo Museum, Tunis, establish that Punic, the Phoenician language, was still spoken here alongside Greek and Latin; there were few signs that Christianity was important although there was a bishopric. Other inscriptions testify to the city's ever-expanding prosperity, and in the 4th cent Gightis became part of Diocletian's new province of Tripolitania, essentially today's coastal Libya.

Vandals. In 430 the Vandals destroyed the city; the Byzantines did little rebuilding, probably adding a fortress, and the Arab invasion in the 7th century saw Gightis wiped off the map, to be lost until excavations began in 1906.

Wind, and wandering sheep, have added to the damage of the centuries, and a tour of the city now offers a sketchy ground plan of the main buildings with virtually nothing original to be seen above chest height.

The baths are at the top of the little valley in which Gightis lies; downhill is the forum, surrounded in the days of Hadrian by porticos and columns. The Great Temple beside the forum could have been the capitol; it has steps leading up to the podium where there are hints of the original columns. Opposite is the Temple of Baal with nearby sanctuaries to Hercules, Apollo and other gods, and a Temple of Mercury on the southern flanks.

Grand houses stood on the southern cliff, matching the fortress, possibly Byzantine, on the northern cliff, both looking out over the port, long since silted up so that only a trace of the jetty remains.

METAMEUR

Six centuries ago the Berber tribe of the Harraza settled here, building the ksar — fortified village — which is now in ruins on the hilltop. Later Arab settlers called the place Oum Tameur from which the name of Metameur derives. The Berbers built many ghorfas, and many ruins are in the village, but only two presentable ghorfas remain — and the police have one of them.

ZARZIS

Zarzis is a tourist town of smart white houses, set on the edge of a large plantation of palms and olives which seem to have overflowed from Jerba. There are 45,000 people in the town yet it is an uninteresting place. The Phoenicians built their Zitha here, the Romans renamed it Gergis, but you needn't bother looking for the ruins. There's *supposed* to be a Roman forum at Ziane, 10km to the west.

There is a good beach a short taxi-drive away, or you could go 4km up the coast to a cluster of three tourist hotels. Beyond that is a large military base putting the last two hotels 9km from town, and incurring a 2,500TD taxi fare each way.

Going to Tataouine? *If you plan to travel to Tataouine and explore the fortified villages in that neighbourhood, take note that public transport is scarce and consider the merits of hiring a car in Zarzis, the most convenient town. Avis, Europcar and Hertz are on the Rte des Hotels and Hertz is also represented at the Hotel Sangho. Or you could take an organised tour: contact Tunisirama at the Sangho or Zarzis Loisirs at the Zita. Or consult the tourist office.*

HOTELS: 3-star: Oamarit, 9km from town, 844 beds in 350 bungalows in self-contained village; Sangho-Club, 9km from town, 722 beds mostly in bungalows in self-contained village in 30-acre oasis; Zarzis, 4km from town, 236r and self-contained; **2-star:** Zita, (formerly Sidi Saad) 4km, in 15-acre oasis, 1012b; **unclass:** Emira, 22b; Zephir, 388b, both on beach; Olivier, began life as restaurant, 20b; de la Station, 51b, both in town.

CAMPING: Sehia, beside Hotel Zita.

RESTAURANTS: Olivier and Souihel, both on Rte des Hotels. In town, Restaurant des Caravanes in souk.

BUSES: Poor services, mainly to Médenine. Bus station Ave Ferhat Hached, west of town.

TOURIST OFFICE: ONT; Route du Port.

BEN GUERDANE

This is a town of 2,500 people created by the French in 1892 to keep the Italians on their side of the Libyan border; the Touazine nomads have settled here since. The large market is the only attraction.

There is a daily **bus** to Gabès and two each week to Tunis and to Tripoli. The **Hotel** Pavillon has 30 beds.

TATAOUINE and the SOUTH

Properly 'Foum Tataouine,' the name is Berber for 'springs,' hinting of natural water in the town. Berbers from the Ouderna and the Ghomrassen tribes settled around the springs which the French administrators later saw as adequate to support a military camp and later a prison.

Tataouine is still a sombre, even a grim town, with the market that the French introduced in 1892 as the only bright spot. Trading on Mondays and Thursdays overflows from the Place Ali Belhouane, surrounded by its arcades like those in Orléans or the smarter quarters of Paris. Here is one of the best places to buy genuine Berber souvenirs knowing they're not made for the tourist trade: take your choice of blankets and shawls in the strong colours the Berbers make from their vegetable dyes or you might also pick up a bargain in perfume, kohl for darkening a lady's face, or henna for dyeing her skin.

Ksar country. In colonial times Tataouine was headquarters for the *Bataillons d'Afrique,* a band of strictly-drilled desert troops who gloried under the names of the *Bat' d'Af* and *Les Joyeux,* 'The Happy Ones,' and had almost a legendary reputation back in France. Nowadays, Europeans use Tataouine as a staging post for expeditions to see the **ksour,** (singular is **ksar**), the fortified villages the Berbers were compelled to live in until this century.

From here on I'm assuming you have hired a car (Zarzis is the most convenient place to get one). If not, you will spend many hours begging for lifts or finding yourself squeezed into a louage that's already overcrowded — or having to pay over the going rate to charter a vehicle and driver. And if two of you plan to travel in this way, forget it.

Beni Barka. If all else fails, you can walk the 2km to the 16th-cent ksar of Beni Barka abandoned early this century when its inhabitants quit this rugged mountainside for the plain. They left some impressive caves as well as a splendid view.

CHENINI — GUERMESSA — GHOMRASSEN — TATAOUINE, 70km

Chenini. Chenini (also known as Chenini Foum Tataouine to avoid confusion with the Chenini at Gabès) is the best-known of the ksour with access along a good road. A white mosque with its square minaret sits on a col on the razorback ridge of hills, and at the foot of the village an underground mosque holds the tomb of the local saint and, according to legend, the entry to another chamber where lie the enormous tombs of the Seven Sleepers.

Seven Sleepers. The Seven Sleepers were Christians who were entombed alive by Roman soldiers. They slept through their 400-year incarceration, but their bodies grew to three metres tall; when they were discovered they agreed to convert to Islam, then they died and were buried here in these overlong coffins. The legend is strikingly similar to that of the Seven Sleepers who were walled up by accident in Ephesus (see *Discover Turkey* in this series) where they slept until they were discovered 200 years later. They proved to Diocletian that there is an afterlife, then they fell asleep again, to be wakened after the Second Coming.

The village itself is a fascinating place, clinging to a rugged and harsh mountainside on which the ksar was built. A few people still live in its ruins but most have homes on the lower slopes, their private quarters being a cave hacked into the hard rock, with conventional rooms built on the front. Several such homes are often enclosed in a communal courtyard.

If you come in spring you may see a hint of green on the terraced gardens where the womenfolk scratch a subsistence living while most of the men go to the towns to earn some cash. The Chenini men are well-known for their business enterprise in Tunis where they distribute the newspapers, The women also make a small income from weaving splendidly-coloured blankets.

Ghorfas. Several ghorfas, the oldest dating from the mid-12th cent, are scattered amid the rocks of the upper cliff, those in the northern part of the village being the closest to total decay. You may also see some ancient olive-oil presses, one of which is said to have been set up in the 11th cent.

The road to Douirat is for four-wheel trucks only; the road to Guermessa, marked by a line of telephone poles, is adequate.

Guermessa. Leave your car at the bottom of the village and walk up the track, the only access to the village. Another white mosque sits on another razorback ridge with a jagged mountain peak on each side. This is almost Himalayan foothill country, except for the heat!

Guermessa, built around 800 years ago, is the oldest ksar in the region. It was impregnable — it still is — but the conservative Berbers still choose to live here, those who cannot find room in the tiny ksar having extended south along the cliffs. The people live off their herds of sheep and camels, supplemented by a few olives, while the menfolk work in the markets of Tunis, coming home for only a few weeks a year.

Ghomrassen. A good road runs north to Ghomrassen, where around 9,000 people live. Some have carved caves in the lower section of this picturesque valley, the locations marked by the clusters of ghorfas. Two-storey ghorfas in good repair line the beginning of a track to the old Ksar Rsifa on a ridge, while to the north the Marabout of Sidi Arfa is on the summit of a rocky pinnacle. And the men of Ghomrassen? They have traditionally run the fritter-stands in Tunis.

Ksar Hadada. Turn north on a good road for Ksar Hadada, (5km), and look for the hotel of that name in a cluster of converted ghorfas: if you like sleeping in unusual places, a disused Tunisian granary should come high on your list, but to make certain of a room in high season you should make a reservation a day or two in advance through the Hotel La Gazelle in Tataouine. Not a bad idea to do it when you hire the car.

Rass El Aïn. Eight km south of Ghomrassen on a poor track, is Rass El Aïn, a ksar built by the Berbers around 263 and restored around 355, for the purpose of protecting the coast road from nomads from the desert. You could risk going straight on to Tataouine or going back to Ghomrassen for the better road.

KSAR OULED DEBBAB — DOUIRAT (22km) — KSAR GHILANE

Ksar Ouled Debbab. Nine km south of Tataouine on the main road south is Ksar Ouled Debbab, occupying a tabletop hill, with ghorfas lining the main street. Part of the old village became a hotel in 1967 but was closed in 1981; rumour claims that the locals were making too much use of the bar. Once you leave the main road the track to Douriat is rough.

Douirat. The original ksar of Douriat was built on the flattish top of a long spur above a near-vertical drop of several hundred feet. The ksar served as a granary and as a refuge for the people until the early 17th cent when the Douiri tribe came under the protection of one Youled Yacoub and felt secure enough to carve their homes near the foot of the cliff. Soon after, they abandoned the old ksar and built fresh ghorfas in front of their new homes, which are the ones worth visiting today.

This more-accessible Douirat prospered as an important resting place on the caravan route north to Gabès, and in 1888 it became an intelligence post for the French. Two years later thet French moved intelligence gathering to their new base at Tataouine, then the new market began drawing trade from Douriat, and when camel trains ceased Douriat's economy crashed. The men moved up to Tunis and became market porters while the stay-at-home women weave, with kilims (carpets, see earlier) among their range of goods.

The children of Douriat and Chenini are among the few in the country who learn Berber at their mothers' knee, adding literary Arabic only if they go to school; French might follow. Not until they go out into the world do they learn colloquial Arabic.

Ksar Ghilane. Ksar Ghilane, 80km to the west on the edge of the Grant Erg, is one of the most remote ksars and one of the most isolated oases in Tunisia. The track is passable for four-wheel-drive trucks (at a marker stone 28km from Tataouine, fork left; another 10km fork right) but liable to be covered by sand at certain times and places. The Roman fortress here is abandoned but there is a welcoming hot spring whose waters nourish clumps of tamarix normally full of small birds, and in spring the nomads from Zaafrane near Douz come here over the dunes.

Caution. *Do not go to Ksar Ghilane without notifying the Garde Nationale or the police: this is real desert travel with all its hazards.*

HOTELS: In Tataouine: 2-star (but unworthy of it) Gazelle, 46b. (Phone 05.60.009 or -913; hotel used for tours and may be booked up. Is also booking agency for Chenini hotel); unclassed Ennour, basic, unaccompanied women not accepted.
In Ksar Haddada — Ghomrassen: unclassed Ksar Haddada, in ghorfa, 72b. (Between the villages but nearer Ghomrassen).
In Chenini: Hotel le Relais, 5b (reservations via Gazelle in Tataouine).

PUBLIC TRANSPORT: Primitive in the extreme. SNT runs a daily bus to Sousse from Tataouine, from the bus stand on road south to Remada. Louages and open pick-up trucks leave from Rue Farhat Hached. For transport to Remada you may have to rely on a military bus.

FESTIVAL: Festival of Saharan Ksour, in Tataouine, Beni Kheddache and Ghomrassen; April.

REMADA and the SOUTH

One quarter of Tunisia's territory lies south of Tataouine yet there is just 130km of asphalted road to Remada and the Libyan border at Dehiba. Beyond that, and for the 350 or so kilometres to Borj El Hattaba (Borj El Khadra on the Michelin map, and also known as Fort Saint) at the southern tip, there are desert tracks, usually over hard-packed earth but occasionally venturing over loose sand — and at times the hard road can be covered with loose sand.

Do not venture south by car or truck without consulting the Garde Nationale or police, and following any advice given.

Remada. Remada is a newish town of 3,000 people clustered in a poor oasis fed by an artesian bore and facing the long-term threat of becoming a salt-pan. The ancient borj (castle) is a ruin and all the ghorfas have been abandoned, for Remada is now an army and air force outpost. There is no hotel, no restaurant, and visiting foreigners are rare.

A louage heads for Dehibat on the Libyan border most afternoons, but there is no scheduled truck to Borj Bourgiba, 41km west, a former military post where the ex-president spent two years imprisonment. There are several ruined and abandoned ksour in this inhospitable countryside.

Final surprise. Around 20km south of Remada on the way to Borj El Hattaba, nomads still occasionally sleep in some caves in the Jebel Segdel as their ancestors have done for centuries. Nearby, so I hear, is a ruined ksar with some wall paintings of ships from the 13th century.

TUNISIAN CHRONOLOGY

c8,000	Capsian Man at Gafsa		sacked; Utica the
814	Founding of Carthage		capital of Ifriqya
310	Agathocles, Tyrant of	112-105	Jugurtha's War
	Syracuse, raids	46	Caesar defeats
	Carthage		Pompey
263-146	Punic Wars; Carthage		

AD 235   Gordian becomes Emperor after Thysdrus revolt

312   Rome accepts Christianity

439   Genseric leads Vandal attack

534   Belisarius leads Byzantine reconquest

647   First Arab invaders defeat Gregory at Sbeïtla

670   Oqba Bin Nafi leads Islamic conquest, founds Kairouan

698   Arabs destroy Carthage

800   Ibrahim Ibn El Aghlab starts Aghlabid dynasty

894   Tunis briefly becomes capital

910   Obaïd Allah proclaims himself the Mahdi, God's chosen

921   Mahdi moves into Mahdia

944-5   Abou Yazid, 'man on a donkey,' besieges Mahdia

1052-57   Beni Hilal leads Hilalian invasion from Egypt

1159-1230   Almohad dynasty; first raids from Normans

1230   Abu Hafs starts Hafcid dynasty

1253   Abu Abd Allah becomes caliph; prosperity grows

1270   Louis IX's crusade fails

1534-81   Spain and Turkey fight for Tunisian spoils

1535   Carlos V of Spain takes Tunis; Dragut appears

1558   Dragut rules Jerba, Gafsa, Kairouan

1569   Ali Pasha of Alger takes Tunis

1571   Battle of Lepanto sees Ottoman Empire's first major defeat

1573   John of Austria takes Tunis

1574   Ottomans rule Tunisia

1580-1702   Hanefite dynasty

1705   Husain Ben Ali starts Husaynid dynasty

1759   Ali Pasha becomes Bey; prosperity returns

1784   French fleet bombards Tunisia

1830   French rule Algeria

1869   Tunisia bankrupt; creditors move in

1881   Bey Sidi Sadok and Jules Ferry, president of the council, sign Bardo agreement

1883   La Marsa Agreement starts French Protectorate

1885   Land registration laws deprive Tunisian farmers; French move in

1886   Philippe Thomas discovers phosphates at Metlaoui

1903   3 August: Habib Bourgiba born in Monastir

1920   Destour Party formed

1934   Neo-Destour takes over from Destour

1942-3   North African campaign of World War Two involves Tunisia

1952   Farhat Hached assassinated

1955   Bourgiba returns to Tunisia

1956   20 March: Independence

1957   Declaration of Republic